AN INTRODUCTION TO JEWISH LAW

Jewish law is a singular legal system that has been evolving for generations. Often conflated with biblical law or Israeli law, Jewish law needs to be studied in its own right. *An Introduction to Jewish Law* expounds the general structure of Jewish law and presents the cardinal principles of this religious legal system. An introduction to modern Jewish law as it applies to the daily life of Jews around the world, this volume presents Jewish law in a way that answers all the questions a student of comparative law would ask when encountering an unfamiliar legal system. Sources of Jewish law such as revelation, rabbinic and communal legislation, judicial decisions, and legal reasoning are defined and analyzed, and the authority of who decides what Jewish law is and why their decisions are binding is investigated.

Dr. François-Xavier Licari is an Associate professor of private and comparative law at the University of Lorraine, France. He has published numerous articles in French, German and US law journals, including *The American Journal of Comparative Law*, *Louisiana Law Review* and *Tulane Law Review*. He has published and edited books on theory of law and an introduction to Jewish law in French, which has received wide appraisal.

An Introduction to Jewish Law

FRANÇOIS-XAVIER LICARI

University of Lorraine

CAMBRIDGE
UNIVERSITY PRESS

University Printing House, Cambridge CB2 8BS, United Kingdom

One Liberty Plaza, 20th Floor, New York, NY 10006, USA

477 Williamstown Road, Port Melbourne, VIC 3207, Australia

314–321, 3rd Floor, Plot 3, Splendor Forum, Jasola District Centre, New Delhi – 110025, India

79 Anson Road, #06–04/06, Singapore 079906

Cambridge University Press is part of the University of Cambridge.

It furthers the University's mission by disseminating knowledge in the pursuit of education, learning, and research at the highest international levels of excellence.

www.cambridge.org
Information on this title: www.cambridge.org/9781108421973
DOI: 10.1017/9781108379878

© François-Xavier Licari 2019

This publication is in copyright. Subject to statutory exception and to the provisions of relevant collective licensing agreements, no reproduction of any part may take place without the written permission of Cambridge University Press.

First published 2019

Printed and bound in Great Britain by Clays Ltd, Elcograf S.p.A.

A catalogue record for this publication is available from the British Library.

Library of Congress Cataloging-in-Publication Data
NAMES: Licari, Francois-Xavier, author.
TITLE: An introduction to Jewish law / Francois-Xavier Licari. University of Lorraine.
OTHER TITLES: Droit talmudique. English
DESCRIPTION: Cambridge, United Kingdom : New York, NY, USA ; Cambridge University Press, 2019.
IDENTIFIERS: LCCN 2018039289 | ISBN 9781108421973
SUBJECTS: LCSH: Mishpat Ivri. | Jewish law – Interpretation and construction. | Jews – Legal status, laws, etc.
CLASSIFICATION: LCC KBM524 .L5313 2019 | DDC 296.1/8–dc23
LC record available at https://lccn.loc.gov/2018039289

ISBN 978-1-108-42197-3 Hardback
ISBN 978-1-108-43311-2 Paperback

Cambridge University Press has no responsibility for the persistence or accuracy of URLs for external or third-party internet websites referred to in this publication and does not guarantee that any content on such websites is, or will remain, accurate or appropriate.

To my wife, Sandy
"She possesses abundant wisdom, so that whatever she does is proper."
Genesis Apocryphon 20:7–8
To my children, Sarah, Henry, Esther and Tania
To my son-in-law, Elie
To my granddaughter, Noa-Haya

Contents

Acknowledgments		*page* xii
Abbreviations		xiii
	An Introduction to Jewish Law	1
1	**Jewish Law As a Subject for Study**	6

SECTION 1 JEWISH LAW

I Which Adjective?	6
II Which Noun?	7
III A Living Law	9
IV Jewish Law and Israeli Law	9

SECTION 2 THE SCIENTIFIC STUDY OF JEWISH LAW

I Jewish Law As a Science	11
II Jewish Law and Comparative Law	12
A In France	12
B In the United States and Israel	12

2	**Jewish Law As a Religious Legal Order**	17

SECTION 1 HALACHAH AS A SYSTEM

I The Juridicity of *Halachah*	17
II The Teleology of the Commandments	18
III The Taxonomy of the Commandments	22
A The Distinction between Matters of Permission and Prohibition (*Issur Veheter*) and Monetary Laws (*Dinei Mamonot*)	22
1 The Distinction	22
2 The Implications of This Distinction	23

vii

		B	Commandments of Biblical Origin and Commandments of Rabbinic Origin	26
			1 The Distinction	26
			2 Consequences of the Distinction	27
	IV	Legislative Drafting (Legistics)		29
	V	Concepts and Terminology		30

SECTION 2 A RELIGIOUS LEGAL SYSTEM

	I	A Fourth Family?		31
		A	A Fluid Family	31
		B	An Ideological Family	32
	II	Some Parameters of a Religious Legal System		33
		A	The Sources of the System	33
		B	The Domain Covered by Jewish Law	35
		C	The *Modus Operandi* of the System	37
			1 General Orientations	37
			2 In the Jewish Tradition, Are the Judgments Divine or Human?	39

SECTION 3 A TRANSNATIONAL LEGAL ORDER — 44

3 The Sources of Jewish Law — 47

SECTION 1 REVELATION
SECTION 2 RABBINIC LEGISLATION (TAKANOT AND GEZEROT) AND COMMUNAL LEGISLATION (TAKANOT HAKAHAL)
SECTION 3 CUSTOMS
SECTION 4 SEVARAH
SECTION 5 THE VIRTUE OF CASUISTICS: EXEMPLUM, RESPONSUM, JUDGMENT

4 Halachic Authority — 64

Introduction — 64

SECTION 1 HALACHIC AUTHORITY: THE RABBINIC PARADIGM

	I	The Holders of Authority: Books and Individuals		67
		A	The Books: The Mishnah, the Talmud and the Codes	67
			1 Typology	67
			2 Authority	70
		B	The Individuals: The *Rav* and the *Posek*	72
			1 Role and Necessary Qualities	72
			2 The Activities of a Rabbi	74

	3	Forum Shopping	75
II		The Sources of Authority	76
	A	Scriptural Sources	76
	B	The Consensual Source	77
III		The Domain of Halachic Authority	77
IV		The Extent of Halachic Authority	79
	A	The Extent of Hermeneutic Authority	79
	B	The Extent of Creative Authority	82
		1 The Exact Scope of the Prohibition on Adding Anything To, or Removing Anything From, the Torah	83
		2 Illustrations	87
V		Halakhic Pluralism	91
		1 An Affirmation of Halachic Pluralism	91
		2 The Limits to Halachic Pluralism	94

SECTION 2 THE NEW PARADIGMS OF HALACHIC AUTHORITY

I	Reform Judaism: *Zeitgeist* as the *Grundnorm*	97
II	The "Counter-Reform" or the Birth of Orthodox Judaism	98
III	"Ultra-Orthodox" Judaism	99
IV	Religious Zionism: The State of Israel as Telos	102

5 Hermeneutics 107

Introduction 107

SECTION 1 EXEGETICAL APPROACHES: THE ORCHARD (HA-PARDES)

I	Four Approaches	107
II	A Famous Controversy: Can the *Peshat* Contradict *Halachah*?	108

SECTION 2 THE PRINCIPAL RULES FOR THE INTERPRETATION OF A BIBLICAL TEXT

I		Analogical Interpretation	112
	A	Rule No. 1: A *Fortiori* Reasoning	112
	B	Rule No. 2: Analogy Based on Identity of Terms	113
	C	Rule No. 3: Inference through Induction	114
II		Explicative Interpretation	115
	A	Rule No. 4: A General Rule and a Particular Case	115
	B	Rule No. 5: A Particular Case and a General Rule	116
	C	Rule No. 6: General Rule + Particular Case + General Rule (a General Law Limited by Specific Instances and Then Again Referred to in General Terms)	117

Contents

D Rule No. 7: The General Rule Requires a Particular Rule
and the Particular Rule Requires a General Rule 117
E Rules Nos. 8–11: "A Law That Was Included in the
Collective Term" 118

III A Few Complementary Rules 121
A Chronological Order Is Not Always Respected in the
Torah 121
B The Torah Is Speaking the Language of Human Beings 121
C The Consonantal Text of the Torah Is Authoritative/the
Vocal Text of the Torah Is Authoritative 122

**6 Jewish Law and the Law of Nations: The Administration of Legal
Pluralism** 124

Introduction 124

SECTION 1 RABBINIC ARBITRATION

I A History Résumé 124
II Rabbinic Arbitration As a Legal Duty, Technical Necessity
and Source of Savings 127
A Rabbinic Arbitration As a Legal Duty 127
B Rabbinic Arbitration As a Technical Necessity 131
C The Economic Advantages of Rabbinic Arbitration 132
III The Arbitration Agreement (*Shtar Beirurin*) and the
Composition of the Arbitration Court 133
A The Arbitration Agreement 133
B The Composition of the Arbitration Court 134
IV Some Procedural Elements 135
A The Summons to Appear before a Rabbinic Court and
the Refusal (*Siruv*) 135
1 The Principles 135
2 The Refusal (*Siruv*) in Non-Jewish Courts 136
B Representation by a Lawyer 137
C The Rabbinic Judgment (*P'sak*) 138
D Strict Adherence to the Law (*Din Torah*) or *Ex Aequo
et Bono* Decision (*Peshara*)? 141

**SECTION 2 "THE LAW OF THE STATE IS THE LAW" ("DINA
D'MALCHUTA DINA")**

I The General Meaning and the Historical Background 143
II Talmudic Sources 143
III A Principle without Any Legal Base? 144

IV	Conditions for the Application of the Rule	145
A	The Nature of the Political Regime	145
B	The Principle of *"Dina D'malchuta Dina"* and the Kingdom of Israel	146
C	The Principle of Equality	146
V	The Domain of the Principle's Application	146
A	Monetary Law but Not the Ritual Domain	147
B	The Interests of the King	147
C	"Non-Jewish Ways" and the New Laws of the King	147
D	State Law and *Halachah*	148
E	Principal Applications	148
1	Taxes	148
2	The Judgments of Non-Jewish Courts	148
3	Changes in the Value of the Local Currency	149
4	Government Appointments to Rabbinic or Judiciary Functions	149
	Concluding Remarks	150
Index		154

Acknowledgments

Many persons offered their support to achieve this book. First, I must acknowledge and thank my dear family, my friends, my colleagues.

I also want to thank my sponsors: Institut François Gény (University of Lorraine, France) and Institut Talmud et Transmission (Strasbourg, France).

As primary sources, I have used the following: Bible, King James Version, https://quod.lib.umich.edu/k/kjv/ (used only for New Testament verses); Talmud of Babylon, Online Soncino Babylonian Talmud Translation for the extracts from the talmud: http://ancientworldonline.blogspot.com/201 2/01/online-soncino-babylonian-talmud.html; Tanakh, JPS (Jewish Publication Society) Tagged Tanakh: http://taggedtanakh.org/Home/ Terms.

Abbreviations

BB	Tractate Bava Batra
BCE	Before the Common Era
Ber.	Tractate Berachot
BK	Tractate Bava Kama
BM	Tractate Bava Metzia
BT	Babylonian Talmud
ca.	circa
CE	Common Era
Deut.	Deuteronomy
Er.	Tractate Eruvin
Exod.	Exodus
Gen.	Gen.
Git.	Tractate Gittin
Guide	Guide for the Perplexed (Maimonides)
Heb.	Hebrews
HM	Hoshen Mishpat
Hor.	Tractate Horayot
JT	Jerusalem Talmud
Ket.	Tractate Ketubot
Kid.	Tractate Kiddushin
Lev.	Leviticus
M	Mishna
Mak.	Tractate Makot
Meg.	Megillat
Men.	Tractate Menachot
MT	Mishneh Torah (Maimonides)
Ned.	Tractate Nedarim
Nid.	Tractate Nida

Num.	Numbers
Pes.	Tractate Pesachim
Pl.	Plural
Prov.	Proverbs
Ps.	Psalms
Resp.	Responsa
RH	Tractate Rosh Hashanah
Shev.	Tractate Shevu'ot
Tem.	Tractate Temura
SA	Shulchan Aruch
San.	Tractate Sanhedrin
Yev.	Tractate Yevamot

An Introduction to Jewish Law

A paper delivered at the first international conference on comparative law (Paris, 1900) contained the following statement: "Everyone, it would seem, is familiar with the Jewish people's laws; however, if you were to ask someone about this or that point, you would discover that this person knows very little, in fact, almost nothing."[1]

More than a century later, the situation has remained pretty much the same. Law students generally complete their program of studies without encountering any aspect of Jewish law, unless they happen to come across the well-known subject of the *get* (Jewish divorce document) or they have to tackle a thorny question involving private international law (conflict of laws). The average educated person usually knows nothing about Jewish law or has only a confused picture distorted by 2,000 years of Christian polemics.

Those who wish to obtain an introduction to Jewish law will discover that works on comparative law are usually silent on this subject and will be unable to find any manuals on Jewish law comparable to those that exist on the laws of other religions, such as canonical or Muslim law.

Why is there such an absence of information? Authors usually do not explain why they exclude an examination of the background of Jewish law. René David, whose groundbreaking work *Les grands systèmes de droit contemporain* has left a lasting imprint on comparativist scholarship, is more eloquent, although one is forced to admit that his words are rather perplexing. According to David, there are three principal families of law: (1) Romano-Germanic – roughly speaking, continental Europe and those countries that

---

[1] M. Rapaport, "L'esprit du Talmud et son influence sur le droit judaïque," in *Congrès international de droit comparé, tenu à Paris du 31 juillet au 4 août 1900, Procès-verbaux des séances et documents*, Tome 1, L.G.D.J., 1905, p. 310.

have adopted the French civil code or the German civil code (Bürgerliches Gesetzbuch [BGB]); (2) common law – England, the United States and those countries that have received this model; (3) the "residual family" or "other concepts of law and social order." The term "other" actually means "non-Western." This family is thus – and unfortunately – defined in negative terms. The definition is particularly unfortunate because David divides this residual family into two totally opposite groups: "Sometimes immense value is attached to law, which, however, is conceived differently than in the West; sometimes, in sharp contrast, the very notion of law itself is rejected and thus social relationships are regulated outside the parameters of law. The first approach is prevalent in Muslim, Hindu and Jewish law, while the second exists in the Far East, Africa and Madagascar." Muslim, Hindu and Jewish law, explains David, are intimately linked to the respective religions. However, readers will not find any further discussion of Jewish law. David clarifies the reason for this exclusion: "Although it is a fascinating subject, Jewish law has not been included in the discussion because its influence is extremely limited." Is he speaking in quantitative terms? Apparently, he is. After all, the 17 million Jews throughout the world constitute a very small global presence; however, the degree of interest in a legal system does not hinge on the number of persons governed by it. If it did, how can one explain the interest shown in the laws of the Principality of Monaco or the Grand Duchy of Luxembourg? The second justification for the exclusion of Jewish law is more mystifying: "The international solidarity existing among Jews, so long as it exists, has never been expressed by a desire to prioritize Hebrew religious law over the laws in effect in the different countries where it could have an influence. Thus, Jewish law has never had the same importance as, for example, Muslim law." Indeed, no Jewish community has ever aspired to assign precedence to its law over the laws of the nation under whose sun it resides. Such a hegemonic ambition has never been congruent with the spirit of Jewish law, which applies to Jews, who have no goal to impose their legal system on other nations but who, quite the contrary, recognize to a great extent the superiority of the laws of those nations (see Chapter 6). Is the desire for legal imperialism a prerequisite for inclusion among the major legal systems in the world today?

At this stage, it is perhaps necessary to show why people should be interested in reading this book. Very simply, note that the Jewish legal system is the oldest legal system still in effect today, that it has left its imprint on numerous legal institutions and that it has influenced authors such as Hugo Grotius (1583–1645) and Hans Kelsen (1881–1973), to cite but two examples. One could also add that the study of Jewish law contributes to a better understanding of legal pluralism because it is a personal legal system that is able to coexist with the legal systems of other nations. Furthermore, Jewish law has several remarkable features: (1) it is religious, non-state law (see Chapter 2); (2) it is dispensed by courts of law that have no coercive authority, which, in any case, can never be manifested because the absence of a state implies the absence of enforcement power; (3) generally speaking, although it lacks any central authority that could guarantee its unity, it manages to function effectively.

In accordance with the editorial nature of a collection, the present work is an essay and not a manual that could provide an overview of the entire context of Jewish law. Emphasis has been placed on the origins, sources and structure of Jewish law. The reader may be guided further by a multilingual selected bibliography.

Further Reading

BIBLICAL LAW

Dozeman, T. B. "The Pentateuch and Israelite Law," in S. B. Chapman (ed.), *The Cambridge Companion to the Hebrew Bible/Old Testament*, Cambridge University Press, 2016, p. 187.

Falk, Z. *Hebrew Law in Biblical Times: An Introduction*, 2nd edn., Brigham Young University Press, 2001.

Knight, D. A. *Law, Power, and Justice in Ancient Israel*, Westminster John Knox Press, 2011.

Morrow, W. S. *An Introduction to Biblical Law*, Eerdmans, 2017.

Strawn, B. (ed.). *The Oxford Encyclopedia of the Bible and Law*. 2 volumes. Oxford University Press, 2015.

Weinfeld, M. *The Place of the Law in the Religion of Ancient Israel*, VT Sup. 100, Leiden and Brill, 2004.

Westbrook, R. and Wells, B. *Everyday Law in Biblical Israel: An Introduction*, Westminster John Knox Press, 2009.

THE INFLUENCE OF JEWISH LAW ON OTHER LEGAL SYSTEMS

Berman, J. A. *Created Equal: How the Bible Broke with Ancient Political Thought*, Oxford University Press, 2008.

Jacobs, J. A. (ed.). *Judaic Sources and Western Thought: Jerusalem's Enduring Presence*, Oxford University Press, 2011.

Leben, C. "La référence aux sources hébraïques dans la doctrine du droit de la nature et des gens au XVIIIe siècle," 56 *Droits* 179 (2012).

Levine, S. J. *Jewish Law and American Law: A Comparative Study*. 2 volumes. Academic Studies Press, 2018.

Rabinowitz, J. J. *Jewish Law: Its Influence on the Development of Legal Institutions*, Bloch Publishing Company, 1956.

Sólon, A. M. "Judaism: Jewish Law in Kelsen," 239 *Revista Brasileira de Filosofia* 97 (2012).

BASIC BOOKS ON JEWISH LAW

Elon, M. *Jewish Law: History, Sources, Principles (Ha-Mishpat Ha-Ivri)*. 4 volumes. Jewish Publication Society, 1994.

Hayes, C. (ed.). *The Cambridge Companion to Judaism and Law*, Cambridge University Press, 2017.

Hecht, N., Jackson, B. S., Piattelli, D., Passamaneck, S. M. and Rabello, A. M. (eds.). *An Introduction to the History and Sources of Jewish Law*, Clarendon Press, 1996.

Resnicoff, S. H. *Understanding Jewish Law*, LexisNexis, 2012.

Urbach, E. E. *The Halakhah: Its Sources and Development*, Yad la-Talmud, 1986.

COLLECTIONS OF FUNDAMENTAL ARTICLES ON JEWISH LAW

Batnitzky, L. and Brafman, Y. (eds.). *Jewish Legal Theories: Writings on State, Religion and Morality*, Brandeis University Press, 2018.

Ben-Menahem, H. and Hecht, N. S. (eds.). *Authority, Process and Method: Studies in Jewish Law*, Harwood Academic Publishers, 1998.

Drey, A. and Hecht, N. S. (eds.). *Windows onto Jewish Legal Culture: Fourteen Exploratory Essays*. 2 volumes. Routledge, 2011.

TEXTBOOKS AND CASEBOOKS

Elon, M., Auerbach, B., Chazin, D. D., and Sykes, M. J. *Jewish Law (Mishpat Ivri): Cases and Materials*, LexisNexis, 1999.

Schiffman, L. H. *Texts and Traditions: A Source Reader for the Study of Second Temple and Rabbinic Judaism*, Ktav Publishing House, 1998.

BIBLIOGRAPHICAL WORKS

Hollander, D. *Legal Scholarship in Jewish Law: An Annotated Bibliography of Journal Articles*, Getzville and William S. Hein & Co., Inc., 2017.

Rakover, N. *The Multi-Language Bibliography of Jewish Law*, Jewish Legal Heritage Society, 1990.

SPECIALIZED LAW JOURNALS AND YEARBOOKS

Dinei Israel: Studies in Halakhah and Jewish Law (Faculty of Law, Tel-Aviv University and Benjamin N. Cardozo School of Law, Yeshiva University) www.cardozo.yu.edu/programs-centers/yeshiva-university-center-jewish-law-and-contemporary-civilization/publications-o)

Hakira: The Flatbush Journal of Jewish Law and Thought (www.Hakira.org)

Jewish Law Annual (Routledge)

Jewish Law Association Studies (www.legaltheory.demon.co.uk/jlas/publications.htm)

Journal of Halachah and Contemporary Society (www.daat.ac.il/daat/english/Journal/index.html)

Oqimta: Studies in Talmudic and Rabbinic Literature (www.oqimta.org.il/english/HomePage.aspx)

Shenaton Hamishpat Ha'ivri (Hebrew University of Jerusalem)

Tsafon: Revue d'études juives du Nord (Université de Lille III) (www.tsafon-revue.com/)

Yod: Revue des études hébraïques et juives (INALCO) (http://yod.revues.org/)

1

Jewish Law As a Subject for Study

SECTION 1 JEWISH LAW

I WHICH ADJECTIVE?

The commonly used terminology for designating the normative legal corpus of the Jewish people is varied: biblical law, Mosaic law, Hebrew law, Jewish law, Judaic law, Talmudic law and rabbinic law. Thus, one must be precise in defining what is Jewish law and what is not.

First of all, the term *Jewish law* should be avoided because it consists, according to Jewish tradition, of two distinct bodies of laws: on one hand, *Sinaitic* law, which God revealed to Moses and which is contained in the Written Law and the Oral Law (see Chapter 3) and applies to Jews; on the other hand, the seven Noahide laws, which God previously gave to all humanity and which some people consider the root of natural law. This is a remarkable example of legal pluralism existing within the context of a legal system. Naturally, that is the first body of laws that interests us throughout this work.

The term *Mosaic law* also leaves much to be desired because it places the emphasis on Moses as legislator. Although Moses has a central role in the Revelation (see Chapter 3), he is considered not the Torah's author, but rather the "mouth" through which God gave Israel the Torah.

Regarding the adjective *Hebrew*, it refers to "a member of or descendant from one of a group of northern Semitic peoples including the Israelites."[1] According to the classical approach, the history of the Hebrews is the chronicle of a political existence that extends over a period of two millennia within the borders of the Land of Israel. The history of the Hebrews begins

---

[1] Merriam-Webster Dictionary, www.merriam-webster.com/dictionary/Hebrew.

with a family led by Abraham, who leaves Sumer and settles in Canaan, located between the Jordan River and the Mediterranean Sea (ca. 1760 BCE). That history came to an end in 135, as a result of a blood war against the Roman Empire: the ancient Jewish state disappears and the second exile begins. The Jewish legal system, whose roots date from this period, shows from its very beginnings the characteristics that will emerge more prominently after the destruction of the Second Temple in Jerusalem (in the year 70 CE), when the spiritual leaders of that period, the Sages or the Rabbis, heirs of the Pharisees, save Judaism by overhauling it. The progressive institutionalization of the Oral Law through its transformation into a written format as expressed in two compilations – the Mishnah and the Gemara (which together constitute the Talmud) – represents a major enterprise, because the Talmud becomes an object of devotion, an object for study and a point of departure for legal reasoning. That is why, when designating the law of the Jewish people, it is preferable to use the term *Talmudic law*, or even *rabbinic law*. These two terms correctly express the fact that this law is the dynamic product of the interpretation and creation of the Talmudic Sages and their successors (see Chapter 4). Although the expression *Talmudic law* seems to me more appropriate, I nevertheless term the object of my study *Jewish law* to conform to the overwhelming American usage. In studying Jewish law one must not overlook the existence of post-Talmudic sources, that is, the numerous commentaries on the Talmud that have flourished to this very day, as well as the responsa (see Chapter 3).

The term *Jewish law* is rendered by the Hebrew word *halachah*, whose etymology is rich in meaning. In the eleventh century, Nathan of Rome gave the word *halachah* two explanations that have become famous. Both explanations take as their point of departure the Hebrew verbal root *heh-lamed-kof*, which means "to walk." Two explanations thus emerge: (1) The *halachah* governs the way the individual and an entire society should proceed and serves as a compass for that individual and that society. (2) The *halachah* is a regime that "walks" or "moves" – that is, it develops and evolves over time (see Chapter 4); it is a dynamic entity. There is a common denominator to these two explanations: the *halachah* is a restraining body of laws imposed on those who accept its yoke.

II WHICH NOUN?

One can harbor doubts as to whether the *halachah* can really be called a body of laws. In point of fact, with a few exceptions (Morocco, Lebanon and Israel, and, even in these three countries, only for those laws related to personal status), the *halachah* has judges (*dayanim*) with no coercive powers, no police officers and no bailiffs at its disposal to ensure that it is respected. In other words, the *halachah* has nothing at its disposal that is generally considered the primary feature of law – namely, state sanctions. However, several arguments support the juridical nature of the *halachah*. First of all, it has an essentially imperative character, commanding individuals to perform or refrain from an entire series of actions from the moment they awake in the morning until they go to bed at night, from the time they are born until the time they die, and accompanies them in their home, in synagogue, in their workplace, even when they go on vacation. Moreover, the legislator is divine and this gives immeasurable weight to the commandments that the *halachah* consists of. Finally, the *halachah* does avail itself of sanctions, whether of a worldly or a divine nature. The worldly sanctions today are essentially social in character: the placing by a community of a ban of greater or lesser degree on those individuals who do not conform to a law judged to be essential by their peers or who refuse to act in accordance with a rabbinic decision.[2] However, it can become a state sanction when the parties submit their dispute to an arbitrator and the decision has been given the validity of a law (see Chapter 6). Furthermore, as G. J. Blidstein aptly points out, one of the major arguments supporting the juridical character of the *halachah* is the legal character of its discourse. The *halachah* reasons on the basis of texts and precedents:[3] it cites authorities, weighs opinions and interpretations and then decides in favor of one of them. Thus, the *halachah* is neither theology nor philosophy, neither morality nor ethics. However, Jewish law is not solely law. Loyalty to it is the very heart of Jewish religiosity. Piety is defined by the degree of obedience to the *halachah*, a fact that reinforces the obligatory character of the *halachah*, at least among observant Jews.

What is the *halachah*'s domain? The *halachah* does not only concern itself with religious or worship issues (such as prayer, ritual slaughter, conversion, etc.) but also embraces the totality of life, including the economic sphere. One area of law concerns obligations – with each category of agreement, sale, lease, loan, torts, etc., regulated with as much attention to detail as the legal system of any country. Jewish law is also concerned with relations between neighbors, with the commission of offenses, with criminal law, etc.

---

[2] For an introduction, see Michael Broyde, "Forming Religious Communities and Respecting Dissenters' Rights," in Michael J. Broyde and John Witte Jr. (eds.), *Human Rights in Judaism: Cultural, Religious, and Political Perspectives*, Jason Aronson, 1998, pp. 35–76.
[3] Here I don't use "precedent" in the common law sense (*stare decisis*). For more explanations, see Chapter 3, Section 5.

III A LIVING LAW

Finally, one must emphasize that Jewish law is not just an object for study or pure intellectual speculation. Jewish law is neither Roman law nor Babylonian law. Quite the contrary, the *halachah* is a living law that is applied every day, at least among observant Jews. With its hallmark, which is personal and not territorial, Jewish law truly establishes a legal order that is both national and transnational. It is national because it regulates the Jewish nation and it is transnational because it regulates a society whose members are distributed among various countries. It is the compass of Jewish communities. For instance, you find an object in the stairwell of your apartment building. You must ask yourself what the *halachah* requires you as a Jew to do in order to locate the object's owner. A friend entrusts you with an object that is stolen during your absence; you will rely on the *halachah* to inform you what is the measure of your responsibility under such circumstances.

Naturally, the relations between the members of any Jewish community are not always tranquil; disputes do sometimes arise. If an amicable solution cannot be found to a dispute, the parties must turn to a rabbinic court. They are urged to avoid bringing their case before a secular court and to instead bring it before a rabbinic court, or *beit din* in Hebrew. The respect Jews display for the *halachah* and for its divine nature means that they cannot bring any dispute that arises before a court that will apply a law that is foreign to the *halachah*.[4] Provided that the arbitration law of the state (e.g., American or French law) is respected, the decision issued by a *beit din* has the force of a state court ruling (see Chapter 6).

IV JEWISH LAW AND ISRAELI LAW

Finally, Jewish law should not be confused with Israeli law. The laws of the State of Israel, which was established in 1948, are generally classified as belonging to the family of "mixed systems," the "third legal family," as distinct from civil law and common law.[5] While certain segments of the Zionist movement envisaged the application of a renovated Jewish law to the newly created State of Israel, they found themselves on a collision course with the country's lawyers, who considered themselves bound by the laws that Israel had inherited from British Mandatory Palestine. Initially, Israeli law, roughly

---

[4] For the nuances and exceptions, see Chapter 6.
[5] On mixed jurisdictions, see Vernon Palmer (ed.), *Mixed Jurisdictions Worldwide: The Third Legal Family*, 2nd edn., Cambridge University Press, 2014.

speaking, presented itself as a mixture of Ottoman law (itself reflecting some civil law influence), common law and religious law, the latter applying to each respective religious community but limited to personal status. Over time, Israeli law has distanced itself from the English model both in substance and in form. From the standpoint of substance, Israeli law now tends toward the continental law model; from the standpoint of form, the Israeli parliament, the Knesset, has adopted numerous laws (laws concerning obligations and contracts, family law, etc.) in order to replace British Mandatory laws wherever possible. The result of this process is an Israeli civil code whose adoption is anticipated in the not-too-distant future. However, the personal status laws deriving from religious law remain unchanged.

Nevertheless, the separation between Jewish law and Israeli law is not absolute. Some Israeli Supreme Court judges use Jewish law even when Israeli law requires the courts to fill lacunae in the law by referring to English common law. This practice gained support when the Knesset adopted the 1980 Foundations of Law Act, which provides in part: "Where the court facing with a legal question requiring [a] decision, finds no answer to it in statute law or case-law or by analogy, it shall decide it in light of the principles of freedom, justice, equity and peace of Israel's heritage."[6] In 1992, the Knesset voted on a basic law on human dignity and freedom that seeks "to establish ... the values of the State of Israel as a Jewish and democratic state."[7] This statute has also been used as the basis for the penetration of Jewish law into Israeli law.[8] More recently, the Knesset adopted the "Basic Law: Israel As the Nation-State of the Jewish People," informally known as the Nation-State Bill or the Nationality Bill. It is a basic law that specifies the nature of the State of Israel as the nation-state of the Jewish people. The law was adopted by the Knesset on July 19, 2018. The law is largely symbolic and declarative. Nevertheless, the statute explicitly refers now to "Jewish law" as a possible source to fill the lacunae of Israeli law.

---

[6] Foundations of Law, 5740–1980, 34 LSI 181 (1979–1980).
[7] Basic Law: Human Dignity and Liberty, 1992, S. H. 1391.
[8] See Steven D. Friedell, "Some Observations about Jewish Law in Israel's Supreme Court," 8 *Washington University Global Studies Law Review* 659 (2009).

SECTION 2 THE SCIENTIFIC STUDY OF JEWISH LAW

I JEWISH LAW AS A SCIENCE

In his *History of the People of Israel* (1887), Ernest Renan writes: "For a philosophical spirit, that is, for a spirit concerned with the origins of things, there are only three histories of prime interest in humanity's past: Greek history, the history of Israel and Roman history. Together, these three histories constitute what one can call the history of civilization, civilization being the result of the alternating collaboration of Greece, Judea and Rome."

If one admits that one of the pillars of civilization is law, one must conclude that there is little room for civilization in faculties of law in France and in most European countries. However, the lack of interest shown toward the study of Jewish law has not always been a fact of life. Jewish law was treated with considerable honor at the first international conference on comparative law, held in Paris (1900). A contribution on Jewish law was inserted in the first section of the conference, which dealt with general theory and with the methodology of comparative law. This contribution attested to the aspiration of some intellectuals to turn Jewish law into an object for scientific study.[9]

About two centuries ago, an intellectual movement of vast importance, *die Wissenschaft des Judentums* ("the science of Judaism"), was founded in Germany. This new science, whose parents were Romanticism and modernism, regarded Judaism as an object for systematic investigation, transferring the study of sacred texts from their traditional context – the house of study (*Beit hamidrash*) – to the critical domain of the university. This new science's ideology was the liberation of Judaism from its "archaisms" and the acceleration of its reform (on Reform Judaism's principles and its approach to the *halachah*, see Chapter 4). When Nazi barbarism dealt it a death blow, this movement could pride itself on its remarkable achievements in all the various domains of Jewish studies, including the methodical study of Jewish law. Between 1822 and 1938, numerous research studies focused on this major element in Jewish civilization. For the survivors and their disciples, this scientific adventure continues to be pursued in Israel and the Diaspora, especially the United States. Today, one can note a dramatic increase of activity in the study of Jewish law.

---

[9] M. Rapaport, "L'esprit du Talmud et son influence sur le droit judaïque," in *Congrès international de droit comparé, tenu à Paris du 31 juillet au 4 août 1900, Procès-verbaux des séances et documents*, Tome 1, L.G.D.J., 1905, p. 310.

II JEWISH LAW AND COMPARATIVE LAW

A In France

When comparative law first saw the light of day in the early years of the twentieth century, some believed that the study of Jewish law was not only of intellectual interest in itself but that it could – and, in fact, should – make its contribution to the new science of comparative law. In France, one of the most notable illustrations of Jewish law's positive impact on comparative law is probably to be found in the writings of Edouard Lambert (1866–1947), one of the French founding fathers of comparative law. In his monumental work *La fonction du droit civil comparé* (*The Function of Comparative Law*) (1903), he devotes an entire chapter to Jewish law, where he presents many arguments in favor of the theses he was developing on the subject of custom.[10] In that domain, Lambert was a unique pioneer: in his era, as in the years that followed, Jewish law was never or almost never considered a subject worthy of research in faculties of law in France.

In recent years, one can note a slight renewal of interest in the scientific study of Jewish law in French universities: a number of doctoral theses are being written today, and Jewish law is slowly finding its place in some seminars and law journals. However, movement in this direction remains marginal.

B In the United States and Israel

In Germany, if the *Wissenschaft des Judentums* has been able to reemerge from its ashes, it has never recovered its initial level of activity either quantitatively or qualitatively. Additionally, in its current state, the *Wissenschaft des Judentums* shows little interest in Jewish law because in Germany today Reform Judaism is dominant and it does not regard the *halachah* as legally binding (see Chapter 4).

Primarily in Israel and the United States, the scientific study of Judaism has today recovered its luster and has expanded its field of research. In these two countries, the scientific study of Judaism is drawing increasing interest, including the legal field, where academic research flourishes: *mishpat ivri* (literally, Hebrew law), according to Israeli terminology, and *Jewish legal studies*, according to American terminology. In the United States, the study of Jewish law is part of a wider movement, *religious legal theory*, and is coming into contact with other fields of research such as *law and economics, critical*

---

[10] E. Lambert, *La fonction du droit civil comparé*, vol. 1, V. Giard & E. Brière, 1903, pp. 231–279.

legal studies and even *feminist legal studies*. The Israeli approach and the American approach are different, although one should note the many convergences, due to the intense exchanges among the scholars of both countries. The Israeli scholarship is focused on the evolution of Jewish law in the course of time and on the multiplicity of its sources, and encompasses the case law of contemporary rabbinic courts. It is concerned only in those branches of law that are of current interest (patrimonial law and matrimonial law) and is not concerned with those domains that are no longer a part of positive law (for example, the laws relating to the sacrifices offered in the Temple in Jerusalem). The material of *mishpat ivri* is assuming a certain ideological dimension because some have not abandoned the idea that a modernized version of Jewish law could, and should, constitute a primary source for the laws of the State of Israel. The treatise of Menachem Elon (1923–2013),[11] a professor of law, a Supreme Court of Israel justice (1977–1988) and, later, a vice president (1988–1993) of that same court, constitutes from this standpoint a model of a unique genre. But there are also many scholars in Israel who do not subscribe to this *mishpat ivri* ideology and so do not confine their studies of the *halachah* in this way.

The American scholarship concentrates on research studies revolving around two themes. First of all, it seeks to identify, and resolve, as much as possible, the conflicts that might arise between a portion of the *halachah* and American law, for example, in the domain of estate law or legal ethics. Another current is placing emphasis on comparative law and on the possible contribution of Jewish law to American law in a variety of domains such as punitive damages, conjugal violence, criminal law or constitutional law. This approach inevitably raises several methodological questions with which comparativists are very familiar, notably the problem of the "transplanting" of a juridical institution produced by one legal system on another. Is it reasonable to adapt the product of non-state law (*halachah*) in the direction of a state law (American or other)? Are the promoters of Jewish law not overlooking the fact that there is often a notable difference between codified Jewish law and the law as applied in practice? Moreover, one should not lose sight of the fact that Jewish law is assuming a marked religious dimension (Chapter 2), which is often erased in order to "export" it more easily to secular systems. To sum up, the comparison of laws is possible, even desirable, but one should reflect more

---

[11] Menachem Elon, *Jewish Law: History, Sources, Principles (Ha-Mishpat Ha-Ivri)*, 4 volumes, Jewish Publication Society, 1994.

profoundly on a methodology suitable for taking into account the different functions and structures of the *halachah* and the Western legal tradition.[12]

To further promote Jewish law, a current in the American scholarship presents it as the paradigm of modernity, even of postmodernity. The public discourse in the United States and Europe has, for several decades, been vaunting the merits of cultural pluralism in order to counter the anonymity of the masses that prevails in our society. For some people, Jewish law seems to be a counter-model to a Western juridical model that is excessively kelsenian, hierarchized, centralized and repressive. The Jewish law system appears to be free of any state authority, to be based on the involvement of the communities and individuals constituting it, to be non-repressive – in short, quasi-libertarian. What is particularly attractive is the pluralism that Jewish law promotes, which tolerates diverse interpretations and which sees the "words of the living God" in each opinion (see Chapter 4). Although this presentation appears tempting, it would be wise to moderate the enthusiasm it arouses because it was only the close relationship between God and human beings that enabled the creation of an order that is both utopian and realistic. It is difficult to see Jewish law, which is saturated with religious thought, serving as a model for a secular society. At least, this is food for thought.

Further Reading

THE NATURE OF JEWISH LAW

Broyde, M. "The Procedures of Jewish Law As the Path to Good-ness and God-ness: Halakhah in the Jewish Tradition," 60 *Jurist: Studies in Church Law and Ministry* 25 (2000).

Elon, M. "The Legal System of Jewish Law," 17 *New York University Journal of International Law and Politics* 221 (1985).

Jackson, B. S. "Jewish Approaches to Law (Religious and Secular)," 164 *Law & Justice: The Christian Law Review* 63 (2010).

---

[12] Another important aspect of methodology can only be briefly alluded to: the tension between internal and external viewpoints. Patrick Glenn has a chapter on Jewish law in his much-discussed *Legal Traditions of the World*. Bernard Jackson addressed this in his "Internal and External Comparisons of Religious Law: Reflections from Jewish Law," in N. H. D. Foster, ed., *A Fresh Start for Comparative Legal Studies? A Collective Review of Patrick Glenn's Legal Traditions of the World*, 2nd edn., Wildy, Simmons and Hill, 2005 = *Journal of Comparative Law* 1.1 (2006), 177–199. The volume also includes Glenn's responses to the various contributions.

Last Stone, S. "Law without Nation? The Ongoing Jewish Discussion," in A. Sarat, L. Douglas, and M. Umphrey (eds.), *Law without Nations*, Stanford Law Books, 2010, p. 101.

Mittelman, A. "Judaism: Covenant, Pluralism and Piety," in B. S. Turner (ed.), *The New Blackwell Companion to the Sociology of Religion*, Wiley-Blackwell, 2010, p. 340.

Saiman, C. N. *Halakhah: The Rabbinic Idea of Law*, Princeton University Press, 2018.

Yuter, A. "Is *Halakhah* Really Law?" 8 *Jewish Law Annual* 35 (1989).

THE SCIENTIFIC STUDY OF JEWISH LAW: FROM THE *WISSENSCHAFT DES JUDENTUMS* TO THE MODERN AMERICAN LAW SCHOOL

Jackson, B. "Modern Research in Jewish Law," *Jewish Law Annual*, Supplement One. Brill, 1980, vii, 157, pp. Fl. 56.

Levine, S. J. "Teaching Jewish Law in American Law Schools: An Emerging Development in Law and Religion," 26 *Fordham Urban Law Journal* 1041 (1998).

Meyer, M. A. "Jewish Religious Reform and *Wissenschaft des Judentums*: The Positions of Zunz, Geiger and Frankel," 16.1 *Leo Baeck Institute Year Book* 19 (1971).

Shilo, S. "The Contrast between *Mishpat Ivri* and Halakah," 20.2 *Tradition: A Journal of Orthodox Jewish Thought* 9 (1982).

THE NOAHIDE LAWS AND NATURAL LAW

Enker, A. N. "Aspects of Interactions between the Torah Law, the King's Law, and the Noahide Law in Jewish Criminal Law," 12 *Cardozo Law Review* 1137 (1990).

Novak, D. *The Image of the Non-Jew in Judaism: The Idea of Noahide Law*, Littman Library of Jewish Civilization, 2011.

JEWISH LAW AND ZIONISM

Last Stone, S. "Law in Light of Zionism: A Comparative View," 19 *Israel Studies* 111 (2014).

Likhovski, A. "The Time Has Not Yet Come to Repair the World in the Kingdom of God: Israeli Lawyers and the Failed Jewish Legal Revolution of 1948," in A. Mermelstein, V. S. Woeste, E. Zadoff and M. Galanter (eds.), *Jews and the Law*, Quid Pro Books, 2014, p. 359.

ISRAELI LAW AND THE INTERACTIONS BETWEEN ISRAELI LAW AND JEWISH LAW

Lifshitz, B. "Israeli Law and Jewish Law: Interaction and Independence," 24 *Israel Law Review* 507 (1990).

Likhovski, A. "The Invention of 'Hebrew Law' in Mandatory Palestine," 46 *American Journal of Comparative Law* 339 (1998).

Sinclair, D. "Halakhah in Israel," in N. de Lange and M. Freud-Kandel (eds.), *Modern Judaism: An Oxford Guide*, Oxford University Press, 2005, p. 353.

Rivlin, E. "Israel As a Mixed Jurisdiction," 57 *McGill Law Journal* 781 (2012).

Shetreet, S. and Homolka, W. *Jewish Law and Israeli Law*, De Gruyter, 2017.

JEWISH LAW AND AMERICAN LAW

Auerbach, C. "The Talmud: A Gateway to the Common Law," 3 *Case Western Reserve Law Review* 5 (1951).

Ashburn, D. G. "Appealing to a Higher Authority: Jewish Law in American Judicial Opinions," 71 *University of Detroit Mercy Law Review* 295 (1993).

Broyde, M. J. "Informing on Others for Violating American Law: A Jewish Law View," 43 *Journal of Halacha and Contemporary Society* 5, 26 (2002).

Cover, R. M. "Foreword: Nomos and Narrative," 97 *Harvard Law Review* 4 (1983).

Goldfeder, M. "Law, Religion, and Culture Intertwined: A Case Study in the Development of American Jewish Law," 4 *Faulkner Law Review* 445 (2013).

Levine, S. J., *Jewish Law and American Law: A Comparative Study*. 2 volumes. Touro College Press, 2018.

Meislin, B. J. *Jewish Law in American Tribunals*, Cambridge University Press, 1972.

Resnicoff, S. H. "Lying and Lawyering: Contrasting American and Jewish Law," 77 *Notre Dame Law Review* 937 (2001).

Stone, S. L. "In Pursuit of the Counter-Text: The Turn to the Jewish Legal Model in Contemporary American Legal Theory," 106 *Harvard Law Review* 813 (1993).

2

Jewish Law As a Religious Legal Order

This chapter seeks to offer a possible answer to two important questions of Jewish legal theory. Does *halachah* constitute a system (Section 1)? Can we describe this system as a "religious" system (Section 2)?

SECTION 1 *HALACHAH* AS A SYSTEM

A legal system (I) presupposes a teleology (II), a taxonomy (III), a methodology (IV) and concepts supported by a terminology (V).

I THE JURIDICITY OF *HALACHAH*

Does *halachah* belong to the category of law? This question, briefly mentioned in Chapter 1, is complex because the very idea of law is elusive. Let us begin with a famous controversy. Is the first of the Ten Commandments ("I am the Lord your God ... ") descriptive or normative? According to Maimonides (Moses ben Maimon, *Rambam*, Cordova, 1138-Fustat [old Cairo], 1204), this is a statement that is prescriptive in nature and that is the first of the 613 commandments in the nomenclature that this author establishes. Nahmanides (Moses ben Nahman, *Ramban*, Gerona, 1194-Acre [Akko], 1270) and Hasdai ben Judah Crescas (Barcelona, ca. 1340–1410 or 1411) consider such a "commandment" self-contradictory. Here we have the question of the source of any normative authority. If the capacity of a person or institution to issue a norm rests on the foundations of a norm, then the most convenient thing to do is to base that norm on another norm, and so on and so forth, ad infinitum. To avoid such a regression, the capacity for enacting a rule must rest on a *fundamental norm* of an axiomatic nature (such as "You must obey God"). The idea of an authority prescribing people to believe in its authority makes no sense because it is because people accept such an authority that one recognizes its power to enact laws.

In the Talmud, the obligation to obey the Torah is founded on a moral argument: the Jewish people accepted the Torah and that acceptance constitutes a binding commitment. This assertion reappears many times, but the most striking, best-known and most ambiguous image can be found in an aggadic (narrative and extralegal) passage in the Talmud (*BT, Shabbat,* 88a): "[It is written:] 'They stood at the foot of the mountain' (*Exod.* 19:17). Rabbi Adimi, son of Hama, the son of Hassa, says: 'This teaches us that God held the mountain above them like a tub and told them: "If you accept the Torah, you will benefit; if not, this place will also be your tomb."'" But this is followed immediately by: "Rav Acha bar Yakov said: 'This is a great refutation against the Torah.'" To meet this objection, in one of the commentaries that immediately follow this passage, we read: "Rava says: 'Nonetheless, they accepted the Torah once more in the time of King Ahasuerus.'" The image of the mountain being held upside down by God probably suggests that, in the face of the divine presence's majesty, free will is simply impossible because one feels a kind of reverential fear. In contrast with this allusion to a lack of consent, Rava cites the *Book of Esther,* where divine intervention is not manifest, but where it is written that the Jewish people accepted the Torah once again. Note that, according to these commentaries, the acceptance of an obligation is binding. One can see here a pre-Sinaitic law that falls under the category of natural law.

II THE TELEOLOGY OF THE COMMANDMENTS

The word *teleology* has at least two meanings: purpose and the study of this purpose.

This purpose is not easy to identify because law is generally apodictic, that is, does not express any justification of its substance (see, for example, the Law of the Twelve Tables for the Roman world and the French or German civil codes for the modern era).

Inversely, as demonstrated by David Weiss Halivni, the Jewish law tradition is justificatory.[1] Thus, in the Pentateuch, there is an abundance of "motive clauses,"[2] such as "for/because," "in order that," "lest," "in consequence," "thus." Sometimes the motive appears without having been introduced by

---

[1] David Weiss Halivni, *Midrash, Mishnah, and Gemara: The Jewish Predilection for Justified Law*, Harvard University Press, 1986.

[2] "Motive clauses" is the standard expression in biblical scholarship.

any particular expression. Deuteronomy alone contains more than 100 such motive clauses. For example, one reads there: "When you build a new house, you shall make a parapet for your roof, *so that* you do not bring bloodguilt on your house if anyone should fall from it" (*Deut.* 22:8). Or: "A woman must not put on man's apparel, nor shall a man wear woman's clothing; *for* whoever does these things is abhorrent to the Lord your God" (*Deut.* 22:5). Or in the Ten Commandments: "Honor your father and your mother, *that* you may long endure on the land that the Lord your God is assigning to you" (*Exod.* 20:12). An analysis of the different motive clauses that the Torah contains reveals that the justification can be more or less precise, or concrete, or spiritual or historical in nature (certain commandments are justified by the fact that God liberated the Israelites from bondage in Egypt). However, the justification presented by the divine legislator does not always permit us to discern the commandment's purpose. Thus, when the Torah declares, "You shall not sow your vineyard with a second kind of seed, else the crop – from the seed you have sown – and the yield of the vineyard may not be used" (*Deut.* 22:9), the intention behind this commandment is unclear, at least at first glance. The prohibitions against mixtures – cooking meat in milk (*Exod.* 23:19, 34:26; *Deut.* 14:21), sewing wool and linen in the same garment (*Lev.* 19:19; *Deut.* 22:11), for example – are tagged as "statutes" (*hukim*), that is, laws the reason for which is not easily discernible. A statute (*hok*) *par excellence* is probably the purifying ritual of the red heifer: the Midrash reports that even King Solomon, despite his wisdom, was unable to discover the ritual's ultimate purpose, although he had discovered the ultimate purpose of all the other commandments (*Midrash Rabba* on Ecclesiastes 7:23). Additionally, note that the Talmud suggests that knowledge of the reason for a commandment (*ta'am hamitzva*) might possibly undermine the effectiveness of the legal system (*BT San.*, 21b). However, on this point, as on many others, the Sages' opinions do not indicate the presence of any systematic attitude: rabbinic literature is full of symbolic or concrete explanations. Thus, the four species that must be shaken during the festival of Sukkoth represent four different types of individuals among the Jewish people who together constitute an organic unity; a husband must avoid all physical contact with his wife when she is menstruating, so that she can return to him as fresh as a bride on her wedding day (*BT Nid.*, 31b). Even today much of post-Talmudic literature is concerned with uncovering the reasons behind the Torah's commandments: depending on the author's philosophy, the explanation will be rationalist, kabbalistic,[3] etc.

---

[3] Kabbalah is a set of esoteric teachings.

Let us take another statute *par excellence*: sacrificial worship within the Temple in Jerusalem. In his *Guide for the Perplexed*,[4] Maimonides presents a revolutionary thesis: this sacrificial worship was nothing but a "ruse" or "detour" employed by God for uprooting the idolatry that was widespread at the time of the Exodus from Egypt: astrolatry,[5] animal sacrifices and incense offerings were common practices among pagans. Since it is impossible for human beings to change their practices or even their nature, God in His wisdom does not command the Israelites to abandon animal sacrifices. Instead of the sacrificial worship being directed toward idols, God redirects it toward Himself. The Temple, the altar and the sacrifices are exclusively reserved for God. Maimonides explains that, in order to channel all remnants of the idolatrous instinct, sacrificial worship abounds in details whose aim is to restrict the field of its application (only one place is possible, only one family can offer the sacrifices, etc.). Through this clever device, God reinforces monotheism without "scaring off" a people familiar with paganism. This theory was not universally accepted in the Jewish world. Nahmanides is strongly opposed to the idea that the sacrifices were nothing but an expedient that God thought up in order to enable the attainment of His principal goal. According to Nahmanides, certain phrases in the Torah clearly demonstrate that the sacrifices are endowed with an intrinsic spiritual value (see, for example, *Lev.* 1:9: "of pleasing odor to the Lord"). Moreover, argues Nahmanides, if sacrificial worship is solely intended to skillfully eradicate idolatry, it should have appeared after the birth of idolatry. However, this is not the case. Noah offers sacrifices when he emerges from the Ark after the Flood (*Gen.* 8:20). Finally, let us consider the symbolic theory that is outlined by Abraham Ibn Ezra (Tudela, Navarre, ca. 1092 – Calahorra, ca. 1167) and that one can also describe as legal because of the idea of representation on which it is based. Ibn Ezra argues that human actions consist of three factors – thought, speech and action. The Torah therefore commands us to place our hands on the head of the animal about to be sacrificed (an action that is a gesture symbolizing the transfer of the sin), and demands that we recognize our sins (an act of speech) as we see the combustion of the animal's internal organs, the seat of thought and instincts; finally, in offering our sacrifices, we acknowledge the fact that we ourselves deserve death.

---

[4] This cardinal book is a treatise of theology and philosophy: *The Guide for the Perplexed* by Moses Maimonides, translated from the original Arabic text by M. Friedlander, PhD, second edition, revised throughout, 1904. Another more recent translation exists by Shlomo Pines, University of Chicago Press, 2 volumes, 1974.
[5] "Worship of the heavenly bodies": www.merriam-webster.com/dictionary/astrolatry.

These approaches, which we can only outline here because of a lack of space, have given way to intellectual duels that are sometimes quite lively.[6] These jousts are, however, more like discussions that complement one another rather than actual conflicts.

So far we have considered the goal of individual commandments. The next step is to ask whether a common denominator can be discovered when Jewish law is viewed in its entirety. Opinions regarding this point vary widely. Consider the following aggadic passage from the Talmud: "Here is another tale about a Gentile who came to Shammai and asked him, 'You can convert me if you can teach me the entire Torah while I am standing on one foot.' Shammai angrily pushed him out of the door with the cubit-rod he held in his hand. The Gentile came to Hillel and asked him, 'Convert me.' Hillel said to him, 'What is hateful to you, do not do to your neighbor. This is the entire Torah; the rest is commentary. Now go and study'" (*BT Shabbat* 31a).

In Maimonides's view (*Guide* 3, 27), the Torah has two goals that complement one another: the soul's well-being and the body's well-being. Through the well-being of our soul, we can attain ultimate perfection in this world and in the next. The well-being of our body is a vehicle for the attainment of the well-being of our soul. To enable us to attain the well-being of our soul, the Law makes use of correct opinions; to enable us to attain the well-being of our body, it establishes norms for the proper conduct of society and the individual. In order to implement correct opinions, the Law promotes two kinds of belief: absolutely true beliefs, such as belief in God's existence and unity, and beliefs that are necessary for society's well-being, such as the belief that God becomes very angry with those who disobey him and that, for this reason, we must fear and respect Him and must take care not to disobey Him (ibid., 3, 28). At the same time, Maimonides repeatedly states that the Law's central goal is to eradicate idolatry. Since idolatry is linked to history, Maimonides's thought apparently considers the Law as a contingent system. However, according to Maimonides, idolatry has two aspects, historical (as elaborated earlier) and ideal: idolatry confuses the end with the means (that is, idolatrous worship is an end in itself) and treats the Law as an end in itself. Meditation on the system's teleology prevents one from succumbing to a particularly subtle form of idolatry – fundamentalism. This explains the cardinal importance of the obligation to study Torah. At the same time, the identification of the Law's

---

[6] Of great interest on this subject are also the thoughts of Rabbi Samson Raphael Hirsch (Germany, 1808–1888, founder of "neo-Orthodoxy"): I. Grunfeld, "Taamei Hamitzvoth in the Jewish Philosophy of Rabbi S. R. Hirsch," in *Rabbi Dr. Joseph Breuer Jubilee Volume*, Philipp Feldheim, Inc., 1962, pp. 95–113.

raison d'être is a necessary means for the demonstration of its divine character. If, Maimonides tells his reader, you find that a given law promotes your physical interests and reinforces your faith, you must conclude that this law emanates from God and that it is divine. However, Maimonides continues, you must still find out whether the person who proclaims that fact is a perfect individual to whom the law was revealed or is simply someone who is falsely boasting of having experienced such a revelation.

Other concepts of the Jewish legal system exist: for example, one that is associated with Judaism's esoteric tradition – Kabbalah.

What should be remembered is that there are a significant number of opinions regarding the goals of Jewish law (evidently no one would dispute the fact that the means are the commandments). However, everyone agrees that Jewish law has a coherent, complex goal, although there is no consensus as to its nature.

III THE TAXONOMY OF THE COMMANDMENTS

There are several modes of classification of the commandments. One consists of distinguishing between the commandments that apply to our relations with others and those that apply to our relationship with God. Another mode distinguishes between, on one hand, matters of permission and prohibitions and, on the other, monetary laws. This mode of distinction permits us to consider various aspects of Jewish law, as can be seen in Section III.A. A distinction between commandments of biblical origin and those of rabbinic origin is also a fruitful approach in terms of its implications (Section III.B).

A *The Distinction between Matters of Permission and Prohibition* (Issur Veheter) *and Monetary Laws* (Dinei Mamonot)

1 The Distinction

Monetary laws essentially include contractual obligations (loans, etc.) and tort law (specifically, physical harm). The category of matters of permission and prohibition includes those applying to the sacrifices offered in the Temple in Jerusalem, agricultural laws (specifically, those relating to the Land of Israel), dietary laws (*kasherut*) and the laws concerning purity within the family unit. This distinction first acquired importance in the Tannaitic era (the era of the Tannaim). In its singular form, the word *tanna* means "one who repeats." In the broad sense of the word, these are the Sages whose opinions are recorded in the Mishnah; in the restricted sense of the word, these are the Sages who compiled the Mishnah. The Tannaitic era extends from the beginning of the Common Era to approximately 190 CE, when the Mishnah's compilation was finalized by the academy of Judah the Prince (Yehuda Hanassi).

2 The Implications of This Distinction

LIBERTY OF CONTRACT The first implication of this distinction relates to the right for individuals to enter into contracts on terms of their own choosing. In Jewish law, one can note here an evolution of the concept of freedom of will. Originally, it was impossible to make any stipulation that was contrary to the Torah's prescriptions – whether regarding monetary or religious issues. Considering this point, the Mishnah in *Tractate Bava Batra* (8:5) states: "If one asserts, 'My eldest son will not receive a double portion of my estate' or 'My son will not inherit, unlike his brothers, any portion of my estate,' such an assertion is meaningless (literally, he has said nothing) because it is a stipulation that has been made contrary to what is commanded in the Torah." The phrase "such an assertion is meaningless" signifies that such a stipulation is invalid because it is contrary to biblical law. From the fourth generation of the Tannaim onward, certain Sages formalized the distinction between monetary and religious laws, recognizing, for example, that a husband can renounce his usufruct with regard to his wife's property although he can inherit her estate after her death (*M Ketubbot* 9:1). The *Tosefta*[7] establishes a rule that obtains formal recognition: "If he says to her, 'I will marry you on condition that, if I die, you will not be eligible for a levirate marriage,' the marriage is valid, although the condition is null and void because the husband has made a stipulation that is contrary to a law established by the Torah. If he says, 'I will marry you on condition that you cannot make any claims on me regarding food, clothing and conjugal rights,' the marriage is valid and so is the condition. The principle here is the following: It is possible to act contrary to a rule in the Torah that concerns a monetary issue but it is impossible to do so if the rule concerns a non-monetary issue" (*Tosefta Kid.* 3:7–8). Levirate marriages (*Deut.* 25:5–6), where a brother-in-law is compelled to marry the wife of his dead brother if the couple had no male offspring, have a spiritual dimension that is expressed by the Torah: "The first son that she bears shall be accounted to the dead brother, that his name may not be blotted out in Israel" (*Deut.* 25:6). For that reason, the brother-in-law cannot *a priori* act contrary to this law (though the Bible there provides a ritual of release, which has come to

---

[7] This commentary, whose title means "addition," consists of the teachings of the Tannaim that were not formally included in the Mishnah.

be recommended by some Jewish communities). The provision of food and clothing to one's wife is also an obligation prescribed by the Bible (*Exod.* 21:10); however, this obligation is essentially pecuniary in nature and that is why the husband can free himself from it by means of a contract.

RABBINIC LEGISLATION The distinction between commandments relating to monetary issues and those relating to nonmonetary issues has ramifications with regard to commandments of a rabbinic origin or those issued by autonomous Jewish institutions (councils or rabbinic courts of law, according to the particular epoch; see Chapter 3). Thus, whereas competent rabbinic authorities recognize that their powers are limited with regard to the issuing of commandments in the religious (that is, nonmonetary) domain, their powers have never been limited with regard to the monetary domain. Similarly, when Jewish communities had autonomous administrative powers at their disposal, their legislative powers were applied only with regard to the civil, criminal or administrative domains but never extended to the religious domain.

SOME SYSTEMIC PRINCIPLES The distinction between monetary and religious (matters of permission and prohibition) domains is expressed in various systemic principles related to the development of *halachah*.

The most important of these principles concerns the prohibition to reason by analogy between these two domains.[8] This rule was formally established in the early years of the Amoraic era (or the era of the Amoraim).[9] When Rabbah wants to use an analogy in order to apply a rule concerning the acts of a rabbinic court to an act of divorce (*get*), Rabbi Amram asks: "How did you, my Master, manage to solve a question relative to a proscription by referring to a rule concerning monetary issues?" (*BT BM* 20b). In effect, the fact that, in monetary matters, the Mishnah permits the return of a document that was lost cannot serve as a reference for the restoration of a document concerning a prohibition, because the Torah's proscriptive laws are in general subject to strict rules, especially with regard to marriage and divorce. The use of analogical reasoning is also forbidden in another sense, as illustrated by a passage from the Talmud that discusses a father's rights regarding his daughter's incomes. According to *halachah*, a father can annul his daughter's vows as long as she has the status of a *na'ara*, that is, before she reaches the age of

---

[8] For an introduction to the use of analogy in Jewish Law, see Bernard S. Jackson, "On the Nature of Analogical Argument in Early Jewish Law," 11 *Jewish Law Annual* 137 (1994).

[9] This generic term in its singular form *amora* refers to Masters of the Talmud who were active between the time of the conclusion of the Mishnah's compilation and the compilation of the Babylonian and Jerusalem Talmuds.

twelve years, six months and one day. Concerning the question whether a father is also entitled to his daughter's incomes as long as she is a *na'ara*, the Talmud examines an entire series of arguments, including an analogy drawn between this issue and a father's right to annul his daughter's vows. The Talmud rejects this analogy-based argument: "The laws concerning monetary affairs cannot be deduced from the laws concerning ritual proscriptions!" (*BT Kid.*, 3b). The discussion that follows teaches another forbidden analogy: "The laws concerning monetary affairs cannot be deduced from the laws concerning fines." Here any analogy is impossible because, in general, the laws concerning monetary affairs relate to the payment of contractual benefits or to reparations for material damages. On the other hand, the laws concerning fines or penalties – *knas* (singular form), *knassot* (plural form) in Hebrew – deal with payments that lack any connection to the damage caused and that might well exceed the amount of that damage.[10] An in-depth study of Talmudic sources shows, however, that the prohibition on extrapolating from the monetary to the religious domain, and vice versa, is not absolute.

This distinction plays a role with regard to various principles that permit the resolution of conflicts of opinion among the Sages. According to a rule expressed in Aramaic, "*halachah* conforms to Rav's opinions in the religious domain and conforms to Samuel's opinions in the monetary domain" ("*Hilcheta ke-Rav b'issurei ve-che-Shmuel b'dinei*"; *BT Nid.* 24b, *BT Bechorot* 49a–b). Rav was a Babylonian Sage (175–247 CE) and was the first and the greatest *amora*; Samuel bar Abba, better known simply as Samuel (Shmuel), was a Babylonian Sage (ca. 165–257 CE) and a member of the first generation of *amoraim* and is considered one of the greatest *amoraim* of that generation.

Finally, this distinction plays an important role in the resolution of a question in the case of doubt. In the monetary domain, the rule is that any doubt is resolved in a lenient manner, in accordance with the principle that the burden of proof lies with the party that seeks to extract money from the other party. The doubt is resolved in a lenient manner for the defendant if the plaintiff is unable to produce proof for the monetary demand being made. This principle is described as a "major rule in law" by the Sages (*BT BK*, 46a). On the other hand, in religious matters, there is no defendant and this general principle regarding the burden of proof becomes irrelevant. The only pertinent principle here is that, when there is doubt regarding a matter of law that is of biblical origin, the question is resolved without any leniency, but when

---

[10] Fines in Jewish law present many analogies with punitive damages. See Elliot Klaymann and Seth Klaymann, "Punitive Damages: Towards a Torah-Based Tort Reform," 23 *Cardozo Law Review* 221 (2001–2002).

there is doubt regarding a matter of law that is of rabbinic origin, the question is resolved in a lenient manner. This leads us to the distinction presented in what follows.

B Commandments of Biblical Origin and Commandments of Rabbinic Origin

1 The Distinction

The distinction between commandments of biblical origin (*d'oraita*) and those of rabbinic origin (*d'rabbanan*) is of major importance. The determination of the criteria for this distinction gave rise to a celebrated dispute between Maimonides and Nahmanides. Before we consider this dispute, let us begin by listing four major elements. First, this distinction is a postulate of the Jewish legal system. Second, the system itself provides neither any precise definition nor any criteria for determining how to apply the taxonomy. Third, there is no defined number of commandments that should be defined as of biblical origin; the number 613, which is referred to in the Talmud, is not considered by the Sages to have any normative authority. Finally, a difference of opinion regarding which category a given commandment belongs to has important halachic consequences, that is, important consequences in terms of Jewish law.

What precisely is this distinction? At first glance, the definition of a commandment of biblical origin would seem a rather simple task: any commandment that comes directly from the Torah. The corollary of that axiom would be that any commandment that cannot be shown to have come directly from the Torah should be of rabbinic order. However, it is well known that the Sages regularly employ familiar hermeneutic principles to interpret the Torah's words (see Chapter 5). Should the norms generated on the basis of these principles be considered as belonging to the biblical or the rabbinic category? A few examples should suffice to demonstrate the importance of this question. The verse from which the daily obligation to lay phylacteries (*Deut.* 6:8: "And thou shalt bind them [the words of the commandments] for a sign upon thy hand, and they shall be for frontlets between thine eyes") neither mentions them specifically nor describes them. Is this obligation therefore of biblical or rabbinic origin? Again, the Book of Exodus (21, 23–25) appears to sanction proportional revenge ("an eye for an eye"); however, the Sages interpreted this revenge as an obligation to provide reparation in the form of compensatory damages in cases of physical harm (*BT BK*, 83b). Are such reparations therefore classified as a biblical or a rabbinic statute? Third, the Torah allows an individual to be punished with forty lashes; however, most of the Sages consider the maximal number that can be administered to be thirty-nine (*BT Mak.*, 22a). Is this form of punishment of biblical or rabbinic origin?

According to Maimonides, a commandment can be defined as being of biblical origin only if (1) it is explicitly mentioned in the Torah (such as, for example, observance of the Sabbath), or (2) it has been derived by means of an exegetical rule and is described as being a commandment of biblical origin by the Sages themselves, who are the transmitters of tradition. All other norms are of rabbinic origin. Nahmanides vigorously challenges Maimonides's position, demonstrating that Maimonides himself does not apply the criteria that he himself has advocated and citing Talmudic sources that contradict him. In contrast, Nahmanides claims that every norm that the Sages of the Talmud deduce with the use of hermeneutic principles is biblical in nature, unless the Sages state that the biblical source is an *asmachta* (which literally means "support"). The Sages of the Talmud sometimes explicitly affirm that the verse cited to support a law alludes to it without constituting the source of that law. Laws in this category are not deduced from a verse but are attached to it by mnemonic means. These laws are thus rabbinic decrees.

2 Consequences of the Distinction

The essential consequence is to treat questions regarding rabbinic origin more leniently than questions regarding biblical origin. This principle breaks down into several sub-principles.

– In case of doubt that concerns an unresolved point and that is a necessary factor in determining *halachah*, one will apply the following systemic principle: *Kol sefeka d'oraita l'chumera, kol sefeka de rabbanan l'kula.*[11] If, for example, I am not sure whether I recited the blessing required before the consumption of a glass of water, I must recite it (or repeat it, if in fact I did recite it in the first place) if the reciting of this blessing is a biblical commandment, and I must avoid reciting it if the reciting of this blessing is a rabbinic commandment. In this particular case, since the reciting of this blessing is a rabbinic commandment, I am excused from reciting it if I am in doubt.

– The loss of a significant amount of money is a motif that is treated leniently in a matter involving a rabbinic commandment but not in a matter involving

---

[11] More or less literally: "If doubt arises on a matter related to a biblical commandment, one must decide on this matter without any leniency. If, however, doubt arises on a matter related to a rabbinic commandment, one must decide on this matter in a lenient manner."

a biblical commandment. The Talmud presents the example of a gutter that is blocked by twigs and that therefore overflows, causing significant damage to the roof of a house. According to the Sages, I could free the gutter's obstruction by pressing my foot on the twigs and by therefore freeing the flow of water in the gutter without violating the Sabbath. Although this kind of action is prohibited in principle on the Sabbath, the prohibition is a rabbinic commandment whose observance one can avoid if the financial loss incurred by the blocked gutter would be significant (*BT Ket.*, 60a).

– The dignity to which every human being is entitled permits leniency in the observance of a rabbinic commandment, but not in the observance of a biblical commandment. The Torah explicitly forbids the wearing of a garment that consists of both woolen and linen threads (*Deut.* 22:11). This is thus a biblical prohibition. According to the Talmud, if I discover that the garment I am wearing is such a prohibited piece of attire, I must remove it immediately, even if I am in a public place, such as a marketplace. In discussing the foundations of this solution, the Talmud cites the following verse: "No wisdom, no prudence, and no counsel can prevail against the Lord" (*Prov.* 31:30). Again, the Torah commands the addition of threads woven in a certain manner to the four corners of a square garment. If I wear such a garment and one of these threads has been damaged to such an extent that the thread no longer conforms to the commandment, it can be considered as if I am "carrying" the other threads and such an action is one of the thirty-nine categories of work prohibited on the Sabbath. Nonetheless, I would not be obligated to remove this garment and I would be able to continue to wear it from a *carmelit* until I reach my home.[12] Since the prohibition on carrying something into a *carmelit* or from a *carmelit* in the direction of a private domain is rabbinic in nature, my dignity as a human being takes precedence over the prohibition of carrying on the Sabbath (*BT Men*, 37b–38a).

– While the Torah demands that pupils must show the utmost respect and deference to their teacher, the parameters of this obligation can vary because of the distinction being considered here. If I am a student and I hear my teacher permitting an act that I know is forbidden and if I can prove that this act is forbidden, I am not obligated to object to my teacher's decision nor am I obligated to ask my teacher about it, as long as the act has not yet been fully performed if the prohibition is rabbinic in

---

[12] A *carmelit* is a type of domain that is not a public domain as prescribed in the Bible but is of rabbinic origin and has been integrated with a public domain in connection with norms related to the prohibition of carrying on the Sabbath.

nature. On the other hand, if the prohibition is biblical in nature, I must intervene before the proscriptive commandment is violated (*BT Er.*, 67b).

IV LEGISLATIVE DRAFTING (LEGISTICS)

The legislative methodology of the "Supreme Regulator" is explained by Maimonides (*Guide*, Part III, Chapter XXXIV): what we must know is that the Law shows no consideration for that which is exceptional. Legislation does not exist for actions that occur rarely. That is, since it seeks to inculcate us with ideas, morals and useful actions, it focuses only on the most frequent cases, without showing regard for actions performed only rarely. Nor does legislation show regard for the potential damage to a single human being from such an arrangement and from such a legal regime. In order to clarify his position, Maimonides explains that, since the Law has a divine nature, one might think that it must provide benefits for humanity viewed in its entirety and for individuals viewed in their singularity. However, if one thinks about nature and its laws, which are also of divine origin, one finds that they contain general advantages, which, however, can cause damage to other individuals. For example, in the natural order, rain is beneficial to humanity because it permits an abundant harvest; however, it can also cause immense damage. Similarly, while the punishment of criminals is necessary in a society, there may be instances where innocent people are punished because of someone's false testimony. It therefore follows, continues Maimonides, that law cannot adapt exactly to all the various circumstances of individuals and of different eras. Quite the contrary, a legal system must be absolute and must embrace all humanity. If it conforms only to individuals, humanity will suffer and "you would be performing an action that is relative in nature." The phrase "you would be performing an action that is relative in nature" is a Talmudic phrase that signifies that if legal arrangements are interpreted in a manner, such would become something that would vary according to the individual and the circumstances; this is a result that the Talmud finds repugnant in principle (*BT Shabbat* 35b; *Hullin* 9a).

According to Maimonides, rabbinic laws must be transparent: rabbinic legislators must clarify that the status of the rules they enact is rabbinic, not biblical. This idea, which is included in the debate over the immutability of the Law, is congruent with the goal that Maimonides pursues as a codifier, namely, the preservation of the Law's formal characteristics. Justifiably, the classification of a law as biblical or rabbinic is one of the most important formal characteristics of *halachah*. This principle of rabbinic legislative drafting is democratic in the sense that legislators must clarify what they are doing and must not manipulate norms in order to endow them with a status that is greater than what their actual status is. With regard to this principle, Maimonides received the assent of many rabbinic masters of the Law (see also Chapter 4).

V CONCEPTS AND TERMINOLOGY

In the Talmud and in post-Talmudic literature (dozens of treatises on Jewish law appear each year), the accounts of debates and solutions base themselves on a precise vocabulary essentially forged by the Sages of the Talmud. However, in the Talmud, which is quintessentially casuistic, the Sages, when they conduct an in-depth discussion of a law and in order to reduce paradoxes, create analogies, etc., hardly offer a definition in the Aristotelian sense of the term, but instead offer criteria of identification, because systemization is foreign to Talmudic thought.

SECTION 2 A RELIGIOUS LEGAL SYSTEM

I A FOURTH FAMILY?

A A *Fluid Family*

Even if the pertinence of the exercise is often denied, it is still common today to classify the laws of the world as "families" or "circles."[13] Is there a family of "religious law"? If so, what are its criteria? This question appears superfluous: everyone knows – or rather intuitively senses – that Jewish law is religious law, which is what one can also say about Islamic law or canon law. Inversely, no one would doubt the fact that Roman law, French law or American law must be considered secular law. Although the notion of religious law is employed in this or that fashion, few take the trouble to define it. If the term *religious* is meant to indicate, as some people think, that which is founded on the divine revelation that took place on Mount Sinai through Moses's intervention, it is uncertain whether Jewish law is entirely religious. In effect, it is traversed by a *summa divisio*, which has already been referred to: *d'oraita* and *d'rabbanan*, namely, among the sources of this law, there is, on one hand, the law that emanates from the written or oral Torah (*d'oraita*) and that has been revealed, and, on the other hand, that which has been decreed by rabbis, that is, creatures of flesh and blood, and not by God.[14] Moreover, Jewish law recognizes the fact that the secular laws can acquire the same value as itself once they ascend to the rank of custom. It also recognizes, in certain conflicts, the superiority of secular over Jewish law, in accordance with the Talmudic maxim, "the law of the state is the law" ("*dina d'malchuta dina*") (see Chapter 6). The religious character of a law is therefore relative. However, its "nonreligious" character is also relative. French law, a paragon of secular law, replicates almost verbatim, in Article 371 of the French Civil Code,[15] the fifth of the Ten Commandments – not to mention the various prerogatives of the President of the Republic, inherited from the kings of France, who were monarchs by divine right.

---

[13] As we saw before, these three families are civil law, common law and mixed jurisdictions.
[14] See supra Section 1.
[15] "A child, at any age, owes honor and respect to his father and mother" (David Gruning, Alain R. Levasseur, John Randy Trahan and Estelle Roy, *Traduction du code civil français en anglais version biligue*. Traduction du code civil français, dans sa version en vigueur le 1er juillet 2013, en anglais, ve. 2015), https://halshs.archives-ouvertes.fr/halshs-01385107/document.

B An Ideological Family

Before we discuss criteria, we need to understand what the term *religious law* suggests. At the very least, the affirmation that a given legal system is of a religious nature indicates that it is part of a certain religion or that it was created within the framework of a certain religion. However, such an affirmation provides no information as to the nature of the system, just as the term *Italian law* indicates nothing more than the fact that this law is practiced in Italy. In contrast, the term *religious law* provides more precise information: it suggests that this category of law differs significantly from Western legal systems, such as the Romano-Germanic legal systems or the common law tradition. Moreover, there is generally an ideological base to the statement that a given legal system can be defined as "religious law." On one hand, such a statement underlines the image of this legal system as a relic of the past that is unsuited for our postmodern world. On the other hand, it expresses the superiority of this legal system as a system of religious law, which is transcendent, immutable, a product of the Divine Word and which happily is not subject to worldly contingencies.

Whether this label is polemical in nature or not, the notion of a system of religious law is commonly regarded as given rather than one that calls for an explanation. However, the notion of religious law is not a given of nature but is rather a product of the human intellect. One cannot explain the notion of religious law by drawing a comparison with a paradigm such as, for example, canon law because no law is evidently religious. The designation is the product of an intellectual operation of taxonomization. A number of propositions emerge from this.

First of all, the "religious" character of a legal system is relative. The notion of religious law involves regrouping elements none of which is necessary or sufficient for characterizing a legal system as a religious legal system and each of which can have a different "weight." At one of the two extremes of the continuum is religious law "in its pure state," that is one that presents all of the traits of religious law; at the other extreme is nonreligious or secular law "in its pure state," that is, one that presents none of these elements. No legal system in the world can be positioned on either of these two poles. In contrast, all of the world's legal systems are situated somewhere between these two extremes and are either more religious or less religious.

Second, a legal system generally uses certain tools for promoting a *Weltanschauung*. The adopted laws reflect or promote a certain worldview. Similarly, a society that supports a religious ideology will have laws regarding the rites that must be performed. However, in order to promote an ideology, a legal system will not only bring into play *laws* but will also forge *tools* and specific *mechanisms* for bringing into play those laws: for example, specific procedures for legislation, interpretation of the laws or the acquisition of the power to judge. Undoubtedly, Talmudic ideology is religious because the Sages of the Talmud place God in the very center of their preoccupation and their thought. However, did they have to develop unique instruments in order to promote such an ideology? This is what we try to discover.

II SOME PARAMETERS OF A RELIGIOUS LEGAL SYSTEM

In order to determine whether a given system is religious or not, three parameters must be considered: the sources of the system, the domain covered by the rules of this system and the *modus operandi* of the system.

A *The Sources of the System*

For Jacques Vanderlinden, this is the sole parameter that really matters. This criterion offers considerable certitude: when a system claims to be of divine origin, it can be considered to have a religious character. Rabbinic literature consistently and unambiguously conveys the message that *halachah*'s origins are divine.[16] Let us recall here the maximalist thesis notably represented by Maimonides: God taught Moses everything – not just the statutes but also their interpretation. A rabbinic commentary on this subject (*Sifra* on *Lev.* 25:1) states: "It is written 'The Lord spoke to Moses on Mount Sinai.' What does the precision used here in this verse – namely, the location, 'on Mount Sinai' – signify?" However, this precision teaches us that, just as God taught Moses the commandment concerning *shmita* (i.e., the Sabbatical year: the obligation to let the land lie fallow every seven years) together with all the laws and details associated with that commandment, similarly He taught Moses on Mount Sinai all of the other commandments together with the various laws and details associated with those commandments. This interpretation leads Maimonides to write that everything that has been deduced with the help of one of the thirteen rules of interpretation[17] was transmitted directly by Moses, our master and teacher, at Sinai (*Preface to the Mishnah*). However, even if

---

[16] See the cardinal contribution of Christine Hayes, *What's Divine about Divine Law? Early Perspectives*, Princeton University Press, 2017.

[17] These rules are exposed in Chapter 5.

one adheres to this maximalist thesis, it does not necessarily follow that the entirety of Jewish law is of divine origin.

Actually, the Written Torah (Written Law) and Oral Torah (Oral Law) are not the sole sources of Jewish law. The Sanhedrin, which was a legislative, executive and judiciary body, enacted obligatory laws. After it vanished in 70 CE, its role in the enactment of decrees or ordinances was taken up by the rabbinic elite and local Jewish communities (see Chapter 3). Jewish law even recognizes that certain elements in the laws of the nations can attain the rank of Jewish law after they have become accepted customs in the Jewish community, as, for example, in commercial law. Furthermore, there is nothing divine in custom, which, by definition, is the product of human interaction. One sees here another illustration of the relative nature of the religious character of what is termed "religious law."

Finally, in certain cases, Jewish law recognizes the preeminence of the laws of a given nation over its own – in keeping with the Talmudic maxim "the law of the state is law" ("*dina d'malchuta dina*") (see Chapter 6).

Another factor that gives *halachah* a resolutely religious color is the place that the esoteric tradition in Judaism, Kabbalah, occupies in *halachah*'s sources. First of all, this tradition gave rise to a significant number of pietistic and austere practices that ultimately acquired the rank of customs. Regarding the question as to whether the Zohar (a kind of kabbalistic Talmud that appeared in the thirteenth century) might be a direct source of Jewish law, opinions are divided. Joseph Karo (Toledo, 1488 – Safed, 1575), author of the *Shulchan Aruch*, the central codification of Jewish law, is of the opinion that the Zohar is more authoritative than the rulings of any rabbinic authority. This position is not unanimously supported; in fact, Jacob Emden, a major eighteenth-century rabbinic authority (Altona, 1697–1776), and Moses Sofer (Frankfurt am Main, 1762 – Presburg, 1862), who tirelessly fought against Reform Judaism, express doubt as to the origins of the Zohar. These thinkers argue that only an infinitesimal part of this work was written by Rabbi Simeon bar Yochai (Galilean rabbi, late first century to early second century CE), who, according to tradition, recorded what was dictated to him by Elijah the Prophet, and the rest was probably the creation of Isaac Luria (Jerusalem, 1534 – Safed, 1572) and his disciples rather than a text "discovered" by Luria. The dispute over the Zohar's origins continues even today. Whereas the rabbinic authorities in Tunisia, Syria and Iraq regard Lurianic Kabbalah as a supremely authoritative source, a leading Ashkenazi rabbinic authority like Moshe Feinstein (Uzda, 1895 – New York, 1986) did not grant the Zohar any particular preponderance.

B The Domain Covered by Jewish Law

One would naturally expect that religious law would concern itself with "religion," a difficult-to-define term whose origin is the Latin word *religio* and whose etymology has been a controversial issue since ancient times.

Following the example of Lactantius and Tertullian, Christian authors are fond of linking the noun *religio* to the verb *religere* (to bind), from the prefix *re-* connoting intensity and the verb *ligare* (to tie). Thus, religion is perceived as having as its goal our relationship with God. Jewish law is, of course, concerned with religion: blessings, sacrifices, prayer, divine reward, divine punishment. However, it is concerned with more than just these subjects and covers all aspects of human life through prescriptive and proscriptive commandments related to dietary matters, clothing, language and sexual relations. Jewish law also includes laws pertaining to the family, bonds (such as bonds of debt), property, neighborly relations, work, commerce, penalties, fiscal and criminal matters, etc. Should we therefore deny that there is a religious character in the civil and criminal aspects of Jewish law? Perhaps, if we adopt an external point of view, that is, a point of view that emphasizes the doxic sense of the word *religion*. However, we must be aware of a certain trait of Western culture (the term *Western* is used here in the absence of any better one): it separates religion from the rest of social life. Although the idioms vary, such as in the Indo-European linguistic group, Western languages have created a special term to distinguish the system of beliefs and rites from all other social institutions. This division and this transfer correspond to the notion of distinct domains – a notion that was never contemplated in earlier epochs. Ancient societies never isolated the sacred from the social because their social formation was intrinsically religious in nature. In fact, the Torah does not designate itself as a "religion." Although the word exists in modern Hebrew (*dat* or *emuna*), the Torah (Pentateuch) refers to itself as the Torah, that is, an entity that teaches or instructs (the word *Torah* is derived from the Hebrew verb root *yod-resh-heh*, to teach). The term *law*, which is a common translation of the word *Torah*, follows the Greek translation *nomos* and conveys the false idea that the entire Torah is of a legal nature. However, the Torah is the source of *halachah*, which conveys the idea of constant movement (the word is derived from the Hebrew verb root *heh-lamed-chaf*, to walk), the notion of a path to follow, the concept of a normative compass where North is invariably God's will.

If we adopt an internal point of view regarding religion, then everything is religion, everything is Torah. Thus, when observant Jews sign a sales contract, employing the modes of acquisition prescribed by Jewish law, they have the sense that the signing of the contract is more than just an act in the business world and that it is also, and more importantly, an expression of obedience to God's will.

Another point illustrates the religious aspect of the point of view relating to the domain covered by religious law. Human legislators cannot govern that which is imperceptible to external observation, notably states of mind, an individual's conscience, etc. In contrast, a divine legislator – that is, God – can and takes a particular interest in such matters because *halachah* aims at the elevation of the soul. Let us take, for example, the tenth commandment: "You shall not covet your neighbor's house: you shall not covet your neighbor's wife, or his male or female slave, or his ox or his ass, or anything that is your neighbor's" (*Exod.* 20:14). Covetousness is a state of mind, nothing more. Although it is by no means unusual for "nonreligious" laws to take into account a state of mind, a distinction exists between the prohibition of an act accompanied by a certain mental disposition and the prohibition of a mental disposition that is not accompanied by any action. Civil law, but also common law, is familiar with the first category, no offense without intention; and there may be aggravations from motive: racism, etc. In contrast, the prohibition of an emotion that does not manifest itself in any external manner is one of the hallmarks of religious law. The Torah prohibits certain thoughts and, inversely, formulates positive commandments that pertain to the intellect or the heart.[18] Many authors draw up a list of these intellectual obligations. Maimonides presents thirteen principles of a theological nature – the "thirteen articles of faith" – and he argues that all Jews must believe them (a highly controversial point).[19] According to Maimonides, it is not necessary for a Jew to acquire any real knowledge of what these principles express. Here again, this is a matter of law, of *halachah*, because failure to believe in one or more of these principles has precise legal consequences in this world. For example, a Jew is prohibited from eating the flesh of an animal that has been ritually slaughtered (in accordance with all the laws pertaining to ritual slaughtering) if the slaughterer rejects these principles. Similarly, a Jew may not consume wine from a bottle opened by an individual who rejects these principles, cannot recite "Amen" to any

---

[18] Steven H. Resnicoff, "Jewish Law: Duties of the Intellect," 1 *University of St. Thomas Law Journal* 386 (2003).

[19] On this particular question, see Menachem Kellner, *Must a Jew Believe Anything ?*, 2nd edn., Littman Library of Jewish Civilization, 2006; Marc B. Shapiro, *The Limits of Orthodox Theology: Maimonide's Thirteen Principles Reappraised*, Littman Library of Jewish Civilization, 2004

blessing uttered by such an individual, etc. Among the obligations of the intellect, cardinal importance is attached to the study of the Torah.

Another characteristic of religious law is that it regulates everything, even things that do not or no longer exist. In *Halachic Man*,[20] Joseph B. Soloveitchik (Proujany, 1903 – Boston, 1993) writes that the inadequacy of many halachic notions in the face of the real world does not at all trouble the halachic individual. Although these notions might not have any practical application, the ideal construction received at Sinai is of eternal value. The author cites a passage from the Talmud (*BT San.* 71a) where the anonymous editor asks why the Torah teaches laws that have no practical application: "An apostate city never existed and will never exist. Why was this law promulgated? So that you will study it and benefit from that study! Similarly, a house stricken with leprosy never existed and will never exist. Why does the Torah mention it? So that you will study it and benefit from that study! A rebellious son never existed and will never exist. Why was this law enacted? So that you will study it and benefit from that study."

Secular law is unfamiliar with such an ideal approach and even rejects such an approach; instead, secular law essentially seeks to be concrete, contingent, adapted to social facts; the existence of laws without any practical application would be a flaw in the system, not a manifestation of its quality.

C The Modus Operandi *of the System*

1 General Orientations

What tools, *lato sensu*, are used by Jewish law to promote the ideology it supports? These tools should express an ideal that is not attained by force but that differentiates between religious and nonreligious law.

The proponents of positivism affirm that three deontic modalities are sufficient for all legal propositions: behavior is regarded by law as required, permissible or forbidden. Jewish law is not happy with this trichotomy: behavior can be recommended – but not required – or disapproved – but not forbidden. On the supererogatory side, we could cite the principle expressed in the phrase *lifnim mishurat hadin* ("beyond the letter of the law").[21] Let us illustrate this question by considering a practical example from the realm of labor law: is an employee entitled to severance pay?

---

[20] Jewish Publication Society, 1983.
[21] On this important principle, see James J. Diamond, "Talmudic Jurisprudence, Equity, and the Concept of Lifnim Meshurat Hadin," 17 *Osgood Hall Law Journal* 616 (1979). See also the bibliography at the end of this chapter.

An employee's right to receive severance pay when the contractual relationship with the employer is severed, whether the reason is the employee's dismissal or the nonrenewal of the employee's contract, is not directly referred to in the Torah or Talmud or in the vast majority of post-Talmudic sources. Only one rabbinic authority, Aharon of Barcelona (1235–1290), in his *Sefer ha-hinukh* (lit. *The Book of Education*), draws an analogy between such a situation and that of a Hebrew servant to whom the master must grant gifts when the latter reaches the end of the six-year period of servitude (*ha'anakah*) (*Deut.* 15:13–15). First he points out what he considers to be the legal reason behind this biblical obligation: "As we have seen with regard to other duties of solidarity, the rationale is to develop in us qualities of goodness and generosity. It is particularly honorable for the master of the house to show his concern for someone who has served him loyally by granting the latter a gift." After reviewing *halachah*'s approach to this question, the author concludes by considering the material and temporal application of these laws in the contemporary world: "Applicable for both men and women during the period of the Temple, the laws concerning Jewish servants were applicable only when the jubilee year was still being observed." Using an analogy, he concludes, "However, even today, a wise man knows how to draw a lesson from this commandment: When a Jew profits over a certain period of time from the services of another, who has been his employee and whose period of employment ends, he must give that person a sign of his gratitude, in accordance with the blessing that God has generously granted the employer." This opinion received a certain echo and the rabbinic authorities of subsequent generations have expressed the opinion that the granting of severance pay constitutes a moral obligation, even if not a legal one. Thus, a *beit din* cannot order someone to make that payment, unless such payment is a legal obligation in that particular place; in that case, the rabbinic court bases its ruling on professional or local customs. Moreover, the granting of severance pay can be validly stipulated in a contract. On the other hand, we can see a precedent for severance pay in the traditional granting of a bonus payment to a worker. In many passages in the Talmud, the Sages, citing passages from the Torah, urge us to exceed our purely legal obligations and to go "beyond the letter of the law." The requirement to exceed our legal obligations is based on a verse from the Torah (*Exod.* 18:20; *BT BM*, 30b). As one can read in the Talmudic passage cited earlier, "Jerusalem was destroyed because legal disputes were judged strictly according to the law of the Torah." The Talmud then asks: "Should legal disputes have been settled instead in accordance with the laws of the tyrannical regime under which they lived? No, what is meant here is that Jerusalem was destroyed because judicial decisions were made in strict accordance with the law of the Torah and no attempt was made to go beyond the letter of the law." In other words, it is an act of piety to show more generosity than what *halachah* requires, for example in the granting of severance pay even if the strict application of *halachah* does not require that payment. The payment can be spontaneous; however, according to many rabbinic authorities, a rabbinic court can compel a party to act "beyond the letter of the law." In such an instance, the rabbinic court must weigh all of the elements in that particular situation, an important element being the employee's loyalty.[22]

Other questions, which are discussed in this book, permit us to position the cursor more precisely: Is the immutability of law a characteristic of Jewish law? Is the judge infallible in this system? What place do God and miracles occupy in the legal and judicial process? Is Jewish law personal or territorial? In Jewish law does the law serve the cause of social peace, or does it also seek to promote moral perfection?

Are the judicial decisions in Jewish law motivated by and based on a body of laws? Are they predictable or can they be appealed? For the moment, we examine the following specific question: according to the Jewish tradition, are the judgments made divine or human?

2 In the Jewish Tradition, Are the Judgments Divine or Human?

The Torah provides a nuanced response to this question. However, if we observe the halachic system from a historical perspective, from the granting of the Torah at Sinai to the present day, we can note that Jewish law has undergone a subtle process of secularization: the cursor has been distanced from the "religious" pole.[23]

In the scriptural sources, God often appears as the supreme judge; this status is closely connected to his status as the supreme legislator. However, this jurisdictional activity is understood not only as an expression of power but also, and first and foremost, as an act of justice: "He will rule the world justly, and its peoples with equity" (*Psalms* 98:9). Nevertheless, the Pentateuch does not limit itself to the subject of divine justice: it postulates and even necessitates the existence of human justice that takes pains to settle interpersonal litigations within the

---

[22] See the interesting judgment (*psak din*) issued by the Beth Din of America (penned by Michael Broyde): *Teacher v. Elementary Yeshiva Day School*, July 30, 2002, *Tradition* 37.4 (2003), pp. 89–100 ("Severance Pay and Jewish Law").

[23] See Bernard Jackson, "Human Law and Divine Justice: Towards the Institutionalisation of Halakhah," 9 *JSIJ: Jewish Studies, an Internet Journal* 223 (2010), www.biu.ac.il/JS/JSIJ/jsij9 .html; see also articles cited in the bibliography, at the end of this chapter.

framework of courts of law and to carry out their judgments. Moses settles legal disputes within his own people even before God grants Israel the Torah at Sinai; thus, the following commandment is clear: "You shall appoint magistrates and officials for your tribes, in all the settlements that the Lord your God is giving you, and they shall govern the people with due justice" (*Deut.* 16:18).

We must now define what we understand by the terms *divine judgment* and *human judgment*. We understand divine judgment as meaning judgment that is the work of human beings but that claims to embody divine will. In this model, the judge is generally a priest or a prophet acting in the name of God. The procedures employed usually lack rationality, for example, the drawing of lots or trial by ordeal. Inversely, human judgment is a judiciary process brought into play by an individual who fulfills no particular religious function and who does not claim to be the instrument of divine will. The judge conducts the trial in a rational manner in accordance with preestablished procedural rules.

Let us now look at manifestations of divine judgment. First, a few words about the drawing of lots.[24] This procedure correctly reflects divine will as expressed in this happy verse from Proverbs: "Lots are cast into the lap; the decision depends on the Lord" (*Prov.* 16:33). In the biblical era, lots were drawn to settle cultural, political, military and judiciary matters.[25] In the judicial context, lots were drawn primarily to locate and identify a person who has committed certain transgressions. This technique is mentioned in the Torah as an institution associated with the priesthood. The instrument in question is called the *Urim* and *Tumim* (*Exod.* 28:30) and is part of the attire of the High Priest, although, in the Pentateuch, we do not find the *Urim* and *Tumim* being employed as an instrument of judgment *stricto sensu*. In any case, this somewhat mysterious system disappeared with the death of the early prophets during the First Temple period (*M Sotah* 9:12).

Trial by ordeal is an often brutal physical test whose goal is to determine the innocence or guilt of someone suspected of having committed a crime. It seems to have been widely used in the medieval period under the name *judicium dei* (judgment of God). Canon law is one of the main factors of the demise of the ordeal in the West.[26]

---

[24] For an introduction, see, e.g., Francis Schmidt, "Gôrâl versus Payîs: Casting Lots at Qumran and in the Rabbinic Tradition," in Florentino García Martínez and Mladen Popović (eds.), *Defining Identities: We, You, and the Other in the Dead Sea Scrolls*, Brill, 2007, pp. 175–186.

[25] See, e.g., Anne M. Kitz, "Undivided Inheritance and Lot Casting in the Book of Joshua," 119.4 *Journal of Biblical Literature* 601 (2000); David Werner Amram, "Chapters from the Biblical Law IX: The Trial of Achan by Lot." 12 *Green Bag* 659 (1900).

[26] Finbarr McAuley, "Canon Law and the End of the Ordeal," 26 *Oxford Journal of Legal Studies* 473 (2006).

The Torah recognizes this mode of divine judgment but in a very limited context. The best-known instance where the technique of trial by ordeal is used is the case of the *sotah*, a woman whose husband suspects her of having committed adultery (*Num.* 5:11–31). An entire tractate in the Talmud is devoted to this subject. The ceremony is conducted by a priest, who has the woman drink bitter water and has her swear that she is innocent. If she is guilty of adultery, she will be punished physically: "May the Lord make you a curse and an imprecation among your people, as the Lord causes your thigh to sag and your belly to distend; may this water that induces the spell enter your body, causing the belly to distend and the thigh to sag" (*Num.* 5:21–22). However, if she is telling the truth and is innocent, the verse informs us: "But if the woman has not defiled herself and is pure, she shall be unharmed and able to retain seed" (*Num.* 5:28). According to the Mishnah (*Sotah* 9:9), this trial by ordeal was abolished during the first century CE by Rabbi Yochanan ben Zakkai. Explanations vary as to the reason for the procedure's abolition. For example, Yochanan ben Zakkai states: "When the cases of adultery increased, the trial by ordeal with bitter water ceased to be employed because the procedure is used only in cases of doubt. However, today many married women meet their lovers in public." The Sages based themselves on certain biblical verses that suggested that the bitter water could not produce any effect if the husband himself was licentious. In any event, it was logical to abandon this practice because, according to *halachah*, this trial by ordeal could only be conducted in the Temple in Jerusalem, which was destroyed in 70 CE. From the historical standpoint, one can question whether this ritual was ever conducted. Some laws are intended to be symbolic, edifying, dissuading and serving as models for proper family conduct.[27] In any case, the drawing of lots and trial by ordeal gradually disappeared. This is what we mean when we refer to the secularization of biblical justice. But it goes far beyond this: judicial activity ceases to be charismatic and becomes purely rational.

This process of secularization, or, if one prefers, humanization, was part of the evolution that took place in the modalities of the administration of justice. This change can be seen clearly in Exodus (18:13–24), which shows a transition from a spontaneous system, in which Moses himself judges the people through an oracular procedure (cf. the word *karav*, "he draws near") from dawn to dusk, to an institutionalized system, administered by judges, where Moses

---

[27] For decades, the Sotah ritual has prompted an incessant flow of scholarship. The student may begin with Ishay Rosen-Zvi, *The Mishnaic Sotah Ritual: Temple, Gender and Midrash*, Brill, 2012; see also Emanuel Rackman, "The Case of the Sotah in Jewish Law: Ordeal or Psychodrama," 3 *National Jewish Law Review* 49 (1988).

deals only with the most difficult cases. Originally, as Moses relates to his father-in-law, Jethro, "the people come to me to inquire of (*lidrosh*) God. When they have a dispute, it comes before me, and I decide between one person and another, and I make known the laws and teachings of God" (*Exod.* 18:15–16). The Hebrew verb that is translated here as "inquire" and whose root is *dalet-resh-shin* signifies an appeal to God through a priest or prophet serving as an oracle. Moses is simply an intermediary between God and His people. Jethro, a Midianite priest who, according to the Rabbis, has just converted to the monotheistic faith of Judaism, criticizes his son-in-law and reproaches him for the inefficiency of this judicial system: "But Moses' father-in-law said to him, 'The thing you are doing is not right; you will surely wear yourself out, and these people as well. For the task is too heavy for you; you cannot do it alone'" (*Exod.* 18:17–18). Jethro exhorts Moses to install a system with judges who are not prophets but simply honest individuals chosen from among the people: "capable men who fear God, trustworthy men who spurn ill-gotten gain" (*Exod.* 18:21).

In Deuteronomy, one can note an additional step taken toward the "humanization" of judgment and its independence in relation to divine will. This process is depicted clearly in the chapter dealing with the appointment of the judges for the new system proposed by Jethro. The passage in Deuteronomy once again relates, with fewer details, the aforementioned episode described in Exodus and indicates how the more difficult cases are to be treated: "And any matter that is too difficult for you, you shall bring to me and I will hear it" (*Deut.* 1:17). We can note here that, contrary to what is depicted in Exodus, Moses unhesitatingly declares that he himself will handle himself the hard cases. The judgment of difficult cases is no longer a prophetic act but rather a "normal" judiciary procedure. However, this does not mean that the process of judgment has become a banal and secular act. The connection between human and divine judgment is maintained: "I charged your magistrates at that time as follows, 'Hear out your fellow men, and decide justly between any man and a fellow Israelite or a stranger. You shall not be partial in judgment: hear out low and high alike. Fear no man, for judgment is God's'" (*Deut.* 1:16–17). Insofar as Moses creates an autonomous system detached from prophecy, as we have noted, these words must be understood as a delegation of authority. The notion of ordination (see Chapter 4) fully illustrates the point that the judges are agents of God; this notion is what permits them to judge all matters in the domains of civil and criminal law. The ordained judges are called *elohim*, which is one of God's names (*Exod.* 21:6 and 22:7–8; MT, *Laws Governing the Sanhedrin*, 4:4). As agents, the judges carry out the mission that God has entrusted to them and are thus accountable to Him (*BT San.* 8a).

This is one interpretation of "for judgment is God's." Rashi (Troyes, 1040–1105) repeats a Talmudic commentary: "If you (the judge) take something from a litigant in an illicit manner (that is, through an unethical judgment), you will then require me to return it to that litigant; it will then emerge that you have acted contrary to my will in your perversion of the act of judging." The Talmud will generate an evolution in the act of representation in the judicial system with regard to God's presence in all human judgments. As we have seen, according to the Deuteronomic approach, God is the supreme judge, while human judges are his representatives. According to the Talmudic approach, the boundaries are fluid and the distance between the human judge and God is reduced: the judge is always a representative of God; moreover, God is seated beside the human judge and is the central participant in the judicial process. This mode of representation is not only theological or symbolic in nature; it has juridical consequences at the level of the judge's ethics and at the level of the litigant's ethics. Although there are many sources pertaining to this subject, here is a brief passage full of imagery, which centers around Rabbi Akiva: "When people presented themselves and wished to have Rabbi Akiva judge their case, he would say to them: 'Know before whom you now find yourselves – you are now before the One who, with his word, created the world, as it is stated in the verse, "And the two litigants will appear before the Lord." You appear before Him, not before Rabbi Akiva, son of Joseph.'" This message was intended not only to remind the litigants to be truthful but also to reinforce the authority of the rabbinic court of law during an epoch when political power passed into the hands of the Romans, who deprived the rabbinic judges of any possibility of forcibly imposing their verdicts. God's presence beside the human judge underlined the heavy burden weighing on their shoulders: the need for rigorous ethical conduct. Maimonides dedicates to this subject no fewer than five chapters (see *MT, Laws Governing the Sanhedrin*, 20–24).[28]

---

[28] On this topic, see also Haim Shapira, "'For the Judgment Is God's': Human Judgment and Divine Justice in the Hebrew Bible and in Jewish Tradition," 27.2 *Journal of Law and Religion* 273 (2012).

SECTION 3 A TRANSNATIONAL LEGAL ORDER

A transnational legal order is one that governs a society whose members are scattered, residing in different countries.[29] Such an order has a "planetary vocation" because it traverses national boundaries; however, it rules over only a part of the world's population. As examples, one can cite sports associations, multinational corporations and the Roman Catholic Church. Nevertheless, canon law is unique in that its field of operation is limited to the spiritual realm. What makes it a legal system is the presence of more clear-cut features: a centralized and hierarchical clergy and a code.

Halachah is also transnational. It is a personal status, applying to the Jewish people, wherever its members happen to reside – whether in the Land of Israel or in the Diaspora. Jews submit to its authority by birth (matrilineal system) or by choice (conversion). Note also that certain prominent features of canon law are less prominent in *halachah* and vice versa. If there ever was a central authority in Judaism (the Great Sanhedrin in Jerusalem), it no longer exists. *Halachah*'s authority is diffuse and its organization is complex (see Chapter 4). There is no longer any clergy, properly speaking; today, the rabbis are first and foremost the administrators and spiritual guides of their communities. Like canon law, *halachah* has courts of law at its disposal. However, their constitution is more subtle than that of their counterparts in the Catholic Church: by force of circumstance, a rabbinical court of law has more affinity with an arbitration court than with an actual court of law (see Chapter 6). As far as a code is concerned, Jewish law is familiar with several, each of which has a different level of authority (see Chapter 4). What essentially distinguishes canon law from *halachah* is its empire: whereas canon law is concerned with the internal regulation of the Church and the Church's relationship with its adherents, *halachah* is concerned not only with the three daily prayer services but also with the sale of furniture and other worldly questions (see supra). It would seem that, in view of its characteristics, Muslim law has a closer affinity with Jewish law. No matter their common features or differences, these systems of law have the following fact in common: they are transnational.

---

[29] For more on this vast topic, see Terrence C. Hallyday and Gregory Shaffer (eds.), *Transnational Legal Orders*, Cambridge University Press, 2015.

Further Reading

COMMANDMENTS (MITZVOT)

Friedberg, A. D. *Crafting the 613 Commandments: Maimonides on the Enumeration, Classification, and Formulation of the Scriptural Commandments*, Academic Studies Press, 2014.

Goldenberg, R. "Commandment and Consciousness in Talmudic Thought," 68 *Harvard Theological Review* 261 (1975).

Greenberg, S. "The Multiplication of the Mitzvot," in *Mordecai M. Kaplan Jubilee Volume, on the Occasion of His Seventieth* Birthday, Jewish Theological Seminary of America, 1953 (English Section), p. 381.

Rabinowitz, A. H. *TaRYaG: A Study of the Tradition That the Written Torah Contains 613 Mitzvot*, Jason Aronson, 1996.

THEOLOGY, PHILOSOPHY AND TELEOLOGY OF JEWISH LAW

Faur, J. "Understanding the Covenant," *Tradition: A Journal of Orthodox Thought*.

Heinemann, I. *The Reasons for the Commandments in Jewish Thought: From the Bible to the Renaissance*, Academic Studies Press, 2008.

Jackson, B. "Philosophy of Law (Secular and Religious)," in A. Diduck et al. (eds.), *Law in Society: Reflections on Children, Family Culture and Philosophy: Essays in Honour of Michael Freeman*, Brill/Nijhoff, 2015.

Kellner, M. *Must a Jew Believe Anything?* 2nd edn., Littmann Library of Jewish Civilization, 2006.

Maimonides, M. *The Guide of the Perplexed*. Translated with an introduction and notes by Shlomo Pines. 1963.

Weiss Halivni, D. *Midrash, Mishnah, and Gemara: The Jewish Predilection for Justified Law*, Harvard University Press, 1986.

HALACHAH AS A RELIGIOUS SYSTEM

Ben-Menahem, H. "Is Talmudic Law a Religious Legal System? A Provisional Analysis," 24 *Journal of Law & Religion* 379 (2008).

Finkelstein, L. "Judaism As a System of Symbols," in *Mordecai M. Kaplan Jubilee Volume, on the Occasion of His Seventieth Birthday*, Jewish Theological Seminary of America, 1953 (English Section), p. 225.

Jackson, B. S. "The Concept of Religious Law in Judaism," in *Aufstieg und Niedergang der römischen Welt*, W. de Gruyter, 1979, Vol. 2, 19.1, p. 33.

Jackson, B. S. "Judaism As a Religious Legal System," in A. Huxley (ed.), *Religion, Law and Tradition*, Routledge, 2002, p. 34.

Radzyner, A. "Talmudic Law As Religious Law: The Source of the Desire to Limit Judicial Powers," 12 *Maarav* 121 (2005).

LEGISLATIVE DRAFTING AND DEONTICS

Novick, T. *What Is Good and What God Demands*, Brill, 2010.

Sinclair, D. "Normative Transparency in Jewish Law: Maimonides, R. Moses Sofer and Isaac Abraham Kook," 19 *Jewish Law Annual* 119 (2012).

METHODOLOGY

Faur, J. "The Fundamental Principles of Jewish Jurisprudence," 12 *New York University Journal of International Law & Policy* 225 (1979).

Milgram, J. S. "Methodological Musings on the Study of 'Kelalei Pesak': 'Hilkheta ke-Rav be-issurei ve-khi-Shemuel be-dinei,'" 61 *Journal of Jewish Studies* 278 (2010).

Moscovitz, L. "'We May Not Infer Civil Law from Ritual Law': Some Observations on the Internal Unity of Rabbinic Law," 22 *Jewish Law Association Studies* 193 (2012).

HUMAN JUSTICE AND DIVINE JUSTICE

Jackson, B. S. "The Administration of Justice in Jewish Law," 4 *Daimon: Annuario di diritto comparato delle religioni* 31 (2004).

Passamaneck, S. M. "Man Proposes, Heaven Disposes," 8 *Jewish Law Annual* 86 (1989).

JEWISH LAW AND MORAL LAW OR EQUITY

Eisen, R. "'Lifnim Mi-shurat Ha-Din' in Maimonides' 'Mishneh Torah,'" 89 *Jewish Quarterly Review* 291 (1999).

Shilo, S. "On One Aspect of Law and Morals in Jewish Law: *Lifnim Mishurat Hadin*," 13 *Israel Law Review* 359 (1978).

HALACHAH AND KABBALAH

Hallamish, M. *Kabbalah: In Liturgy, Halakhah and Customs*, Bar-Ilan University Press, 2000.

Katz, J. *Halakhah and Kabbalah: Studies in the History of Jewish Religion, Its Various Faces and Social Relevance*, Magnes Press, 1986.

3

The Sources of Jewish Law

SECTION 1 REVELATION

Revelation is one of law's sources. In this respect, Jewish law is revealed law *par excellence*. According to Jewish tradition, God spoke to Moses on Mount Sinai and, at this unprecedented and completely unique event, the entire Jewish nation was present. Jewish tradition designates this formative event as the "granting of the Torah at Sinai." The sacred text resulting from it, the Torah, is a text that has a high normative density because it contains no fewer than 613 commandments, some of which are positive and the rest of which are negative; if does not matter if there are certain doctrinal differences regarding their nature and classification (see previous chapter). In addition to the Written Torah or Written Law, God transmitted to Moses an entire body of instructions that was not fixed as a written text and that is referred to as the Oral Torah or Oral Law, although it was ultimately – and contrary to an express prohibition – to be written down in order to save it from the turmoil of the Diaspora. The *raison d'être* of this Oral Law is to clarify the Written Law. Often a biblical verse presents a certain degree of ambiguity or a gap. The Oral Law's role is to clarify or complete that verse. *Mutatis mutandis*, the relationship between the Written Law and the Oral Law is the relationship between a statute and the decrees issued for its implementation. Essentially, the Oral Law consists of the Mishnah and a special category of laws referred to as "those laws which were transmitted to Moses at Sinai" (*halachah l'Moshe mi-Sinai*) – laws that God conveyed orally to Moses simultaneously with the Written Law but that were not integrated with it. The laws in this category have the same authority as biblical laws. In order to illustrate this function of the Oral Law, let us take, for example, the phylacteries, which every Jewish male is obligated to daily put on his forearm and forehead (as in the ten laws concerning how phylacteries are to be made in MT, *The Laws Governing Phylacteries*, 1:3). The Torah (that is, the Written Law) transmits only this positive commandment but transmits neither the form of the phylacteries nor their color nor the material of which they must be made. Similarly, the Torah does not indicate whether the phylacteries must contain parchment and, if so, what should be written on that parchment. All of this information is conveyed by the Oral Law, which, according to Jewish tradition, was transmitted directly from God's mouth to Moses's ear, and was subsequently transmitted orally by Moses to the members of his inner circle and then passed on from master to student and from one generation to the next until it was set down in written form, this being dictated by the circumstances under which the Jews lived. Happily using a Kelsenian vocabulary, some modern scholars of the Talmud such as Menachem Elon have designated the Torah (the Written and Oral Torah, or Laws, taken as a single entity) as the *Grundnorm*, the source from which all of Jewish law derives – an incontestable and intangible source.

Before proceeding any further, we must define what precisely is meant by the term *revelation*. Dictionaries confirm the common sense of this word, namely, that every revelation is unilateral. Thus, for example, in *Merriam-Webster*, we find the following definition: 1a: an act of revealing or communicating divine truth; b: something that is revealed by God to humans.

It could also be defined as an act that can be carried in various ways and through which God or the Divinity manifests Himself to a human being and communicates to that human being the knowledge of truths that are partially or totally inaccessible to reason; a body of truths that are made known to a human being and which constitute the foundations of the religion in question. In other words, revelation is generally understood to be a unilateral process: God is the transmitter and the recipient – in this case, the Jewish people or Moses – is completely passive. Rabbinic literature suggests a model that is less absolutist and more nuanced. Readers might perhaps think that the determination of the exact roles of the divine and the human in the Torah's revelation is a question that is more theological than legal. However, in our view, it is clearly legal because it serves to define more precisely the nature of this source of law. Moreover, it permits comparativists to know whether this is the same thing as saying that Muslim law is "revealed law" and, or broadly, to know whether we can classify Jewish law as part of the family of "religious laws" (see Chapter 2). According to one famous passage, here is "how the voice of God [in the revelation at Mount Sinai] was heard by all Israel and by every Jew according to their capacity: the elderly according to their capacity, the adolescents according to their capacity, the children according to their capacity, the infants according to their capacity, the women according to their capacity, even Moses according to his capacity ... Everyone received the divine message according to their capacity" (*Midrash Rabbah Ex.* 5). From this *midrash*, we can deduce that the "recipients" were not passive, that the revelation had many facets and that it was not monolithic. And it was something they explicitly accepted (*na'aseh venishmah*), whether entirely voluntarily or not (*BT, Shabbat*, 88a, discussed in Chapter 2).

SECTION 2 RABBINIC LEGISLATION (TAKANOT AND GEZEROT) AND COMMUNAL LEGISLATION (TAKANOT HAKAHAL)

Among the sources listed by Maimonides, we find decrees (*gezerot*), ordinances (*takanot*) and practices, measures that were adopted by the Sages to serve as "a barrier around the Torah," and that were conceived in order to adapt to the necessities of the epoch. Rabbinic legislation thus essentially has two functions: to fill in lacunae in the system, when it cannot provide a response adapted to the socioeconomic needs of that particular moment in time; and to issue preventive or restrictive laws in order to preserve the observance of the written law. In the laws of nations, however, the hierarchy of norms wants secondary legislation to submit itself to the authority of primary legislation: secondary legislation cannot contradict or even repeal primary legislation because the former derives its authority from the latter. In Jewish law, on the other hand, the primary legislation is the Torah: it is the *Grundnorm* – immutable and eternal. The legislation derived from the Torah draws its authority from the Torah, but it can, to a certain extent, deviate from it (see Chapter 4).

The Talmud reports that the first ordinances date back as far as Moses, who passed many (*BT Shabbat* 30a), such as, for example, the obligation to observe a seven-day period of mourning for a relative (*JT Ket.* 1:1). Important ordinances were proclaimed by Joshua, King David, King Solomon, Ezra, the members of the Grand Sanhedrin and the rabbinic court of the Hasmoneans.[1] Note also that these ordinances and decrees preceded the mishnaic period, which began with Hillel and Shammai. During the mishnaic period, the Sages also passed ordinances; Hillel and Shammai introduced thirty-six (*BT Shabbat* 15a). Joshua ben Gamla is praised for having decreed that an elementary education must be provided to all children in all cities in Israel (*BT BB* 21a). The Sages of Yavneh and Usha also promulgated numerous decrees on points of detail, the essential legislation having been fixed many years before.

This legislative power was then passed on to various councils and assemblies of Diaspora communities, which enjoyed administrative or constitutional autonomy, for example, Spire, Worms and Mayence (acronym : Shum) in Germany. In these three cities during the Middle Ages, the highest Ashkenazi rabbinic authorities held a synod and passed a number of ordinances that

---

[1] Arthur Marmorstein and Solomon Zeitlin, "The Takkanot of Ezra" (v. "JQR.," ns, VIII, pp. 61–74) 10.2/3 *Jewish Quarterly Review* 367 (1919).

applied to their communities.[2] Among the rules they issued and that touched on several questions of civil law, these authorities reiterated the absolute obligation that all disputes must be submitted to rabbinic courts of law and the strict prohibition against any Jew applying to a secular court of law (on this last point, see Chapter 6).

Essentially, rabbinic legislation intervened in four domains: religion, family, national awareness and society. Regarding religion, rabbinic legislation sought to erect a hedge around the Torah. Thus, for example, the Sages instituted the regular public readings of the Torah, fast days, etc. Regarding family, the aim was to safeguard the well-being of women. Thus, for example, since, according to the Torah, a daughter cannot in principle inherit all or part of an estate, a rabbinic decree stipulated that her brothers must support her materially until she marries. From the rabbinic principle that a husband must love his wife as much as he loves himself and must honor her even more than he honors himself, it was deduced that a husband must pay for all medical treatment necessitated by his wife's illness, must pay the ransom demanded for her release and must pay the expenses of her funeral. Some ordinances were passed to protect widows and divorced women. Other ordinances spelled out a wife's obligations toward her husband, the obligations of parents toward their children, etc.

The decrees and ordinances passed for the maintenance of national awareness included the various laws related to two holidays: Hanukkah and Purim. Hanukkah is an eight-day holiday that commemorates the Maccabees' victory in 163 BCE over the Syrians who wanted to destroy Judaism and to Hellenize their entire kingdom, while Purim is a one-day holiday instituted to commemorate the providential rescue of the Jews of the Persian Empire who narrowly escaped the lethal plans of the grand vizier of King Ahasuerus (Xerxes I), Haman. These events in the Persian Empire, which apparently took place toward the middle of the fifth century BCE, are depicted in the Book of Esther.

Society's well-being is expressed through ordinances that promote honesty and social equality. Thus, for example, the definition of the crime of theft was expanded to include playing dice, betting on pigeon races, attracting a swarm of bees in order to distance it from its owner, etc. The aim of this rabbinic legislation was analyzed earlier in this volume (Chapter 2).

Note that the popular will limited the Sages' legislative power. Maimonides codifies this rule: "Before issuing a decree, passing an ordinance or enacting a

---

[2] Louis Finkelstein, *Jewish Self-Government in the Middle Ages*, Jewish Theological Society of America, 1924.

custom, a rabbinic court must weigh the matter carefully and must know beforehand whether or not the majority of the public can accept that decree, ordinance or custom. A decree can never be issued unless it is known that the majority of the public can accept it" (*MT, Laws Governing Rebels*, 2:5). Moreover, if a decree or an ordinance is not observed extensively in the Jewish world, a rabbinic court can retroactively repeal it (ibid., 2:6–7). Ordinances passed by rabbinic authorities have the status of rabbinic laws (*mitzvot de-rabbanan*).

SECTION 3 CUSTOMS

Customs (*minhagim*) are a manifestation of *halachah*'s human aspects.[3] A custom can be defined as an anonymous rule established by constant popular practice. Jewish law has always recognized the capacity of collective habit to create a norm in the ritual or monetary domain, in accordance with the saying "a custom adopted by our ancestors has the same validity as the Law." The halachic authorities found various sources in Scripture to provide support for the binding force of custom. "Do not remove the ancient boundary stone that your ancestors set up" (*Prov.* 22: 28).[4] A verse of the Torah is sometimes referred to: "You shall not move your neighbor's landmarks, set up by previous generations" (*Deut.* 19:14).

Customs are generally limited to a specific community; however, some customs link up the entire Jewish people. A custom practiced in a given community can be a source of law when the *halachah* has not yet been formalized. Thus, we read in the Talmud: "Regarding any law that is not clear and concerning which the rabbinic court does not know which path is preferable, go and see how the community acts and then follow the community's example" (*JT Pe'ah* 25:3). Implicitly, the corollary is that, when a rabbinic court comes to a decision, its decision takes precedence over established custom. Here is how Hillel explains this reference to popular practice: "Let the Jews do what they think best. If they are not prophets, then at least they are the children of prophets" (*BT Pes.* 66a). This affirmation by Hillel tends toward the recognition of the divine origin of customs.

In sum, custom performs three functions in Jewish law. First, custom determines which opinion is to be accepted when the halachic authorities disagree as to what the law is with regard to a particular issue. Second, custom supplements existing law when new questions arise that existing law doesn't solve. Third, custom establishes new rules that are contrary to existing law, i.e., norms that modify or abrogate existing *halachah* (*minhag mevattel halachah*; lit. "custom annuls" or "override the law"). Nevertheless, the rule that custom overrides the law is fully effective only in monetary matters (*dinei mamonot*). In the area of matter prohibitions and permissions (*issur veheter*),[5] only in particular and limited cases may the law authorize what the law prohibits.

---

[3] The root of the word *minhag*, usually translated "custom," is the verb *nahog*, "to conduct oneself."

[4] See also, in the same vein, *Prov.* 1:8: "My son, heed the discipline of your father, and do not forsake the instruction of your mother."

[5] For this distinction, see Chapter 2.

The major contribution of customs to Jewish law has been in the following domains: transfer of movable property, the creation of obligations, and labor law. One principle at the heart of Jewish law is that the ownership of an object cannot be transferred solely through an exchange of consent between two parties. In order to effect a transfer, an act of conveyance must take place. This act is called *kinyan* (literally, acquisition, or, to be more precise, a legal bond).[6] Jewish law recognizes several forms of *kinyan*, depending on the nature of the goods involved. The act of *kinyan* is required not only in the transfer of real rights but also in the creation of a contractual bond. One form of *kinyan* is called *kinyan halifin* (lit., an acquisition through an exchange);[7] in this category of acquisition, an object is exchanged in order to carry out a certain transaction. Traditionally, the object exchanged is a handkerchief (*soudar*). In *kinyan halifin*, the recipient of an object must give the object's donor a handkerchief. The Book of Ruth relates (4:7–8) an episode in which a field is acquired through *kinyan*.[8] For some goods, the act of *kinyan* is carried out when the object acquired is pushed a tiny distance. The act of *kinyan* is required for the transfer of ownership or for the creation of a legal bond; it also determines the birth of a personal right or a real right. One question that can be asked here is whether a custom could have given rise to alternative modes of *kinyan*, in other words, acts of acquisition that were not foreseen by either the Mishnah or the Talmud. The Talmud's response to this question is positive and sets in motion several consequences (*BT BM* 74 a). At this point in the text, a discussion related to the transfer of ownership of a barrel of wine is initiated: "Rabbi Pappi says in Rava's name: 'The affixing of a seal (*situmta*) is a valid mode of acquisition.'" The Gemarah then asks: "By virtue of what rule is this acquisition rendered valid?" Rabbi Haviva replies: "In order to carry out a valid acquisition (i.e., an act of acquisition that produces a binding commitment)." The rabbis say, "Solely to have the effect that the party that withdraws from the transaction will incur the rabbinic court's sanctions." After hearing the various opinions, the Talmud states: "This is the *halachah*: 'Solely to have the effect that the party that withdraws from the transaction will incur the rabbinic court's sanctions. However, wherever the custom is such that this

---

[6] For an introduction to this topic, see J. David Bleich, "The Metaphysics of Property Interests in Jewish Law: An Analysis of Kinyan," 43.2 *Tradition: A Journal of Orthodox Jewish Thought* 49 (2010).

[7] This is an amoraic institution.

[8] The object here is not a handkerchief but a shoe. For the legal issues raised by this particular *kinyan*, see Louis M. Epstein, *The Jewish Marriage Contract: A Study in the Status of the Woman in Jewish Law*, Jewish Theological Society, 1927, pp. 33–34, FN 5.

(namely, the fixing of a seal) has the effect of transferring ownership, the acquisition is rendered valid.'"

Some clarification is needed here. In the fourth century, during the era of Rava (approximately 280–352), it was common practice among Babylonian merchants to use a mode of acquisition called *situmta*. Wine merchants customarily went to their supplier in order to choose the wine they wished to acquire. Since the merchants did not have enough room for storing the barrels of wine, they would acquire and would arrange for the delivery of the barrel of wine only when they needed to do so. Since the barrels of wine remained meanwhile with the vendor, the purchaser affixed a mark or seal as evidence of his ownership. However, from Jewish law's standpoint, the vendor remained the wine's owner because no act of *kinyan* had taken place (here the tradition is driving forward the act of possession, where the object is "pulled," in accordance with rabbinic legal terminology). Rabbi Pappi reports Rava's opinion that the mark or seal on the barrel constitutes a valid mode of acquisition in the view of *halachah*. Rabbi Haviva is of a similar opinion; however, that cannot be said of a group of anonymous Sages. According to these anonymous Sages, this mode of acquisition is flawed because it imposes on the purchaser only the moral and religious obligation not to cancel the transaction; if the purchaser does cancel the transaction, the purchaser will be incurring the curse of the rabbinic court and the transaction will not be enforceable. The Talmud approves the first opinion, declaring that, if local custom accepts marking as a valid mode of acquisition, then *halachah* must be fixed in the same sense and must admit *situmta*, granting it the same status as other modes of acquisition recognized by *halachah*.

The case of the seal opens the door to the multiplication of modes for the transfer of ownership, permitting the integration of Diaspora Jewish communities. In addition to different markings, one can cite the transfer of keys (*traditio clavium*), a practice borrowed from Roman law, or a handshake.[9]

Finally, all modes of acquisition are recognized on condition that they constitute a custom. Annotating the Talmudic passage we have just analyzed, Rashba (Solomon ben Aderet, Spain, 1235–1310) baldly states: "From this we learn that custom takes precedence over the law in all similar situations and that custom determines the validity of acquisitions and transfers in all matters

---

[9] Ron S. Kleinman, "Delivery of Keys ('Traditio clavium') As a Mode of Acquisition: Between Jewish and Roman Law," 16 *Jewish Law Association Studies* 123 (2007).

related to monetary law. Thus, merchants can acquire any object in any manner that conforms to their usual practice." The *Shulchan Aruch* receives *halachah* as fixed by the Talmud (SA HM 201:2). Later rabbinic authorities debate whether mercantile customs can also deviate from Jewish law in acquisitions of real estate. Most of them are in favor of such a possibility.

SECTION 4 *SEVARAH*

Sevarah (lit., logic) is a sensible, logical idea that does not rely on any text – neither a verse nor a mishnah nor a *baraita*. "Why do I need a biblical verse to teach me this idea? We should let logic guide us!" Through this interrogative statement, the Talmud teaches us that *sevarah* has an obligatory force (*BT BM* 46b; *Ket.* 22a; *Nid.* 25a). *Sevarah* is based on the profound belief that human reason, when practiced by the Sages, assumes the same authority as the Torah. For example, in response to the question asked in the Talmud (*BT San.* 47a) – How can we know that it is better to let yourself be killed than to kill someone? – the following anecdote is introduced: "We should let logic guide us! One day, someone came before Raba, seeking his counsel: 'The governor of the city has ordered me to kill a certain person and said, that if I fail to do so, I will be killed.' Raba replied, 'Then, you must let yourself be killed; you must not kill that person. Who says that your blood is redder than this man's? Perhaps his blood is redder.'" Several cases are decided in the Talmud on the basis of logical thinking with regard to monetary matters (see, for example, *BT BM* 46b) and to ritual matters (see, for example, *BT Kid.* 13b). According to Jewish tradition, this method of interpretation was revealed to Moses as a reliable method for discovering the Torah's message. Using this method correctly, the Sages in the following generations were able to reestablish elements of Jewish law that had become obscured or had been erased by time. Thus, the laws arrived at by logical deduction have the status of biblical laws (*d'oraita*).

A number of mechanisms in civil law are based on logic: for example, the presumption of ownership created by adverse possession (*hazaka*, *BT BM*, 100a; *BT Ket.* 20a), the presumption that a borrower need not pay back a loan before its due date (*BT BB* 5a/5b), or the presumption that agents must strictly follow the instructions of those whom they are representing (*BT Er.* 31b; *Git.* 64a). One should also mention here the concept of *migo* (an Aramaic word that literally means "from within"), according to which, in certain circumstances, a judge can admit the veracity of an argument on the logical ground that, had the litigant wanted to lie, he or she could have advanced a more plausible argument.[10]

---

[10] The *migo* doctrine is a very complex topic. For an introduction, see Yuval Sinai, "The Doctrine of Affirmative Defense in Civil Cases: Between Common Law and Jewish Law," 34 *North Carolina Journal of International Law & Commercial Regulation*, 111, 150 seq. (2008).

SECTION 5 THE VIRTUE OF CASUISTICS: EXEMPLUM, RESPONSUM, JUDGMENT

The example (exemplum; *ma'aseh* in Hebrew) is an event from which a law or principle in Jewish law can be deduced. As such, it constitutes a source of Jewish law. A law or principle derived from a *ma'aseh* is formally distinct from other sources of Jewish law, such as *midrash* (interpretation), ordinances, custom or logical reasoning. Unlike a *ma'aseh*, in all these other sources, *halachah* dons an apparently independent form; in a *ma'aseh*, it is tied to a particular set of concrete facts from which it must be separated and abstracted in order to be expounded. A *ma'aseh* can assume two different forms. It can be a judgment rendered in a concrete case by a rabbinic court of law or by a rabbinic authority (see Chapter 4) that is described in the Mishnah or Talmud. It can also be an act or a pattern of behavior instituted by a Sage or any person recognized as an authority in matters relating to *halachah*. A *ma'aseh* can be a source of law in both monetary and ritual matters.

The recognition of *ma'aseh* as a source of law is connected to the very nature of the system, that is, to the fact that authority in Jewish law has been placed in the hands of the Sages and their successors (see Chapter 4). It must be acknowledged here that a judicial decision or a pattern of behavior instituted in daily life by a competent authority in Jewish law is the result of the mastery or internalization of *halachah*.

The Sages were keenly aware that they were embodying the Law in its practical, active dimension: they were consequently acting with a high degree of circumspection (*BT Git.* 19a and 37a); their close association with Jewish law is the means for the acquisition of the Torah (*Pirkei Avot* 6:6). The idea that a specific case can clarify or supplement the legal system appears in the Torah itself (*Lev.* 24:10–23; *Num.* 9: 1–8, 15:32–36, 27:1–11). However, the force of a *ma'aseh* does not stem from the fact that Jewish law embraces the doctrine of the binding precedent (see below), but rather from the fact that the Sages recognize its power to create law.

In order to legitimately deduce a principle or law from a *ma'aseh*, one must make two distinctions. First, the factual aspect of the *ma'aseh* must be carefully distinguished from its legal aspect. Second, one must distinguish those elements that are not pertinent and that have no influence on the conclusion from the standpoint of *halachah* from those elements that *are* pertinent and that lead to the result in terms of *halachah*(see, for example, *BT BM*, 36a). Most of these *ma'asim* (the plural of *ma'aseh*) appear in the Mishnah or Talmud; one reads there how, in this or that circumstance, a certain Sage made such-and-such decision or behaved in such-and-such manner. In the post-Talmudic epoch, the *ma'aseh* continued to play its role as a source of law. People wrote books about the decisions or behavior of their masters and teachers in this or that situation. By its very nature, the responsum closely resembles the *ma'aseh*.

The term *responsum* (pl. *responsa*) designates responses that were written on questions of religious law referred to a rabbinic authority by colleagues, by rabbinic courts of law or by Jewish communities. This practice of "questions and answers" (*Heb.* "she'elot u-teshuvot") began in the Talmudic period and was institutionalized during the period of the *Geonim*. If originally, the responses were concisely phrased, this custom was gradually abandoned in order to provide responses that were motivated by and based on traditional Jewish sources. The responsa permitted the maintenance of a certain degree of uniformity in the *halachah* despite the dispersion of Jewish communities, without, however, avoiding the differences in practice between the Ashkenazi and Sephardi worlds. This constant communication contributed to the perpetuation of feelings on national unity among the Jews of the world.

The editing of responsa can be divided into three major periods. The first period was that of the *Geonim* (the seventh to the eleventh centuries). The questions were addressed to the *Geonim* of Babylon because of their superior education in Jewish law matters. During that period, the themes varied and touched not just on religious questions in the strict sense but also on questions concerning the administration of the various local Jewish communities. Many of these responsa have been lost because they were not published systematically. The second period is that of the *Rishonim* (the twelfth to the fifteenth centuries). During that period, the themes centered around religious practice but also on questions related to the emergence of modernity. The *Rishonim* wrote responses that were longer and more carefully reasoned than those of their predecessors. The last period is that of the *Aharonim* (the seventeenth century to the present). Although, during this period, the themes remain diversified, one can note the appearance of questions related to the disruption of previous moral codes and to the loss of communal homogeneity; in addition to earlier questions connected with emancipation, there are now questions related to technical progress along with essentially religious questions, such as how to use electricity on the Sabbath. Closer to the issues of our present era, the astounding progress of modern medicine has given rise to questions on topics such as organ transplants, medically assisted procreation, etc. Note here that Orthodox rabbinic authorities are not the only ones to produce responsa. Hundreds of thousands of responsa are now accessible electronically thanks to the immense work carried out by Bar-Ilan University's Responsa Project over the past four decades.

What precisely is the authority of this doctrinal and legal literature? It cannot be compared to the binding precedents of common law. In fact, the doctrine of *stare decisis* in the strict sense could never have been adopted in Jewish law for two reasons. First, in principle, no judgment in Jewish law is final as long as it is uncertain whether the truth has actually been attained as far as the facts and the law are concerned. Thus, if one of the parties can introduce new evidence, the rabbinic court of law is obligated to reexamine the case. Since such a possibility could undermine both legal security and commerce, it is an established practice to negate in advance by an appropriate stipulation the validity of new evidence that might surface later (*BT San.* 31a; *MT Laws Governing the Sanhedrin* 7:6–8; *SA HM* 20). Secondly, any judgment containing an error is nullified when the law on this point is clear and well established. Here as well, a way was found to assure the stability and definitive character of a judgment (*BT San.* 33a; *MT Laws Governing the Sanhedrin* 6:1; *SA HM* 25:1–3). The theoretical nature of a judgment in Jewish law has necessarily led to the conclusion that a judgment cannot be endowed with the force of a binding precedent. In addition, the doctrine of the binding precedent conflicts with the method of Jewish law concerning the elaboration of *halachah*. The existence of a divergence of opinions in matters related to *halachah* (for a detailed discussion of this point, see Chapter 4) is regarded as a phenomenon that is not only legitimate but also desirable and indicative of *halachah*'s vitality, of the possibility of different approaches, based on common general principles, toward a search for solutions to new questions that may emerge. The decisive criterion in the case of divergences in the area of Jewish law is the soundness of each opinion "in accordance with the Talmud of Rav Ashi" (that is, the Babylonian Talmud) (*Piskei ha-Rosh San.* 4:6) or "in accordance with the Talmud of Jerusalem or the *Tosefta*, if there is no decisive element in the Talmud of Babylon" (*Yam Shel Shlomo* Intro. to *BT BK*). For this reason, no codification of Jewish law can be considered as furnishing an absolute, definitive response. The acceptance of the *Shulchan Aruch* (see Chapter 4) does not signify that rabbinic judges are deprived of the discretion that *halachah* always provide them to take into consideration, when reaching a legal decision, all of the pertinent human and social factors in the particular case. Thus, one can say that exempla, responsa and judgments are a point of departure, not a point of arrival, when a rabbinic authority or a rabbinic judge weighs issues in a case.

Two systemic principles reinforce the rejection of the principle of *stare decisis*. The first is expressed in the maxim "the law is according to what has been decided by the most recent Talmudic scholars" ("*hilcheta ke-vatrei*"), which was formulated to emphasize the freedom of contemporary rabbinic authorities to reach their own decisions, notwithstanding the respect they should show toward the positions of their predecessors. According to one source, contemporary rabbinic authorities or rabbinic judges should adopt the following attitude toward their precursors: if they do not accept the correctness of their precursors' judgments and if they can support their own view with evidence that will be acceptable to their contemporaries, they can overrule these judgments because all matters that have not been clarified in the Talmud of Rav Ashi and Ravina can be reexamined and decided anew by anyone; it is even possible to deviate from the decisions of the *Geonim* just as the last *Amoraim* distanced themselves from the decisions of the first *Amoraim*. In contrast, one can consider the judgments of contemporary rabbinic authorities as having supreme authority because they are familiar not only with the doctrines of their contemporaries but also with those of the rabbinic authorities of previous generations; thus, in their decision regarding which of the various opinions to follow, the contemporary rabbinic authorities are able to reach the heart of the matter (*Piskei ha-Rosh*, ibid.).

Similarly, the second systemic principle is expressed in a Talmudic maxim, "judges must rely solely on what they see" ("Ein lo le-dayan ella ma she-einav ro'ot"), which appears in the following Talmudic passage: "Rabba said to Rav Papa and Rav Huna, son of Rabbi Joshua, 'If you should come upon a judgment I have issued and you see that it can be refuted, do not tear it up until you see me. If I can justify it, I will tell you; if not, I will reverse my decision. After my death, do not tear it up and do not pass any judgment based on it. Do not tear it up because, had I been alive, I might have been able to justify it to you. Do not base any judgment on it because "Judges must rely solely on what they see"'" (*BT BB* 130b). The principle according to which rabbinic judges should be solely guided by what they see is a systemic legitimization of the right of all rabbinic judges to exercise their discretion in order to reach decisions that they consider appropriate. According to some commentators, one can even go one step further in interpreting this right: the Talmud does not demand that rabbinic judges (or rabbinic authorities) merely recognize the theoretical possibility of exercising their discretion but instead demands that they do so, because the exercising of one's discretion in this case is not an option but is rather something that must be carried out.

Further Reading

OVERALL STUDIES ON THE SOURCES OF JEWISH LAW

Elon, M. *Jewish Law: History, Sources, Principles (Ha-Mishpat Ha-Ivri)*, Vol. 2. Jewish Publication Society, 1994.

Hecht, N. S., B. S. Jackson, S. M. Passamaneck, D. Piatelli and A. M. Rabello. *An Introduction to the History and Sources of Jewish Law*, Oxford University Press, 1996.

Lopes Cardozo, N. T. *The Written and Oral Torah*, Rowman & Littlefield, 2004.

Roth, J. *The Halakhic Process: A Systemic Analysis*, Jewish Theological Seminary of America, 1986.

Schimmel, H. C. *The Oral Law*, 3rd edn., Feldheim Publishers, 2006.

STUDIES ON SPECIFIC SUBJECTS RELATED TO THE SOURCES OF JEWISH LAW

Revelation

Blidstein, P. "In the Shadow of the Mountain: Consent and Coercion at Sinai," 4.1 *Jewish Political Review Studies* 41 (1992).

Halivni, D. W. "On Man's Role in Revelation," in J. Neusner, E. S. Frerichs and N. M. Sarna (eds.), *From Ancient Israel to Modern Judaism: Essays in Honor of M. Fox*, Scholars Press, 1989, p. 29.

Halivni, D. W. *Revelation Restored*, Routledge, 1997.

Landman, L. "Aspects of Traditions Received from Moses at Sinai: *Halakha le-Mosheh mi Sinai*," 67 *Jewish Quarterly Review* 111 (1976/1977).

Rabbinic and Communal Legislation

Elon, M. "Modes of Halachic Creativity in the Solution of Legal and Social Problems in the Jewish Community (Heb.)," 44 *Zion* 241 (1979).

Guttmann, A. "Participation of the Common People in Pharisaic and Rabbinic Legislative Processes," 1 *Jewish Law Association Studies* 41 (1985).

Nachalon, A. "The Communal Enactments ('*Takkanot HaKahal*') (Heb.): Their Legal Nature According to the Tashbetz," *Shenaton ha-Mishpat ha-Ivri* 271 (1976/1977).

Customs

Bedzow, I. "*Minhag Israel Torah He* (The Custom of Israel Is Torah): The Role of Custom in the Formation of Orthodoxy," 57 *Leo Beck Institute Yearbook* 121 (2012).

Gutman, A. "Die Stellung des Minhag im Talmud," 83 *Monatsschrift für Geschichte und Wissenschaft des Judentums* (N. F. 47) 226 (1939).

Kleinman, R. S. "Do the Parties to a Contract Need Actual Knowledge of Civil Laws or Commercial Practices in Order for These Laws or Practices to Function as Valid Customs in Jewish Law?" 23 *Jewish Law Association Studies* 93 (2012).

Exemplum (Ma'aseh)

Goldberg, A. "Form und Funktion des Ma'ase in der Mischna," 2 *Frankfurter Judaistische Beiträge* 1 (1974).

Reichman, R. "Die Stellung des Ma'ase (Präjudizes) im Talmud" (November 8, 2000), *Forum historiae iuris*, www.forhistiur.de/2000–11-reichman/.

Responsa

Zohar, Z. "Le processus du responsum," in S. Trigano (ed.), *La société juive à travers l'histoire*, Vol. 4, Fayard, 1993, p. 179.

Persuasive Authority

Ta-Shma, I. "The Law Is in Accord with the Later Authority – *Hilkhata Kebatrai*: Historical Observations on a Legal Rule," in H. Ben-Menahem and N. S. Hecht (eds.), *Authority, Process and Method: Studies in Jewish Law*, Harwood Academic Publishers, 1998, p. 101.

Warhaftig, Z. "Precedent in Jewish Law," in H. Ben-Menahem and N. S. Hecht (eds.), *Authority, Process and Method: Studies in Jewish Law*, Harwood Academic Publishers, 1998, p. 1.

Logic

Jacobs, L. "Hazakah: Presumptive State," in L. Jacobs (ed.), *The Talmudic Argument*, Cambridge University Press, 1984, p. 110.

Wiederblank, N. "How Are We to Determine What God Wants? Reason, Revelation, or Both," 18 *Hakirah* 107 (2018).

4

Halachic Authority

INTRODUCTION

The construction of Jewish law took a relatively long time, so much so that one must take into account what preceded it, what scholars call "biblical law," in order to understand the phenomenon of authority in Jewish law.

The Torah, in the manner in which its legal verses are formulated, presupposes that it does not contain all of the information necessary for their application. There are, in effect, five cases where the law is promulgated in the wake of incidents that reveal a lacuna (*Lev.* 24:12–16; *Num.* 9:6–11, 15:34–35, 27:1–11, 36). In each instance, the lacuna is filled by God Himself. Naturally, such situations could be expected to multiply after the death of Moses, the sole individual capable of asking God questions and transmitting God's response to the Jewish nation.

The solution to this problem can be found in the Torah itself:

> If a case is too baffling for you to decide, be it a controversy over homicide, civil law, or affliction [that is, ritually pure or impure] – matters of dispute in your courts – you shall promptly repair to the place that the Lord your God will have chosen, and appear before the levitical priests, or the magistrate in charge at the time, and present your problem. When they have announced to you the verdict in the case, you shall carry out the verdict that is announced to you from that place that the Lord chose, observing scrupulously all their instructions to you. You shall act in accordance with the instructions given you and the ruling handed down to you; you must not deviate from the verdict that they announce to you either to the right or to the left. (*Deut.* 17:8–11)

These verses ultimately created a central court of law, the Great Sanhedrin, and, at the same time, established its authority to decide on all "matters of dispute in your courts," that is, all questions that the local courts of law have not managed to settle. This central court of law had a triple function: to teach, to legislate and to judge. If one sticks to the literal sense of these verses, this court of law was composed of "levitical priests" and "the magistrate[s]."

Control of the Temple in Jerusalem and of the rites that evolved there was placed in the hands of the members of priestly families, descendants of Aaron, Moses' brother – a group known as the Great Sanhedrin or the "Great Rabbinic Court of Law."[1] Thus, the Temple was the cultural and legal center and retained this status until the waning years of the Hasmonean dynasty. The Sanhedrin consisted of seventy-one rabbinic judges-legislators. Since the Sanhedrin was regarded as legally competent to settle all questions brought before it, its members had to be experts in all domains of the Torah. They also had to be sufficiently versed in the secular sciences in order to be able to apply the law to concrete cases. To become a member of the Sanhedrin, one had to receive ordination (*s'micha*), the authority for which directly dated back to Moses. The seat of the Sanhedrin was located in that part of the Temple that was called the Chamber of the Hewn Stone (*Lishkat ha-gazit*). The wars with Rome undermined the Sanhedrin's authority, and, in 28 CE, it renounced its power to judge in cases involving crimes punishable by death and moved to a new location, installing itself in a quarter of Jerusalem. In 70 CE, when the Temple and Jerusalem were destroyed, the Sanhedrin established itself in Yavneh in Judea. It successively installed itself in various cities (Usha, Beit She'arim and Sephoris), finally establishing its permanent seat in Tiberias, where it continued to function until the completion of the Jerusalem Talmud's editing (ca. 375 CE). During the persecutions under Constantine (337–361 CE), its members were forced to go into hiding. The Sanhedrin was ultimately dissolved. Ordination was abolished in 388 CE.

A prominent characteristic of rabbinic law is its uniformity. This feature is due to the concentration of interpretation and legislation in the hands of the Great Sanhedrin, which enjoyed total authority in these matters. However, after the first century CE, following the destruction of the Temple in Jerusalem (70 CE) and the decline in the Sanhedrin's authority, halachic doctrine split into two major schools of thought, the schools of Shammai (50 BCE-30 CE) and Hillel the Elder (70 BCE-10 CE).[2] Shammai was a Talmudic scholar and served as the Sanhedrin's vice president. He and

---

[1] Hugo Mantel, *Studies in the History of the Sanhedrin*, Harvard University Press, 1965.
[2] Alfredo M. Rabello, "Civil Justice in Palestine from 63 BCE to 70 CE," in Ranon Katzoff (ed.), *Classical Studies in Honor of David Sohlberg*, Bar Ilan University Press, 1996, p. 293; ibid., "Jewish and Roman Jurisdiction," in Neil S. Hecht, Bernard S. Jackson, Stephen M. Passamaneck, Daniela Piattelli, and Alfredo M. Rabello (eds.), *An Introduction to the History and Sources of Jewish Law*, Oxford University Press, 1996, pp. 141–167.

Hillel the Elder were the last of the five pairs of Sages (*zugot*) who transmitted the Oral Law during the last century of the Second Temple in Jerusalem. Whereas Shammai was a proponent of a rigorous approach to *halachah* (*BT Shabbat* 31a), Hillel, who was of Babylonian origin, was the leader of the Pharisees during the reign of Herod and was an eminent Sage during the period of the Second Temple. According to Jewish tradition, he generally opted for a less lenient interpretation of the Law. Each school taught and practiced Jewish law in accordance with its respective viewpoint. The Talmud relates that the increase in the number of disputes between these two schools of thought led to the existence in practice of "two bodies of Jewish law" (*BT San.* 88b), a situation that was diametrically opposed to what the Torah requires: "There shall be one law for you and for the resident stranger" (*Num.* 15:16). This ongoing dispute took a dramatic turn and, if the situation had been allowed to continue, would probably have ultimately ended in a schism. Gamliel II (middle of the first century) undertook to restore *halachah*'s uniformity or, at least, to define or redefine the parameters of halachic authority, in the absence of a Temple that would never be reconstructed. He managed to preserve the authority of the Sanhedrin and of the Yavneh academy, turning them into rallying points for numerous Talmudic scholars. This community of Sages, representing diverse opinions, gradually developed an orally transmitted body of halachic and ethical precepts. Gamliel's grandson Judah the Prince (Yehuda Ha-Nassi) compiled these teachings, and the result was the Mishnah.

The Judaism of Yavneh and its successors has retained its validity to this very day (Section 1). However, from the nineteenth century onward, what we customarily call "rabbinic Judaism" and its concept of authority have become the target of attempts (some major, some minor) to alter them (Section 2).

SECTION 1 HALACHIC AUTHORITY: THE RABBINIC PARADIGM

In order to understand rabbinic Judaism, we should study (1) the individuals who fill the positions of authority, (2) the sources of that authority, (3) its areas of jurisdiction and (4) the extent of that authority. By studying these questions, we can better understand (5) halachic pluralism.

I THE HOLDERS OF AUTHORITY: BOOKS AND INDIVIDUALS

A *The Books: The Mishnah, the Talmud and the Codes*

1 Typology

According to Jewish tradition, God directly transmitted the Oral Torah (Oral Law) to Moses, who then transmitted it to Joshua, who transmitted it to the Elders, who transmitted it to the Prophets, who transmitted it to the members of the Grand Assembly (*Pirkei Avot* [*Ethics of the Fathers* or *Chapters of Principles*] 1:1). The term *Grand Assembly* was the name given to the Sanhedrin led by Ezra at the beginning of the Second Temple period. The Grand Assembly undertook the job of formalizing the biblical canon and the liturgy, and arranged the Oral Torah (Oral Law) in a format that could be more easily memorized by students; this corpus is called the Mishnah. The word *Mishnah* denotes that this compilation had to be reviewed (as indicated by the Hebrew verbal root, *shin-nun-heh*) by students repeatedly and that it was of secondary status (*sheni*, which means "second" in Hebrew) in comparison with the Written Torah (Written Law). The Sages who taught this first Mishnah were called *Tannaim* (plural form of *Tanna*); this word is Aramaic and its verbal root is the equivalent of the aforementioned Hebrew verbal root, *shin-nun-heh*, to review, to repeat.

Although it was forbidden to write out the Oral Law, it was permissible to preserve the notes taken by the students of the academies (*yeshivot*). The directors of these academies similarly saved their notes in order to keep the tradition intact. None of these writings, however, was ever published; hence the term given to them – the "Secret Scrolls." Succeeding generations memorized and studied the Mishnah, which was augmented by rabbinic legislation and by casuistry. The entire *oeuvre* is known as the First Mishnah. In the course of time, controversies arose and several versions of the Mishnah circulated orally, reflecting respectively the particular standpoints of the masters and teachers in the academies.

Rabbi Akiva (45–135 CE) undertook the task of upgrading the Mishnah's organization. Due to the political circumstances of the times – the Roman invasion and the beginning of the Second Exile – the Sages reached the conclusion that the Mishnah must be written down; the Mishnah's editor-anthologist was Judah the Prince. Although it is commonly thought that the work of editing was completed circa 190 CE, the Mishnah was published only thirty years later.

The Mishnah is divided into six sections (*sedarim*, pl. of *seder*, which literally means "order"), which in turn are divided into tractates (*masechtot*, pl. of *masechet*); there are altogether sixty-three tractates in the Mishnah. The six *sedarim* are *Zera'im* (Seeds), which is concerned with the laws governing agriculture in the Land of Israel; *Mo'ed* (Festival), which is concerned with the Jewish festivals and with the triannual pilgrimage to the Temple in Jerusalem associated with them; *Nashim* (Women), on family law; *Nezikin* (Damages), which is concerned with the laws governing bonds and debentures, criminal law and the legal procedures associated with it; *Kodashim* (Holy Things), which is concerned with the sacrifices offered in the Temple in Jerusalem and with the rituals associated with them; *Toharot* (Purity), which is concerned with the subject of ritual purity.

Although the material of the Mishnah is almost exclusively legal, it cannot be considered a code, at least in the modern sense of the term; instead, it should be seen as a compilation or an anthology. It presents diverse opinions, including minority ones, and has few scriptural references; it also contains narrative or historical elements. Thus, by its very nature, it resembles, *mutatis mutandis*, The Digest of Justinian (533 CE). Initially using categories that often appear theoretical or abstruse, the Mishnah then presents, generally with considerable detail, the concrete consequences of those categories. It creates lists of analogous legal phenomena and proceeds to analyze each element in the list.

The opinions that are not included in this compilation are called the *Braitot* (plural of *baraita*; Aramaic, lit. "exterior"). Some of these *Braitot* appear in the *Tosefta* (Aramaic, lit. "addition"), which follows the order of the Mishnah and consists of teachings judged to be of insufficient authority.

Another important source for understanding Jewish law is the *halachic midrashim*. The Hebrew verbal root of the word *midrash* (the singular form of *midrashim*) is *dalet-resh-shin* (to demand, to seek). There are two kinds of *midrashim*: *aggadic midrashim*, which are of a narrative character, and *halachic midrashim*, which are of a legal character. Whereas aggadic *midrashim* contain homiletic and allegorical commentaries, halachic *midrashim* are a legal commentary on the Torah and follow the order of the Torah, explicitly citing biblical verses. They represent an oral tradition that preceded the Mishnah and were also compiled in various texts. The *Mechilta*, which contains commentary on the Book of Exodus; *Sifra* on Leviticus; and *Sifri* (or *Sifrei*) on Numbers and Deuteronomy are amongst the *halachic midrashim*.

The study of the Mishnah cannot be considered an end in itself. Its conciseness and apodictic character call for an analysis of sources and arguments in relation to their respective merit. This analysis is called the *Gemara*, from the Hebrew verbal root *gimel-mem-resh*, which denotes both "to study" and "to finish." The Gemara, which was born when the Oral Torah (Oral Law) was still transmitted orally and had not yet been written down, expanded after the Oral Law was formalized and was written down. This clarification of the Mishnah took place over a period of three centuries. When the danger of the Gemara's disappearance in view of the dispersion of Jewish communities throughout the Diaspora loomed over the horizon, Rav Ashi (352–427 CE) and the Babylonian academies of Sura, Pumbedita and Nehardea undertook the task of collecting all of the discussions appearing in the Gemara and arranging them in an orderly format. The Babylonian Talmud focuses on thirty-seven of the Mishnah's sixty-three tractates. It is not a code of law in the modern sense of the term but instead represents a unique literary genre: it clarifies (but not always) which opinions are binding and identifies sources and evaluates arguments, presenting homilies and stories that elevate the level of the discussions. There is an evident intellectual affinity between the Talmud's discursive part (the Gemara) and halachic *midrashim*. Both are of a dialectical nature with a tendency toward rhetoric, which is rarely encountered in the Mishnah. Another common trait shared by halachic *midrashim* and the Gemara is prolixity. Although the essential part of the Talmud was formalized in the fifth century, the contents were apparently stabilized only in the eighth.

The Jerusalem Talmud was written down before the Babylonian Talmud. The name "Jerusalem Talmud," which Jewish tradition has retained, is not appropriate because, when the Jerusalem Talmud was written down, around the years 220–375 CE, Jerusalem had already been transformed into a pagan city by the Roman occupier (the city, renamed Aelia Capitolina, was "founded" – i.e., refounded – by Hadrian in 131 CE) and access to it was barred to Jews. The Jerusalem Talmud was written in Roman Palestine in the academies of Sepphoris, Tiberias, Caesarea and Lydda. For this reason, the Jerusalem Talmud is sometimes called the "Caesarian Talmud" or the "Palestinian Talmud." Thus, although there were many editors-anthologists, they all worked under the guidance of Rabbi Yohanan bar Nappaha, who was one of the most important of the second-generation *Amoraim*. Generally referred to simply as "Rabbi Yohanan," he lived in the third century CE (Sepphoris, ca. 200 – Tiberias, ca. 280).

In the course of time, there were many compilations whose goal was to achieve a synthesis of *halachah* on the basis of the decisions of succeeding generations. The most notable were the works of the *Rif* (Rabbi Isaac Alfasi, Morocco, 1013–1103); of the *Rosh* (Rabbi Asher ben Yechiel, Cologne, 1250 – Toledo, 1328); of *Maimonides* (1135–1204), specifically, his *Mishneh Torah*; and of Yosef Karo (1488–1575), who published the *Shulchan Aruch* (1528). The latter two works constituted codes of Jewish law, strictly speaking. The publication of these works closed the era of the *Rishonim*, lit., the "First" (Codifiers), and opened the era of the *Acharonim*, the later codifiers. Their principal activity was to comment on the *Shulchan Aruch*, whether to clarify obscure points in the text or to question its conclusions.

2 Authority

What authority do these books have? In his introduction to his code (Mishneh Torah), Maimonides writes, "[b]ut all Jews must observe everything that is written in the Babylonian Talmud ... because the entire Jewish people have accepted everything that appears in the Talmud" (*MT* Introduction). Since this opinion is commonly accepted, the upshot is that, if a position taken by another work written prior to, or in the same era as, the Talmud – such as the Tosefta, the Midrash and the Jerusalem Talmud – contradicts the Babylonian Talmud's position, the Babylonian Talmud's position must take precedence.

Similarly, it is generally understood that the decisions taken by the *Geonim* (589–1038), who headed the major Babylonian academies, are almost universally accepted and that, for this reason, those decisions can never be contradicted by subsequent authorities unless the latter can present persuasive arguments. Similarly, this is the attitude adopted toward the *Shulchan Aruch*, which was also almost universally accepted. This acceptance of classical Jewish sources of law commands is essentially unanimous, or nearly unanimous, support. However, with regard to the opinions of the *Geonim* and those appearing in the *Shulchan Aruch*, the support stemmed from those who held positions of authority in that particular era rather than from universal acceptance by the Jewish people as a whole. This state of affairs closely resembled a concept in Islamic law – the *ijma'a*, the consensus of religious teachers.[3]

---

[3] *Ijma'a* means "consensus of the Muslims" or "consensus of the doctors." It is a well-established source of Islamic law even if its exact contours are still highly controversial (Ahmad Asan, "The

In reality, however, a decision dating from ancient times can always be questioned (unless it appears in the Talmud). The more ancient the law, the more familiar the rabbinic authority who challenges it must be with the pairs of Talmudic scholars associated with that law (see also Chapter 2).

Majority rule (*rov*) is the guiding principle when a decision must be taken in the face of several diverse halachic authorities. The Talmud deduces from the Torah (*Exod.* 23:2) that this principle applies in the case of diverse opinions on a question of law as well as on a question of fact. The immense majority of authors agrees that majority rule is of biblical origin. Some rabbinic authorities maintain that the majority rule is in the category of a biblical precept only when the conflicting opinions have been issued by contemporaries debating with one another face to face. However, in cases where these authorities could never have met in order to engage in a dispute, whether due to historical factors or whether due to geographical ones, serious doubts arise as to whether the status of the majority rule. In such cases, the majority rule would have the force of a rabbinic, rather than a biblical, precept. The ground for this distinction is the fact that we can never be certain that, had the members of the majority been able to discuss the matter with the members of the minority, they would not have changed their point of view to such an extent that the majority camp would have turned into the minority camp.

Majority rule seems to have the simplicity of an arithmetic rule. We must quickly banish this illusion. The first difficulty centers on the manner by which we determine the connotation of "majority."[4] In effect, when the members of the body that holds the authority are identified, the next step is simply to count votes. For example, the US Supreme Court consists of nine justices, the opinion of each of whom is known. Thus, the majority in this instance is easy to establish. However, in the Jewish legal system, which has not had a central institution for more than 2,000 years, the difficulty is to decide what voices really count in order to reach a majority. In other words, it is difficult to determine who are in the positions of authority and to then determine the respective merits of those who are the most eminent among these individuals. *Halachah* imposes criteria that enable us to identify those

---

Classical Definition of Ijma: The Nature of Consensus," 14 *Islamic Studies* 261 [1975]). To the best of our knowledge, the analogy between the "acceptance by the total community" evoked by Maimonides and the source of Islamic law called *ijma'a* has been elaborated for the first time by a German scholar: Ludwig Blau, "Das Gestezbuch des Maimonides historisch betrachtet," in Wilhelm Bacher, Marcus Brann and David Simonsen (eds.), *Moses ben Maimon: Sein Leben, seine Werke und sein Einfluss*, Band II, Leipzig, 1914, pp. 331, 351 seq.

[4] It is worth noting that an anonymous opinion (*stam*) in the Talmud is assumed to be the majority.

holders of positions of authority who must show certain intellectual and ethical qualities. However, there is the danger that manipulation can be employed in this system because, from among those who really count, it is easy to exclude those whose opinion does not accord with the opinion that one wants to prevail in the particular dispute. It could be suggested that the preeminence that renders a certain rabbinic authority worthy of being counted among the various rabbinic authorities is itself determined by some form of communal or rabbinic consensus. Such a tautology is evidently inadmissible.

From the practical standpoint, we find that the characteristics of the system are based on tradition and on hierarchy: a subtle dose of deference to intellectual authority and to the past, of conservatism (a feature peculiar to legal systems), of power relations, of mimicry, of gradual evolution, of social acceptance, of chance or of Providence. If we want to make a comparison, we should draw a comparison with the *jurisprudence constante* of French law: a discreet shift from the status of persuasive authority to the status of a binding one. This phenomenon of sedimentation can be clearly seen if we analyze the codification of law in the Jewish law system.

B The Individuals: The Rav and the Posek

The oral tradition, after it had been written down, could exercise its authority only through the medium of human beings. In the majority of modern communities, the human being serving as this medium is the *rav* (rabbi), interpreter of the law, or the *posek*. Posek (pl. *poskim*) is the term in Jewish law for "decisor": a legal scholar who decides the *halachah* in cases of law where previous authorities are inconclusive or in those situations where no halachic precedent exists. These qualities can be found in the same person, although this is not always the case.

1 Role and Necessary Qualities

In the system of Jewish law, the rabbi today occupies an eminent place as someone who settles major or minor day-to-day questions and contributes to the transformation of *halachah* into a living law.

The *Tractate Avot (Fathers* or *Principles)*, better known as the *Pirkei Avot (Ethics of the Fathers* or *Chapters of Principles)*, helps us to understand both the role of the rabbi as a halachic authority and the responsibility incumbent upon the individual to solicit the rabbi's counsel: "Joshua son of Prachia (Yehoshua ben Prachia) says: 'Acquire for yourself a rabbi, attain for yourself a friend and give everyone the benefit of the doubt'" (1:6). Later in this same chapter of that tractate, this injunction is repeated: "Rabbi Gamliel would say, 'Procure a master and teacher for yourself and liberate yourself from doubts'" (1:16). Why this redundancy? Most commentators explain that the first mishnah refers to a rabbi with whom one can learn Torah while the second refers to someone who can be consulted on halachic questions. In practice, there are two types of rabbi: the rabbi who serves as a teacher or master and the rabbi of a city (in Aramaic, *mara d'atra*, lit., "master of the place") who answers legal questions that arise in the community. The latter's competence, because of the nature of the matter, is not limited, but *halachah* provides this type of rabbi with particular responsibility in certain areas. For example, the rabbis of cities must warn their communities concerning cases where it is permissible to desecrate the Sabbath in order to save a human life; they must be especially versed in the laws relating to persons who are ailing on the Day of Atonement (Yom Kippur), which is a twenty-four-hour-long fast and which is the most solemn day on the Jewish calendar, because the issues associated with these laws are questions of life and death.

The criteria for service in the position of rabbi are rigorous. One often wrongly thinks that what qualifies someone to function as rabbi is the granting of *semichah* or rabbinic ordination. This was the case at a certain point in Jewish history, but it is no longer the case today. In the modern era, *semichah* is not classical *semichah*, which, according to Jewish tradition, dates back to Moses. During the period when classical ordination existed, a rabbi was not permitted to decide in a matter for which the Torah required a judgment delivered by a *beit din* (rabbinic court of law), unless this rabbi was ordained by his rabbi, who himself was ordained by *his* rabbi, according to an unbroken chain of authority traceable to Moses. The date when this chain was disrupted – and thus terminated – is a subject of controversy. The most commonly held opinion is that this interruption occurred during the era of Hillel II, that is, circa 360 CE.

Regarding the title "rabbi," one should not give too much thought to the fact that, in a single community, many people might bear the title "rabbi" (in some communities, the title in Hebrew is "rabbi," while, in others, it is "rav"). The title might be a mark of respect for someone who is recognized as a scholar in sacred matters or as an individual enjoying a certain measure of moral authority. The title can also apply to someone who has been granted a limited ordination, that is, someone who is authorized to respond to questions only in a certain specific area of *halachah*. In Jewish law, several conditions must be in place for one to be granted the title of rabbi. A person is forbidden from providing decisions in matters of *halachah* without first having attained the level of someone who is qualified to provide such decisions. Proof that an individual has attained this level of expertise is expressed in the granting of a license to serve as a rabbi (*semichah* in the modern sense of the term). This type of ordination is granted by the rabbi who personally ordinates the candidate or by a recognized authorized body following an exam in which the candidate must demonstrate profound knowledge and that is preceded by a long period of internship with an experienced rabbinic authority. The basic license to serve as rabbi is called *Yoreh Yoreh* and it provides its recipient with the authority to decide in matters relating to daily life. More advanced students receive a license called *Yadin Yadin*, which authorizes its recipient to decide in financial matters. Recipients of these licenses – whether *Yoreh Yoreh* or *Yadin Yadin* – are obliged to provide answers to questions in halachic matters so that they can prevent their coreligionists from going down the "wrong path" in halachic terms. An individual who has not attained this level of expertise and who nonetheless settles halachic questions is referred to in rabbinic literature as a fool who is also a wicked person and a charlatan.

Opinions vary as to the minimum age when one can serve as a rabbi. Some rabbinic authorities cite forty or over as the minimum age, although everyone agrees that a child who has not yet reached the age of thirteen cannot function as a rabbi. Finally, a rabbi must not only be learned in halachic matters and an experienced practitioner but must also be a God-fearing person and be an individual of exemplary character.

2 The Activities of a Rabbi

Rabbis responding to a halachic question deliver a decision that is a ruling (*p'sak halachah*). The response is also called an instruction (*hora'ah*). Not all rabbis provide – or even want to provide – rulings (*piskei halachah*); those who do are called *poskim*, which literally means "decision makers" or "decisors." This type of response is a decision because, in principle, it is imposed upon the person who asked the question. However, one should not confuse a rabbi with a rabbinic court of law or with the rabbinic judges composing that court. Here there is no question of a lawsuit nor does this ruling have the status of a judgment. I ask my rabbi how to proceed because I am facing a certain difficulty: for example, the *kashrut* of an animal (in other words, whether, in terms of Jewish dietary laws, the animal's flesh is kosher, that is, can be eaten), what should be my attitude toward a difficult neighbor, whether this or that investment conforms with the requirements of *halachah*, what illness would exempt someone from fasting on Yom Kippur, etc. However, not every question is appropriate for consultation with a rabbi for the purpose of obtaining a ruling. The consultation with a rabbi must concern a practical question that the questioner must settle within a reasonable period of time. A theoretical question or a question that was decided in the past does not fall under this category. This does not mean that it is forbidden to ask such questions. A theoretical question or a question *a posteriori* comes under another category: the category of sacred studies. This distinction is important because the study of the Torah is one of Judaism's 613 commandments and is subject to other rules than is a halachic decision (see, for example, *MT, Laws Governing the Study of the Torah*). In short, the relationship between the questioner and the rabbi issuing the ruling resembles the relationship between an individual or a company that consults a renowned lawyer or university professor on a delicate point of law in order to know what direction should be taken in the business affairs of that individual or company. However, there is a considerable difference between this kind of consultation and a rabbinic ruling: whereas the former is not binding on the questioner, the latter is.

3 Forum Shopping

After I have asked a rabbi a halachic question, am I permitted to consult with a second rabbi regarding this same question? Generally speaking, *halachah* forbids such behavior. The principle underlying this prohibition is known as "the Sage who prohibits," and the source in the Talmud is the following passage: "If a Sage rules that something is ritually impure, another Sage is not permitted to rule that it is ritually pure; similarly, if a Sage rules that something is forbidden, another Sage is not permitted to rule that it is permissible" (*BT* Nid. 20b). The *Rishonim* advance three reasons behind this prohibition. First, the moment a rabbi declares that something is ritually impure, the object in question becomes a prohibited item, almost intrinsically so, and for that reason another rabbi cannot declare that it is ritually pure. Second, it is inappropriate for a Jew to ask a second rabbi the same question he asked the first rabbi because, by doing so, he is undermining the first rabbi's status. Third, if the second rabbi's response is different from the first rabbi's response, one might be tempted to wrongly think that there are actually two Torahs, that is, two separate legal systems in Judaism, and this kind of thinking is strictly forbidden by the Torah itself (see above). Most of the *Rishonim* favor the first reason. Although opinions vary regarding the modalities of this prohibition, everyone agrees that, if the second rabbi permits what the first rabbi prohibited (something that the second rabbi has no right to do), the second rabbi's decision has no validity.

II THE SOURCES OF AUTHORITY

Regarding the sources of authority, we can think of two different models: an epistemological model and a deontic one. According to the epistemological model, authority draws its legitimacy from the possession of knowledge in a certain area and, in principle, all the members of a community are equal and are capable of attaining that authority because everything depends on the knowledge one acquires after making the necessary effort. According to the deontic model, where the authority can legitimately order the execution of certain acts and can similarly oblige the members of a community to execute those acts. The source of such authority is not knowledge but rather the power conferred on the holder of authority to establish binding norms. This implies an absolute obligation to obey those who are in positions of authority even when they err. Naturally, each model is an ideal type that cannot precisely reflect the idiosyncrasies of empirical reality. Nonetheless, a model is important because it has a heuristic function: it offers a construction that enables us to make comparisons with Jewish law. In rabbinic literature, the deontic model is predominant, although it is tempered there by the epistemological model.

The deontic model can be applied equally when we discuss hermeneutic authority and legislative authority. It is based principally on two arguments: the divine commandment that is embodied in scriptural sources and the consent of the community.

A *Scriptural Sources*

Rabbinic literature as a whole considers the verse in Deuteronomy cited earlier (17:9) as the source of halachic authority. We have already seen that it is regarded as the basis for the Sanhedrin's authority. However, once the Sanhedrin was destroyed, the verse's "center of gravity" is displaced and is established by the expression "the magistrate in charge" (*Deut.* 17:9). The Talmud questions whether it is possible for a questioner to "go to" – that is, to consult – a rabbinic judge who lived in another era in the same way that the questioner can consult with a contemporary rabbinic judge. Why, then, does the Torah use the phrase "the magistrate in charge"? Basing itself on the hermeneutic principle that there is no superfluous word in the Torah, the Talmud responds that the phrase teaches us that the rabbinic judges of every epoch have absolute, incontestable authority, even if they are inferior in terms of quality and knowledge when compared with the rabbinic judges of previous generations. I am not permitted to diminish the reputation of those who are in authority during my epoch by comparing them with prominent figures in the past. Thus, "Jerubaal in his generation is the equal of Moses in his generation... Jephtha in his generation is the equal of Samuel in his generation" (*BT RH* 25b).

However, this transfer of authority is not limited to rabbinic judges in the strict sense of the term but also applies to the Sages and their descendants, the "doctors of law," to use Maimonides's expression. This transfer of authority would permit the Sages of Yavneh and their successors to regenerate Judaism and to develop Jewish law.

B *The Consensual Source*

See above regarding the acceptance of the Talmud and the *Shulchan Aruch*.

III THE DOMAIN OF HALACHIC AUTHORITY

Like other works of rabbinic literature, the Talmud contains subjects that cannot, strictly speaking, be classified as legal. For example, one can find in the Talmud statements that belong respectively to the categories of history, medicine, psychology, zoology, astronomy, even sorcery. One can also find there lessons in ethics deduced from verses in the Torah, the Prophets and even the Hagiographa.[5] These instructions concern our relations with God and also teach readers how to relate to their neighbors. Finally, one finds there parables and allegories, which, if correctly interpreted, deliver important messages regarding the Sages' vision of the world (*hashkafah*, lit., "perspective," which is often translated as "Jewish thought" or "Jewish philosophy").

These three types of information are called *aggada*, as opposed to *halachah*. Do the opinions expressed in *aggadot* (pl. of *aggada*) enjoy the same authority as those issued on subjects related to Jewish law? Do they enjoy an inferior level of authority or do they lack all authority? This question is an important one because, in the course of the past two decades, we have witnessed the publication of works that advance a common thesis: *all* the words of the Sages are divinely inspired, are thus absolutely true and must therefore be considered binding, even if they contradict the latest scientific data. Those who reject the Sages' words are simply heretics. In other words, *everything* is *halachah*. Nevertheless, it is reasonable to assume that the Sages' statements apply only to halachic matters, as indicated by the verse cited earlier.

---

[5] The third section of the Jewish Scriptures, the first two being the Torah (or Pentateuch) and the Prophets.

First of all, note that, in Deuteronomy, in the original Hebrew text, verses 17:8–9 use the word *mishpat*, which, according to the context, can also signify the "law" or a "question of law," i.e., *halachah*. We should recall that this verse focuses on three areas in which the Sanhedrin is competent ("be it a controversy over homicide, civil law, or affliction [that is, ritually pure or impure]"), all of which most certainly come under the category of law.

Were the Sages endowed with the divine spirit and was their knowledge of the natural sciences derived from it? The Talmud leads us in the direction of an emphatic negative response to this question. We can read there: "The Sages have taught us: 'When the Last Prophets, Haggai, Zechariah and Malachi died, the divine spirit departed from Israel'" (*BT San.* 11a). In the same tractate, we read: "Rav said: 'I spent 18 months with a cowherd in order to learn which blemish is permanent and which is temporary [in firstborn animals]'" (*BT San.* 5b). If the Sages' knowledge of the natural sciences comes directly from God, what need did Rav have for an internship of observation with a cowherd in order to acquire the experience needed for settling questions of *halachah*? In another passage (*BT Pesachim* 94b), we read that, in matters of astronomy, Judah the Prince preferred the opinion of the (Gentile) learned of the nations to that of the Sages of Israel.

In his *Guide for the Perplexed*, Maimonides adopts a similar position:

> You must not find it strange that Aristotle differs here from the opinion of our Sages. The theory of the music of the spheres is connected with the theory of the motion of the stars in a fixed sphere, and our Sages have, in this astronomical question, abandoned their own theory in favor of the theory of others. Thus, it is distinctly stated, "The wise men of other nations have defeated the wise men of Israel." It is quite right that our Sages have abandoned their own theory: for speculative matters every one treats according to the results of his own study, and every one accepts that which appears to him established by proof (Part II, ch. 8).[6]

Later in this work, Maimonides again states that the scientific knowledge of the Sages of the Talmud reflects the knowledge that existed in their era:

> You must, however, not expect that everything our Sages say respecting astronomical matters should agree with observation, for mathematics were not fully developed in those days: and their statements were not based on the authority of the Prophets, but on the knowledge which they either themselves possessed or derived from contemporary men of science (Part III, ch. 14).[7]

---

[6] Moses Maimonides, *The Guide for the Perplexed*, translated from the original Arabic text by M. Friedländer, 4th edn., E. P., 1904, p. 163.

[7] Ibid., p. 278.

Prominent representatives of Neo-Orthodoxy, such as Samson Raphael Hirsch (Germany, 1808–1888), stated similar views. The Sanhedrin and the Sages of the Talmud enjoyed authority only in halachic matters, and the same can be said for their successors, the rabbinic authorities who are actively making rabbinic rulings today: they can certainly make their opinion known on the age of the universe or on other scientific or philosophical questions, but such an opinion cannot be considered a *p'sak halachah*, that is, a binding legal decision.

IV THE EXTENT OF HALACHIC AUTHORITY

A *The Extent of Hermeneutic Authority*

The last of the verses cited earlier determines the extent of rabbinic authority: "you must not deviate from the verdict that they announce to you either to the right or to the left" (*Deut*. 17:11). In this context, the *Sifrei* (or *Sifri*) comments: "Even if they (contemporary rabbinic authorities) declare that what you see as right is really left or that what you see as left is really right, you must obey them." Regarding that same verse, Nahmanides (Moses ben Nahman, 1194–1270) writes:

> Even if you think that they [the rabbinic authorities] are wrong and the matter is a simple one in your eyes because you can distinguish between right and left, you must do what they command you to do and you must not say, "How can I eat this forbidden piece of fat?" Or "How can I kill this innocent person?" Instead you must say to yourself, "This is what I have been commanded by the Lord who gives us the commandments. He commands me, with regard to all of His commandments, to act strictly in accordance with what I am instructed to do by those who stand before Him in the place that He will choose. He has given me the Torah so that I will always obey what they tell me even when they are mistaken ... in accordance with everything they will tell us regarding the Torah's interpretation, whether they received that interpretation from a direct chain of interpretation beginning with what God transmitted to Moses or whether they are interpreting the text in accordance with the Torah's meaning or intention. Because God gives us the Torah so that we will obey the Torah according to what they tell us, even if you think that they are calling left what you see as right. Certainly this is the case when they are calling right what you are calling right. God's spirit hovers above those who serve in His Temple and He will never abandon his followers; thus, they will always be spared from making mistakes and from stumbling over obstacles.

The basis of rabbinic authority is that the development of Jewish law is guided by Providence. Thus, even what seems to be a misinterpretation of God's will is actually an expression of that will.

Are the Sages and their successors willing to accept competition? According to Jewish tradition, God has continued to communicate with His people after the Revelation on Mount Sinai – whether indirectly and abundantly, during the era of the Prophets, or indirectly, but sparingly, through an intermediary, namely, a celestial voice, a voice from heaven (*bat kol*, "echo," lit. "daughter of a voice"). The Talmud reports that this celestial voice became the sole possible means of communication between God and human beings once the era of prophecy ended (*BT Yoma* 9b). In the post-prophetic era, can the Supreme Legislator Himself still intervene *directly* in the halachic process? This question is of cardinal importance because it allows us to precisely measure the Sages' authority.

In order to answer this question, we may look at a celebrated passage in the Talmud that begins with a discussion of the ritual purity of an oven with a unique structure, referred to in this passage as the oven of Achnai[8] (*BT BM* 59b):

> We learned the following: "On that day, Rabbi Eliezer gave every possible response; however, they [the Sages] did not accept any of them. He said to them, 'If the law here is in accordance with my opinion, this carob-tree will prove that fact,' whereupon the carob-tree was uprooted and transferred to another spot located at a distance of one hundred cubits[9] from the original site; some say that the distance was, in fact, 400 cubits. The Sages answered, 'A carob-tree cannot be presented as evidence.' Rabbi Eliezer then said to them, 'If the law here is in accordance with my opinion, this stream will prove that fact,' whereupon the stream began to flow in the opposite direction. The Sages answered, 'A stream cannot be presented as evidence.' Rabbi Eliezer then said to them, 'If the law here is in accordance with my opinion, the walls of this academy will prove that fact,' whereupon the walls of the academy began to tilt inwards, threatening to fall altogether. Rabbi Joshua rebuked them and told them, 'When talmudic scholars debate with one another on a halachic question, who gave you permission to interfere?' Out of deference to Rabbi Joshua, the walls did not fall and, out of deference to Rabbi Eliezer, they did not return to their original erect position. Instead, they simply continued to tilt inwards, remaining motionless. Rabbi Eliezer then said to

---

[8] Where the translation could perhaps be a "snake-like oven" – which could refer to the fact that it is made of separate coils of clay – or a term that perhaps refers not to the oven's shape but to the snake-like, that is, circumlocutory, discussion concerning this type of oven.

[9] An ancient unit of measure, equivalent to the length of an average person's forearm.

the Sages, 'If the *halachah* is in accordance with my opinion, the heavens will prove that fact,' whereupon an echo was heard [from heaven]: 'Why are you arguing with Rabbi Eliezer? The law here is, indeed, in accordance with his opinion.' Nonetheless, Rabbi Joshua stood up and said, citing the Torah, 'It is not in the heavens' (*Deut.* 30:12). What is the meaning of these words, 'It is not in the heavens'? Rabbi Jeremiah replied, 'Since the Torah was given to us on Mount Sinai, we pay no attention to any echoes from heaven. After all, You, the God of Israel, wrote [in the Torah] on Mount Sinai, 'you shall not give perverse testimony in a dispute so as to pervert it in favor of the mighty' (*Exod.* 23:2) – that is, one must follow the majority.' The Talmud continues: 'Rabbi Nathan encountered Elijah [the Prophet] and asked him, "What did God do at that time [that is, during this dispute]?" Elijah answered, "He laughed and said, 'My children have defeated me, my children have defeated me.'"'

This Talmudic passage indicates that, from the systemic standpoint, celestial intervention cannot decide on points of law. The revelation took place only once and, since that time, God has decided not to intervene in halachic disputes. It is significant that God Himself approves His exclusion from the halachic process and, in doing so, God Himself subscribes to Rabbi Jeremiah's interpretation of the verse "It is not in the heavens." Since God revealed His will on Mount Sinai in the text of the Torah and since the interpretation of the Torah has been entrusted to the Sages, God's participation in the hermeneutic process would constitute a violation of His own will. Nonetheless, He does intervene in order to prove that Rabbi Eliezer was right in his dispute with the majority; in doing so, God seems to be flagrantly violating an essential systemic rule that is issued by the Torah itself and according to which conflicts of opinion must be regulated by majority rule (see earlier in this volume).[10]

According to one commentator, Nissim Gaon (ca. 990–1060, a Tunisian rabbi and exegetist), God, in doing so, actually wanted to put the Sages to the test: would they agree to question their own decision, supported by the majority and thus valid, in the face of a celestial intervention? In this test, they refused to be intimidated and that is why God is so happy: the Sages understood that the Torah is immutable! The authority of both the prophecies (see later in this volume) and the celestial voice is not the only item that is excluded; in principle, divine inspiration, dreams and all other supernatural manifestations cannot serve as the basis for the determination of *halachah*.[11]

---

[10] But the Talmud is not consistent on the status of a *bat kol*. See, e.g., BT Eruvin 13b, "The things that both schools are saying are the living words of God," discussed later in this volume.

[11] On this fascinating topic, see Ephraim Kanarfogel, "Dreams As a Determinant of Jewish Law and Practice in Northern Europe during the High Middle Ages," in David Engel, Lawrence H.

The midrash on the oven of Akhnai conveys another lesson: *it emerges that theoretically, rabbinic authority recognizes no limits.* It is the sole interpreter of the Torah and it tells us what the Torah wants to say to us. What the rabbinic authority says, *in each generation,* is approved by God Himself, even if this is not what He wanted to say originally or ultimately. The reader will easily reach the conclusion that, in view of the extent of the authority conferred on the Sages or on the rabbis, Jewish law was able, and was even obligated, to develop in such a manner as to ensure that its most recent products had only a distant connection with its first products. This possibility was ratified by the Sages themselves in another famous midrashic passage in the Talmud. The episode relates how Moses ascends to heaven, just after his having received the Torah. In heaven, Moses finds himself seated at the back of a classroom (sitting in an imaginary eighth row, the seventh one being the one with the worst students!). Rabbi Akiva, whom the same passage praises for his prowess in exegesis, is conveying to his students a class based on an interpretation of the Torah. As he listens to this lesson, Moses is profoundly annoyed because he cannot understand anything that is being said by this future Sage (Rabbi Akiva belongs to the third generation of Sages of the Mishnah, ca. first–second centuries CE). Nonetheless, he is reassured when, replying to a question posed by one of the students, Rabbi Akiva states, with regard to one of his assertions, that the source of that assertion is a law that God gave to Moses on Mount Sinai. What the editor of the Talmud is suggesting here is that the law that was transmitted by the Sages, and that we know today, is the result of interpretation and that this result might seem very distant from the Supreme Legislator's intention. However, in the same breath, the Sages affirm that, just as this interpretation is something that has long been rooted in the Torah, the later states of *halachah* are not a debasement of the system but are rather its legitimate development.

Any discussion on development invites us to ask what are the limits of that development. Can the holders of rabbinic authority add or abolish a commandment? In other words, can they touch the very substance of the Torah? This question calls for a nuanced response.

B The Extent of Creative Authority

The Torah forbids any additions to, or deletions from, its text. According to the Sages' interpretation, this prohibition applied exclusively to the Prophets.

Schiffman and Elliot R. Wolfson (eds.), *Studies in Medieval Jewish Intellectual and Social History: Festschrift in Honor of Robert Chazan*, Brill, 2012, p. 111.

Regarding themselves, the Sages retained an interpretation that gave them immense latitude.

1 The Exact Scope of the Prohibition on Adding Anything To, or Removing Anything From, the Torah

Generally speaking, the Torah itself apparently prohibits any activity that is not purely interpretative. Or, if one prefers, explicative interpretation is permitted while creative interpretation is not. Deuteronomy expresses this idea in two different places: "You shall not add anything to what I command you or take anything away from it, but keep the commandments of the Lord your God that I enjoin upon you" (*Deut.* 4:2), and "Be careful to observe only that which I enjoin upon you: neither add to it nor take away from it" (*Deut.* 13:1). Thus, we can never find a source that permits the Sages to amend or repeal anything in the Torah; on the other hand, there is a prohibition on adding or removing commandments. The Talmud understands these verses and invokes them to justify the prohibition according to which a priest serving in the Temple cannot utter a blessing that he himself devised (*BT RH* 28b). In his commentary on these verses, Rashi provides an illustration of these prohibitions: it is forbidden to add (or detract) a compartment in the phylacteries. However, we must admit that the Talmud itself contains several amendments to, or abrogations of, laws contained in the Torah. The verses regarding capital punishment for the "rebellious son" are interpreted in such a way as to render the punishment's application absolutely impossible; the forty lashes of the whip for certain violations are reduced to thirty-nine; the ordeal to which a woman suspected of adultery must be submitted disappears as a result of the lowering of moral standards (see Chapter 2 regarding the *sotah*). More generally, everyone agrees that the Sages contributed to the elaboration of norms. In order to emerge from this apparent paradox, we must distinguish the power of the prophets, which is nonexistent in this domain, and the power of the Sages and their successors.

THE REJECTION OF PROPHECY IN THE HALACHIC PROCESS Regarding the Prophets, the closing verse of Leviticus (27:34) serves as the basis for denying the Prophets the power to *innovate* in the domain of *halachah*: "'These are the commandments that the Lord gave Moses for the Israelite people on Mount Sinai." *Targum Yonatan* interprets this verse: "without their being able to add anything to the commandments, God ordered Moses to transmit them to the Children of Israel on Mount Sinai." Thus, the expression "these are the commandments" indicates that these were God's commandments, no more, no less. The Talmud also categorically excludes prophecy as a source of law (BT *Shabbat* 104a, BT *Yoma* 80a, BT *Meg.* 2b, BT *Tem.* 16a). In his code, Maimonides, invoking other scriptural sources to support this exclusion, develops the range of the rule:

> It is written, "It is a law for all time throughout the ages" (*Lev.* 3:17, 23:14; *Num.* 10–18) and "It is not in the heavens" (*Deut.* 30:12). We thus learn from these verses that no prophet is permitted to add any new commandments from now on. For this reason, if a person, whether a Gentile or a Jew, gives a sign or portent and says that God has sent him to add or retract a commandment or to give any of the commandments an interpretation that we have not heard from Moses, or who says that the commandments given to Israel are not eternal and for all succeeding generations but are rather commandments that are to be observed only for a limited period of time, this is a false prophet who has come to deny Moses' prophecy. He must be put to death by strangulation because he has maliciously plotted to speak on behalf of God, although he was not commanded to do so. (*MT, The Laws Governing the Foundations of the Torah* 9:1).

The remainder of this chapter elaborates on this rule, which is designed to enable us to determine what a prophet can legitimately decide in exceptional circumstances. The prophets' lack of authorization to deal with halachic matters has a hermeneutical corollary according to which we cannot learn the laws of the Torah from the words of tradition (*divrei kabbalah*). In other words, it is forbidden to deduce the rules of Jewish law from the Prophets or the Hagiographa because the prophets were not authorized to promulgate new laws. However, it is permissible to detect in these writings an allusion to or a simple confirmation of halachic norms.

THE SAGES AND THEIR SUCCESSORS The Sages were very conscious of their creative powers. Thus Rava says: "How foolish most human beings are! They will stand up in order to honor a scroll of Torah but they will not do so in the presence of a great individual! [Yet they should realize the following:] Whereas it is written in the Torah that, when a person is punished with lashes of the whip, 40 lashes are required, the rabbis reduced that number by one [to 39]" (*BT Mak.* 22b).

On this subject, two explanations confront each other: the explanation given by Salomon ben Aderet (Barcelona, 1235–1310, better known as Rashba) and the one given by Maimonides in order to clarify what, a priori, constitutes an anomaly. In commenting on a passage from the Talmud, according to which the ram's horn (*shofar*) is sounded twice during the *Amidah* prayer of the additional (*Mussaf*) service on Rosh Hashanah (Jewish New Year), Rashba reveals his doctrine. He notes that certain commentators (the Tosafists, French and German commentators, twelfth–fourteenth centuries) justified this double sounding of the *shofar* with an argument that is not very convincing: the repeated performance of a commandment does not contravene the prohibition of adding to what is written in the Torah. In reality, according to Rashba, it is reasonable to think that there is no problem because the Sages never maintained that the prohibition on adding to what is written in the Torah applies except in cases where we add something on our own authority – for example, a priest (*kohen*) who decides to add a blessing to the three standard priestly blessings. However, argues Rashba, the prohibition does not apply to any additional commandments issued by rabbinic authorities because the Torah states: "You shall act in accordance with the instructions they will give you" (*Deut.* 17:11). Thus, emphasizes Rashba, the rabbinic authorities have the power to make additions to what the Torah says for whatever reason that seems legitimate in their opinion, and this holds true as well with regard to the Torah's prohibition on suppressing a commandment: for example, when the Jewish New Year falls on a Sabbath, the rabbis justly decided that the ram's horn should not be sounded, although the Torah requires its sounding on that holiday. In fact, observes Rashba, Jews are commanded to heed the words of their rabbis: "you must not deviate" (*Deut.* 17:11). According to Rashba, the injunction "you must not deviate" is not only a source of the Sages' interpretive powers but also a source of their legislative powers. No antinomy can arise from the confrontation between this verse and those that forbid amending or repealing anything in the Torah. Thus, no rabbinic amendment or repeal of a commandment in the Torah can be considered a violation of the Torah. Only amendments decreed by an individual or a rabbinic authority that is not recognized are illegitimate. Here is the problematic nature of Reform Judaism, as is discussed briefly in what follows. Finally, it is important to note that Rashba insists on the need for a valid reason for any piece of rabbinic legislation. The power of the Sages is immense, but it is not arbitrary.

Maimonides offers another approach. In his view, the prohibition to add to or detract from any of the Torah's commandments is not limited to individuals. Even when decided by rabbinic authorities, the question whether an amendment or a repeal of a commandment in the Torah is permissible or not depends on the manner in which this piece of rabbinic legislation was adopted:

> A rabbinic court of law is authorized to issue a decree and to forbid what is permitted in the Torah and this prohibition can be in effect for many generations to come. Similarly, a rabbinic court of law is authorized to temporarily permit what the Torah prohibits. Thus, we can ask ourselves

what the Torah means when it warns us, "neither add to it nor take away from it" (*Deut.* 13:1). The meaning of that warning is that it is forbidden to add to, or to detract from, what is written in the Torah and to declare that this is what the Torah commands – whether the reference is to the Written Torah (or Written Law) or to the Oral Torah (or Oral Law). How is this principle expressed in practical terms? It is written in the Torah, "You shall not boil a kid in its mother's milk" (*Exod.* 23:19, 34:26; *Deut.* 14:21). According to our tradition, we understand that the Torah is prohibiting the preparation or consumption of any dish in which milk and meat are mixed together – whether the meat is that of a domesticated or an undomesticated animal. The Torah, however, does allow the preparation or consumption of a dish in which milk and chicken are mixed together. If a rabbinic court of law permits the preparation or consumption of a dish in which milk and the meat of an undomesticated animal are mixed together, that action would amount to a detraction of one of the Torah's commandments. If a rabbinic court of law prohibits the preparation or consumption of a dish in which milk and chicken are mixed together and declares that chicken falls under the same category as the meat of a kid (young goat) and that this is a prohibition issued by the Torah, that action would amount to an addition to the Torah's already existing commandments. However, that rabbinic court of law could state, "The Torah does permit the preparation or consumption of a dish in which milk and chicken are mixed together; however, we are prohibiting the preparation or consumption of such a dish and we will notify our fellow Jews that this is a decree designed to prevent them from mistakenly committing a sin. For example, some of our fellow Jews might say 'Chicken is permitted because it is not explicitly prohibited in the Torah; thus, the meat of an undomesticated animal is similarly permissible because it is not explicitly prohibited.' Other Jews might also say, 'The meat of a domesticated animal is permissible, except for the meat of young goats.' Still others might say, 'The meat of a domesticated animal is permissible, except for the meat of young goats.' Then again, others might say, 'It is permissible to prepare or consume a dish in which the meat of a young goat and the milk of a cow or lamb are mixed together because the Torah states "its mother's milk" – in other words, the prohibition only applies if the milk is from the same breed of animal as the meat.' Other Jews might say, 'It is permissible to mix milk and meat together, if the milk is that of a young goat and if the meat is that of another breed of animal because the Torah states "its mother's milk" – in other words, the prohibition only applies if the milk is from the same breed of animal as the meat.' Therefore, this rabbinic court has decided to prohibit the preparation or consumption of any dish in which any kind of meat – including chicken – and milk are mixed together." This kind of action amounts not to the addition of a commandment to the Torah's already existing commandments but is rather the establishment of a fence around the Torah's prohibitions that is designed to serve as an extra precaution that will help prevent Jews from mistakenly committing sins. And this holds true for other instances as well. (*MT Laws Governing Rebels* 2:9)

Thus, according to Maimonides, the manner in which the rabbinic decree is issued permits us to draw a distinction between a legitimate rabbinic measure and an illegitimate one. If the amendment or repeal are declared to have been prescribed by the Torah, such a measure would constitute a violation of the prohibition of adding to or detracting from the Torah's commandments. If, however, the measure that is adopted – whether it adds to or detracts from one or more of the Torah's commandments – is clearly presented as not having been prescribed by the Torah, such a measure is valid.

We should underline here other points in the Maimonidean doctrine. First of all, Maimonides draws a distinction with regard to the duration of a particular piece of rabbinic legislation. Whereas a decree prohibiting what is permitted can be allowed to remain in effect on a permanent basis, a decree allowing what has been forbidden can remain in effect only on a temporary basis. Maimonides does not explain this differentiation. One might suggest that the reason might be that the preservation of a Torah commandment can necessitate a definitive prohibition of what in principle is permissible (such as in the case of the prohibition on the mixing of milk and chicken, a prohibition still in effect today); however, it is more difficult to imagine that the permanent lifting of a prohibition can constitute the indispensable means of safeguarding that prohibition. Second, note that Maimonides is more precise on the subject of the grounds for rabbinic legislation: it erects a fence or a hedge around the Torah – a concept that we encounter, for example, in the Mishnah (*Pirkei Avot* 1:1). In other words, what legitimates a given piece of rabbinic legislation is the desire to preserve a Torah commandment. Finally, the legislative intervention must be proportional to the goal that is being aimed for.

2 Illustrations

Let us now look at a few examples of cases where the Sages or the rabbinic authorities have intervened. A convenient way of examining such cases of rabbinic intervention is to group them under three categories, each of which expresses a different guiding principle.

IT IS TIME FOR GOD TO ACT/IT IS TIME FOR US TO ACT ON BEHALF OF GOD We read in the Psalms: "For the Lord, it is time to act, for they have violated Your teaching" (Psalms 119:126). The translation provided earlier clearly reflects the ambiguity of the original Hebrew (*et la'assot lashem heferu toratecha*), which can be read as "it is time for the Lord to act" or "it is time to act on behalf of the Lord" (*BT Ber.* 63a). The rabbinic literature has retained both readings. Nonetheless, a reading according to which it is God who must act when His Torah is threatened cannot serve as a guiding principle for the Sages' legal action. Only the second reading, according to which we must act when the Law is violated, can indicate what circumstances would legitimate the Sages' legislative intervention. Thus, for example, to thwart the heretics, it is permissible to change the formulation of a blessing (*M Ber.* 9:5). The lifting of the prohibition on writing down the Oral Torah certainly falls under this same category: the Exile from the Holy Land and its harmful consequences for knowledge of the Law urgently required that what had not been lost must be saved.

We find in the rabbinic literature two other sayings that express the same idea and that we can regard as subcategories of the previous category. The first one begins: "It is preferable that a letter in the Torah be uprooted" ("*Mutav te'aker ot ah'at min ha-Torah*"). The latter half of the saying varies according to the source. For example, "It is preferable that a letter in the Torah be uprooted rather than the name of God should be desecrated in public" (*BT Yev.* 79a). The second is phrased as follows: "Sometimes the cancellation of the Torah actually serves as its foundations." This saying, which can be found only once in the Talmud (*BT Men.* 99a), serves as a justification for the breaking of the Tablets of the Law by Moses (*Exod.* 32:19), when he descended from Mount Sinai only to find the Golden Calf that the Israelites had fashioned. The Law has no place in such an ambiance of renunciation. Here, the destruction of the Tablets, even temporarily, assured the Law's existence.

We should note that these maxims, in accordance with their function in the general theory of law, provide only directives and do not permit us to determine with any certainty when the suspension of the *Grundnorm* is possible. We might feel embarrassed by the fact that a question of such cardinal importance should be regulated by such loosely worded principles. The judge-legislator appears to have complete power – for better or worse. Regarding this point, we can present a number of contrary observations. In principle, rabbinic intervention is exceptional when we consider a norm whose fundamental element, the Torah, is both legal and theological. Since this power was conceived to protect the Torah in extraordinary cases (emergencies of any kind, deterioration of the socioeconomic fabric, exile, etc.), we cannot expect this system to be capable of offering a precise, even a rigid, norm. The second major principle, however, offers cleaner contours.

IT IS WRITTEN "BY THE PURSUIT OF WHICH MAN SHALL LIVE" There is a saying that we find in many passages in the rabbinic literature and that, contrary to the sayings discussed earlier in this volume, draws its source from the Torah itself: "You shall keep My laws and My rules, by the pursuit of which man shall live: I am the Lord" (*Lev.* 18:5). The Sages deduced from this verse that the commandments should not be applied in a manner that could threaten human life. For example, the commandments linked to the observance of the Sabbath can be violated in order to save a human life (*BT Yoma* 85b). The study of another Talmudic passage allows us to define more precisely this principle and the exceptions to it:

> If I am told to commit a sin or die, I should commit the sin and save my life unless the sin is idolatry, incest or murder... Rabbi Ishmael says: "How do we know that, if I am told to commit the sin of idolatry or die, I should commit this sin and save my life? Because it is written 'by the pursuit of which man shall live' [*Lev.* 18:5] – that is, we should live and not die. Does this principle apply even when I am told to commit the sin of idolatry in public? No, because it is written in the Torah, 'You shall not profane My holy name, that I may be sanctified' [*Lev.* 22:32] ... When Rabbi Dimi came, he cited Rabbi Yohanan who said, '[The principle according to which I must choose death rather than commit the sin of idolatry, incest or murder applies] only when there is no royal decree; however, if there is a royal decree, I must choose death rather than commit even a minor sin.' When Rabin came, he cited Rabbi Yohanan who said, 'Even if there is no royal decree, I can commit a sin as long as I do so in private; however, if there is a royal decree, I must choose death rather than commit even a minor sin.'" (*BT San.* 74a)

The explanation given by Rabbi Yohanan has been codified by Maimonides (*MT Laws of the Foundations of the Torah*, ch. 5). The guiding principle that is common to the cases where I must choose death rather than commit a sin is that the Torah will be better served if I die rather than if I survive. For example, when there is a royal decree, I must do whatever I can to strengthen the Jewish community's commitment to the Torah. The Sages consider martyrdom preferable to the repealing of the Torah. If there is no royal decree and the violence takes place in private, the martyrdom will not serve the cause of the Torah and that is why the maxim "*Va-hai bahem*" – "by the pursuit of which man shall live" – is applied.

DEROGATORY CRIMINAL LAWS: THE "NEED OF THE HOUR" (HORA'AT SHA'AH) The examples we have encountered essentially concern civil or ritual law. We can also find in Talmudic literature an exemplum (see Chapter 2) that is of cardinal importance: the authority of rabbinic courts to decide *contra legem* in criminal matters and not only to inflict "light" physical punishment (such as flogging) but also to hand down and execute death sentences. This point is so important that we find parallel – but not identical – texts referring to it in three different sources: *BT, JT* and *Megillat Ta'anit (Scroll of Fasting)*. Although the variations between the three texts are instructive, we concentrate on the version that appears in the Babylonian Talmud:

> The following has been learned: Rabbi Eliezer, son of Jacob, said: "I have heard about a rabbinic court of law flogging and punishing individuals not because of what is written in the Torah and not because they committed a sin but rather to build a fence around the Torah (in order to prevent people from sinning). There was the case of someone who rode a horse on the Sabbath during the Greek era; he was brought before a rabbinic court and was stoned to death – not because this was a fitting punishment but rather because this was the need of the hour [*hora'at sha'ah*]. There was another case of a man who had sexual relations with his wife under a fig tree; he was brought before a rabbinic court and was flogged – not because this was a fitting punishment but rather because this was the need of the hour." (*BT San.* 46a)

The Talmud provides us with other examples that are rather startling and that are not prescribed by the Torah, such as piercing the eyes of a murderer (*BT San.* 27a), cutting off the hand of a chronic sinner (*BT San.* 58b), burning alive a woman found guilty of adultery (*BT San.* 52b) and burning alive eighty witches in a single day (*BT San.* 44b). The systemization of these cases raises many questions: Was this authority granted only to the original Sanhedrin or was it also granted to the rabbinic courts that succeeded it in subsequent generations in Palestine as well as in the Diaspora? Was this authority solely judicial or was it also legislative? What was the nature of the penalties that a rabbinic tribunal was authorized to mete out? Rabbinic authorities have given a broad interpretation to these precedents, arguing that the jurisdiction granted to the Sanhedrin was both judiciary and legislative and that the latter can be exercised by communities in exile (on communal ordinances, see Chapter 3), expressing itself across an entire spectrum of penalties, ranging from fines to the death penalty and including excommunication and the confiscation of assets (see *MT, Laws Governing the Sanhedrin* 24:6–10). The authority exercised by the rabbinic courts of law in Diaspora Jewish communities was not unlimited: as we have seen, it had to be justified by the urgency of the hour and it had to be motivated by a desire to assure the Torah's eternal character. According to Maimonides, the measures adopted by these courts were only temporary. The justification for emergency measures was provided by the verse "the magistrate in charge" (*Deut.* 17:9), the nature and domain of the "need of the hour" (*hora'at sha'ah*) depending, as the verse suggests, on what the particular circumstances and epoch required. Justification for the confiscation of assets, which generally consisted of the expropriation from one individual of a sum of money that was then granted to another individual, was provided by a passage in the Prophets (*Ezek.* 10:8).

V HALACHIC PLURALISM

The Talmud's legal pluralism is often affirmed, even vaunted. Without pretending to exhaust the question, we may discuss this subject in order to clarify it further.

1 An Affirmation of Halachic Pluralism

The Sages tell us what Jewish law is and they have total latitude to do so. Nonetheless, it is evident, when we read the Talmud even superficially, that there are few subjects on which the Sages agree. The Talmud is fertile ground for the production of varieties of fruit all of which bear the same name: controversy. A vivid controversy that aims at methodically discussing subjects in a profound manner. We have already seen that the rule for definitively establishing the *halachah* in a given case in the event of a plurality of opinions is majority rule (*Exod.* 23:2). However, the passage in Deuteronomy that has been cited earlier and that is the source of rabbinic authority expresses the existence of a supreme legal instance that is empowered to render final decisions. Should we therefore conclude that the disappearance of the Sanhedrin has opened the door to the more general availability of controversies, whereas, before its disappearance, the Sages spoke with a single voice? Maimonides teaches us that this is a subject that must be nuanced. Disputes and conflicts were always present – to such an extent that a decision adopted by the Great Sanhedrin can be revoked by a later Sanhedrin that has adopted a different interpretation (*MT, Laws Governing Rebels* 2:1).

Controversy is not evil; it is good as long as it is being conducted in the name of heaven (*Pirkei Avot* 5:17). Nevertheless, laws must be established definitively and legal disputes must be settled; thus, choices must be made between contrary opinions, in accordance with the methods presented elsewhere. These choices, which necessarily imply the rejection of one of the opinions, are problematic because the opinion that was rejected is divine. Another passage in the Talmud tackles this issue:

Rabbi Abba cited Samuel who said: For three years the School of Shammai and the School of Hillel debated with one another. The School of Shammai declared: "The *halachah* in this case conforms with our opinion," while the School of Hillel declared: "The *halachah* in this case conforms with our opinion." An echo from heaven (*bat kol*) was heard: "The things that both schools are saying are the living words of God; however, the religious law in this case conforms with the opinion of the School of Hillel". If the things that both schools are saying are "the living words of God," why was it decided that the religious law in this case conformed with the opinion of the School of Hillel? Because the members of the School of Hillel were pleasant and soft-spoken and because they would mention not only their opinion but also that of the School of Shammai. Moreover, they would mention the School of Shammai's opinion before their own. (*BT Er.* 13b)

This midrash is often commented on in rabbinic literature as well as in the writings of contemporary authors.[12] Quite simply, this midrash expresses the idea that no antagonistic opinion is, by its very nature, "true" or "false." Positions that do not go beyond the limits of pluralism (on these limits, see later in this volume) are both *correct* and *incorrect* because they are equally divine, even after the normative character of one of them has been rejected.

This is how the midrash is understood by Ritva (Rabbi Yom Tov ben Avraham Asevilli, Seville, 1250–1330), as can be seen in his gloss on the aforementioned Talmudic passage. In that gloss, he notes that the French Sages of blessed memory asked how it was possible that "the things that both schools are saying are the living words of God" when one school forbade something while the other permitted it. The French Sages, says Ritva, explained that, when Moses ascended to heaven to receive the Torah, he was shown, one by one, forty-nine arguments for declaring that something is forbidden or permitted. When Moses questioned God regarding what he was shown, God responded that the determination of the law was entrusted to the Sages of Israel in each generation and that the decision had to be theirs. From the midrashic standpoint, this explanation is correct, concludes Ritva, although, ultimately, it does assume an esoteric meaning.

However, no matter how convincing it appears to be, this understanding of this Talmudic passage poses a major difficulty from a logical standpoint: how can we affirm that both A and non-A are equally true? Some classical commentators found it difficult to accept the evident, but excessively metaphysical, meaning of this Talmudic passage.

---

[12] For a very fine discussion of the issues, see Avi Sagi, *The Open Canon: On the Meaning of Halachic Discourse*, Continuum, 2007.

Thus, the author of the principal code of Jewish law, Joseph Karo, proposes a more rationalist interpretation. He admits that he finds the basic message of that Talmudic passage surprising. If, asks Karo, the law in that particular case was not really what the members of the School of Hillel said it was, was the law made to conform with their opinion simply because of the virtues of their character? Perhaps, he suggests, the intention of this passage was to ask: on what basis were they privileged to hold positions that were always correct to such an extent that, because of the correctness of their positions, the religious law in this particular instance was established in accordance with their opinion? Karo denies that two antagonistic positions can both be true; however, he is obliged to distance himself from the clear sense of this Talmudic passage.

We owe a debt of thanks to Salomon Nissim Algazi (ca. 1610–1683, rabbi in Smyrne [present-day Izmir] and Jerusalem) for his synthesis of the metaphysical and rationalist positions. Commenting on the aforementioned work by Karo and citing Hananel ben Houchiel (990–1053), better known as Rabbenu Hananel, who was a Tunisian rabbi and a commentator on the Talmud and on the Torah, Algazi explains the meaning of "the things that both schools are saying are the living words of God" as follows: like Ritva, he notes that Moses was shown by God forty-nine arguments for declaring something as ritually pure and forty-nine arguments for declaring something as ritually impure *without settling the question*. The decision was left to the opinion of the majority, in accordance with what is written in the Torah (*Exod.* 23:2). This, in essence, says Algazi, is the significance of the question in the Talmudic passage: since "the things that both schools are saying are the living words of God," and since both points of view were communicated to Moses on Mount Sinai, on what basis, asks Algazi, did the School of Hillel merit the honor of the law being determined according to its opinion, as declared by an echo from heaven?

Thus, according to Algazi, God refrained from revealing His will and left it up to the Sages to choose from among the various interpretations. Although the logical problem is thus resolved, from a practical standpoint there is a difference between the idea that God never revealed His will and the idea that He did not reveal it in a definitive manner (thus His will can vary in the course of time and will always be correct). On the other hand, this idea shows that there are at least two different approaches to the concept of Revelation.

In any event, the Sages' interpretation is always authentic. The Torah is what they say it is, just as "the Constitution is what the judges say it is," as was stated by Charles Evans Hughes (1862–1948), who served as US Supreme Court justice from 1930 to 1941.

2 The Limits to Halachic Pluralism

We should clarify here a question that has caused a huge quantity of ink to flow: is there a limit to halachic pluralism? In other words, does every opinion belong *ipso facto* or even *ipso iure* to the category of "the living words of God," or is it possible to argue that halachic pluralism does not apply, for instance, to an opinion that presents an entirely new solution? We have seen in the preceding developments that, if the Torah is in itself intangible, that meaning must be determined by the Sages and can legitimately vary in the course of time. Thus, logically, it seems impossible that we can ever identify an interpretation or a decision that might be *contrary* to the Torah. Thus, if the Sages interpret "an eye for an eye, a tooth for a tooth" (*Exod.* 21:24) as the payment of reparations commensurate with the extent of the physical loss – in other words, as monetary compensation – it is unacceptable, from a systemic standpoint, to assert that the Sages have changed the meaning of this verse and have repealed the *lex talionis*, replacing it with a measure that is far less harsh.

Similarly, if "bind them as a sign on your hand" (*Deut.* 6:8) is interpreted as designating a phylactery, any other interpretation, regardless of its value, has no legal importance whatsoever. However, what we have here are verses that present a certain degree of equivocality, which therefore calls for exegesis. Are there no verses that are sufficiently univocal and that can therefore enable us to qualify an interpretation (or a decision) that is *contra legem*? This point is admitted in the Babylonian Talmud by a mishnah in Tractate Horayot that deals with the sacrifices that the Great Sanhedrin must offer if it has committed an error with regard to law:

> If a rabbinic court decides to uproot a commandment entirely – declaring, for example, "The Torah does not command us to observe the laws of religious purity in conjugal relations," "The Torah does not command us to observe the Sabbath," and "The Torah does not forbid us to worship idols" – the members of the Sanhedrin are exempt from offering a sacrifice [i.e., a sin-offering]. If a rabbinic court decides that part of a commandment should be canceled while the rest of the commandment should continue to be observed, the members of the Sanhedrin are obligated to offer a sacrifice [i.e., a sin-offering]. How would such a decision be expressed? For example, the court declares, "The Torah commands us to observe the laws of religious purity in conjugal relations; however, if a man has sexual relations with his wife, who saw some menstrual blood after the seven days of purity [which must be counted each month after the disappearance of menstrual blood, and with whom he can have sexual relationships only after the absence of all menstrual blood for a period of twenty-four hours], he is exempt from the

punishment of *karet*."[13] Or the court declares "The Torah commands us to observe the Sabbath; however, a person who removes an article from the private domain and transfers it to the public domain is exempt from the punishment of *karet*." Or the court declares "The Torah forbids us to worship idols; however, a person who bows down before an idol is exempt from *karet*." The members of a court that makes such decisions are obligated to offer a sacrifice [i.e., a sin-offering], as it is written, "and the matter escapes the notice" [*Lev.* 13:4] – in other words, if they cancel part of a commandment but not the entire commandment. (1:3)

It is not necessary to explain in detail each of the cases mentioned in this mishnah in order to understand what is expressed there. Let us simply say that, whereas the prohibition on "working" on the Sabbath is mentioned many times and from different aspects, the prohibition on carrying an article from the private domain to the public domain is not explicitly referred to in the Torah. The reason for the exemption from offering a sacrifice (namely, a sin-offering) is that the "uprooted" commandment – the observance of the Sabbath – is so explicit that it is impossible for someone to rely on such an erroneous decision made by a rabbinic court and not that it is permitted to issue an interpretation *contra legem*. Conversely, a sacrifice must be offered when the Sanhedrin does not completely negate a verse but rather denies an accepted interpretation of a given verse.

The Talmud presents the *ratio legis*:

Rabbi Judah cited Samuel, who said: "A rabbinic court is not obligated to bring a sacrifice unless it commands something that the Sadducees do not accept; however, if it commands something that the Sadducees do accept, the tribunal is exempt from bringing a sacrifice. What is the reason for this distinction? [Because such an error belongs to the category of] 'Go and learn it in school' [i.e., any schoolchild knows the answer to that question]." (*BT Hor.* 4a)

This category of errors designates a question that is so clear that even a schoolchild knows the answer – that is, the issue is explicitly presented in the verse(s) in question. In other words, a rabbinic court is not obliged to bring a sacrifice to the Temple for an erroneous decision because such a decision is not a "decision"! The allusion to the Sadducees' approval is intended to underline the Torah's explicit character, because the Sadducees were a sect that rejected both the Oral Torah and the Sages' authority.

---

[13] A premature death as decreed by heaven.

However, one is tempted to reason *a fortiori*. If an erroneous decision obligates the presentation of a sacrifice, in this case a sin-offering (namely, a bull sacrificed for an unintentional sin committed by the entire community), does it not stand to reason that a grossly mistaken decision should also obligate the presentation of a sin-offering? In his commentary on "go and learn it in school," Rashi clarifies: since the rabbinic court could learn about and become familiar with this law, any error in the decision-making process regarding that law could not be deemed unintentional; in fact, Rashi argues, such a decision can be viewed as an intentional act. Yet, he notes, the possibility of atoning for an intentional error by means of a sacrifice does not exist in principle (except in four instances). We may cite other examples. A decision to allow a priest (*kohen*) to marry a divorced woman would constitute an "uprooting of the Torah" because there is a verse in the Torah that explicitly forbids such a union (*Lev.* 21:7). Similarly, a denial that the Torah recognize the concept of *mamzer* (an illegitimate child born of an adulterous or incestuous relationship) would obligate the rabbinic authority making that decision to "go back to school" because, although the definition of a *mamzer* is not explicitly given, the existence of *mamzerim* (pl. of *mamzer*) cannot be doubted (*Deut.* 23:3).

SECTION 2 THE NEW PARADIGMS OF HALACHIC AUTHORITY

The paradigm of halachic authority, which was patiently forged in the course of 2,000 years of rabbinic Judaism, began to be questioned, more or less radically, from the nineteenth century onward.

I REFORM JUDAISM: *ZEITGEIST* AS THE *GRUNDNORM*

In the course of its long history, Judaism has known sects or heresies that have partially or totally questioned the authority of the sources of Jewish law. First, there were the Sadducees during the Second Temple period. They rejected the Pharisees' interpretation of the Torah. Historian Josephus Flavius, a member of a priestly family that had close ties with the Sadducees, summarized their opposition. The Pharisees, he wrote in *The Antiquities of the Jews*, transmitted to the Jewish people certain laws that they received from the Sages and that they observed; these laws were not included in Moses' written laws – that is, the Written Torah or Written Law – and for that reason they were rejected by the Sadducees, who believed that (a) the only laws that were valid and that thus must be observed were those that were included in the Written Law, and (b) the laws received according to the tradition of the Sages did not have to be observed.[14] Nonetheless, we cannot consider the Sadducees to be literalists: the Talmud refers to "The Sadducees' Book of Decrees." The Sadducees' doctrine can be summarized in the following manner: while possessing their own oral exegesis, the Sadducees rejected certain traditions that were external to the Written Law and, especially, the external traditions of other movements.[15]

Another challenge to Judaism has come from the Karaites, who are essentially distinguished by their rejection of the Oral Torah or Oral Law and by their scripturalism. This dissident sect in Judaism was born in Babylon in the eighth century and exists today as a rather small community.[16]

Reform Judaism is a movement in Judaism that denies the immutable character of the Written Law. According to Reform Judaism's doctrine, *halachah* must be adapted to the spirit of the times and to its demands.

---

[14] www.gutenberg.org/files/2848/2848-h/2848-h.htm.
[15] Anthony J. Saldarini, *Pharisees, Scribes and Sadducees in Palestinian Society*, W. Eerdmans, 2001.
[16] Meira Polliack, *Karaite Judaism: A Guide to Its History and Literary Sources*, Brill, 2003.

Reform Judaism quickly cultivated subgroups that were more or less radical in their rewriting of the Written Law and their changes in Jewish practices, specifically, subgroups such as Liberal Judaism and Reconstructionist Judaism. Reform Judaism arose in Germany in the nineteenth century in the wake of the Emancipation and the philosophy of the Enlightenment (*Haskalah*); it was closely associated with *die Wissenschaft des Judentums* (the "science of Judaism"; see Chapter 1).[17] In the late nineteenth century, it spread to France, where it continued to flourish, although it was practiced by only a small percentage of French Jews. In this same era, it established roots in the United States and became the largest religious movement in the American Jewish community.[18] The basic approach of Liberal or Reform Judaism is that, step by stop, *halachah* must adapt (for example, by lifting most of the prohibitions related to the Sabbath, by permitting intermarriage, etc.) from a legal system whose source and authority originate in the Torah to a moral and ethical system whose sources are a universalistic and secular philosophy. Reform Judaism represents a genuine change in the paradigm of halachic authority: the dejuridicization of *halachah*.

II THE "COUNTER-REFORM" OR THE BIRTH OF ORTHODOX JUDAISM

Although it presents itself as the legitimate heir of "traditional" Judaism, that is, rabbinic Judaism, which we have already analyzed, Orthodox Judaism is a relatively recent development in the Jewish world. Orthodox Judaism first appeared in the nineteenth century as a reaction to the growth of Reform Judaism. Like Reform Judaism, Orthodox Judaism is not a unified religious movement. We can think of at least two subgroups in Orthodox Judaism. In the center, we should mention German Jewry's version of Neo-Orthodoxy, which was founded by Rabbi Samson Raphael Hirsch (1808–1888), and Hungarian Jewry's version of Neo-Orthodoxy, which was founded by Rabbi Ezriel Hildesheimer (1820–1899). We must distinguish between Neo-Orthodox Judaism and "right-wing" Orthodox Judaism, which originated in Eastern Europe and which opposed the Emancipation. Right-wing Orthodox Judaism was decidedly Orthodox: its founders advocated a strict adherence to *halachah*, as we know it today. Hirsch and

---

[17] W. Gunther Plaut, *The Rise of Reform Judaism: A Sourcebook of Its European Origins*, Jewish Publication Society, 2015.

[18] Dana Evan Kaplan, *American Reform Judaism: An Introduction*, Rutgers University Press, 2003.

Hildesheimer also advocated a strict adherence to *halachah* and Neo-Orthodox Judaism waged a merciless battle against Reform Judaism but, unlike Eastern European Orthodox Judaism, was open to the world and sought to integrate into society – in this case, German society.[19] In this regard, it is particularly revealing that all of Neo-Orthodox Judaism's leaders held doctorates conferred on them by a German university and they were proud of that fact. This was the era of the "Rabbi Dr." Moreover, German was recognized as a legitimate language for rabbinic commentaries, and this recognition represented an attempt to break the monopoly of Hebrew and Yiddish.

We should mention here the three major characteristics of Orthodox Judaism: traditionalism, separatism (with regard to Reform Judaism) and legalism (strict adherence to *halachah*). In our opinion, Orthodox Judaism, even the right-wing variety, does not really constitute a change in the paradigm of halachic authority; instead it represents a hardening of the attitude toward *halachah*, as expressed by the slogan "innovation is forbidden." The Eastern European variety of Orthodox Judaism was strongly opposed to secular studies, and this aspect would become one of the hallmarks of ultra-Orthodox Jewry. Orthodox Jewry opened the door for the emergence of ultra-Orthodox Jewry, which, paradoxically, we regard as constituting a real change in this paradigm.

III "ULTRA-ORTHODOX" JUDAISM

Although the term is not that satisfying, we use it because it is often employed to designate right-wing Orthodox Judaism. Those who adhere to this doctrine are called *Hareidim* (lit., those who fear God). The use of the term *ultra-Orthodox* in the media is often abusive, even caricatural. The term requires clarification. "Ultra-Orthodoxy" is not a stricter reaction to Reform Judaism (whose members in any case are considered by ultra-Orthodoxy to be lost to Judaism) or even to the Zionist enterprise, held in contempt for its secularism. In reality, ultra-Orthodoxy is a reaction to German Neo-Orthodoxy, as attested by the fact that ultra-Orthodoxy's "manifesto" (actually a rabbinic decision) represented a decision that was taken to protest any changes in the organization of the synagogue. The changes vilified in that decision were those that were introduced in the synagogue in Presburg, which belonged to the Neo-Orthodox

---

[19] The motto was "Torah im derech eretz," lit. "Torah in the way of the land." See Mordechai Breuer, "The 'Torah-im-Derekh-Eretz' of Samson Raphael Hirsch," *New York: Feldheim* (1970); Mordechai Eliav, "Various Approaches to Torah Im Derekh Eretz: Ideal and Reality," 26.2 *Tradition: A Journal of Orthodox Jewish Thought* 99 (1992).

community. Ultra-Orthodoxy can be characterized by several traits that clearly distinguish it from "mainstream" Orthodoxy. The first is the preeminent role of Talmudic academies – *yeshivot* (pl. of *yeshiva*) for non-married men and the *kollelim* (pl. of *kollel*) for married men – which are considered the community's major institution, like the preeminent role given to the *Rosh Yeshiva*, the director of such a Talmudic institution, who enjoys greater authority and prestige than the rabbi of that community. The second trait is the preeminence of written sources on community and family life. This trait is not only the product of ultra-Orthodoxy's highly conservative attitude but is also the result of the Holocaust: the disintegration of most of Europe's Jewish communities during the Holocaust disrupted oral transmission forever. However, the most salient trait of ultra-Orthodoxy is the concept of *Da'at Torah* (lit., "the Torah's point of view"). This concept expresses a veritable modification of the paradigm of authority in the contemporary Jewish society. However, the concept did not emerge *ex nihilo*. The origin of the concept can be found in the Mishnah: "Delve into the Torah and continue to delve into it because it contains everything" (*Tractate Avot or Pirkei Avot* 5:22).

The Maharal of Prague (Rabbi Yehuda Loew ben Bezalel [1520–1609]), better known as the Maharal, an acronym for *Morenu Ha-Rav Loew*, "our master and teacher, Rabbi Loew", comments on this Mishnah in his *Derech Haim (Path of Life)* that this statement requires further clarification.[20] He asks whether the words "because it contains everything" signify that the Torah truly contains everything, whereupon he himself answers this question: "God consulted the Torah and created the universe" (*Genesis Rabba* 1:2). God established the universe, argues the Maharal, in accordance with the order in the Torah; thus, everything that happens follows the order in the Torah. This, says the Maharal, is the meaning of the midrash: God looked at the Torah and used that blueprint to create the world, which means that order in the world follows the order in the Torah. This is the Mishnah's meaning. The injunction "delve into the Torah and continue to delve into it because it contains everything" signifies that, when we explore the Torah's profound meaning, this study can lead us to a comprehension of the entire world. Moreover, study of the Torah teaches us that everything that occurs in the world has its roots in the Torah. In other words, concludes the Maharal, everything originates in the Torah, which is humanity's blueprint.

---

[20] Meir Sadler (ed.), *Rabbinic Theology and Jewish Intellectual History: The Great Rabbi Loew of Prague*, Routledge, 2013.

However, this philosophical conception has gradually been given a normative content of an almost infinite field: (unchanged) those individuals who are designated *Gedolei Hador* (the "Leaders of Their Generation," who are, so it seems, exclusively Ashkenazi Jews) regularly give their opinion on all areas of life, even on social and political questions that have no apparent connection with the Torah. Their opinion is not a simple piece of advice, but is often understood as a commandment that all pious Jews must observe without even attempting to understand the reason for this opinion. Actually, they have no choice but to obey because, contrary to responsa, no explanations are given for these decisions. In short, the notion of *Da'at Torah* leads to a concentration of power: traditionally, political or social decisions were made by the monarch, or the Exilarch (leader of the Diaspora Jewish communities), or even the leaders of a local Jewish community, while halachic decisions were made by the rabbi of a city (in Aramaic, *mara d'atra*, lit., "master of the place"; see earlier in this volume) or the renowned rabbinic authority who had been consulted. According to the doctrine of *Da'at Torah*, everything or nearly everything falls under the jurisdiction of the "Leaders of Their Generation." However, the mutation of the paradigm does not stop there. In reality, it assumes many aspects.

First of all, *Da'at Torah* tends toward a kind of "panjurism" (Heinrich Rommen): everything or nearly everything falls under the category of *halachah* and can be the subject of a rabbinic decision (*psak din*). Traditional areas of ethics (*mussar*), of Jewish thought or even of science, have surreptitiously slid into the orbit of law (see above on the domain of authority). Second, in the modern era, the recognized power of rabbinic authorities has never gone past the circle of their own local community or of the persons who consulted with them on a particular halachic question. The claim of nearly total authority from the holders of *Da'at Torah* thus assumes a legitimacy that is, at the very least, questionable. Third, what one author has described as a "culture of submission" is justified by the fact that the "Leaders of Their Generation" are regarded as infallible or, at least, divinely inspired. Yet infallibility is alien to Jewish law: even the most learned of the Sages could be mistaken. Thus, as we have already seen, the Talmud discusses important developments relative to the expiatory sacrifices that essential institutions of the Jewish nation, including the Great Sanhedrin, are obligated to bring if they have committed a substantive error in the area of *halachah* (see earlier in this volume). One manifestation of *Da'at Torah* was the ban placed on *The Challenge of Creation* (2006), a book written by Natan Slifkin, an Orthodox rabbi, that is an essay on the compatibility of the Darwinian theory of evolution and the Torah.[21] Slifkin in particular calls our attention to an opinion that has long been admitted in rabbinic literature, namely, the Bible's description of the creation of the world in the Book of Genesis need not be taken literally. We are currently witnessing *halachah*'s hypertrophy.

IV RELIGIOUS ZIONISM: THE STATE OF ISRAEL AS TELOS

In the nineteenth century, the vast majority of Orthodox rabbis opposed the Zionist movement. Of course, there were some notable exceptions. Nonetheless, the predominantly secularist and socialist nature of Zionism led the leaders of Religious Zionism to create in 1902 a rival organization to the World Zionist Organization; the new body was called the *Mercaz Ruhani* ("spiritual center") or *Mizrahi*.

The most learned and influential figure in the Religious Zionist movement was the chief Ashkenazi rabbi of Mandatory Palestine, Abraham Isaac Kook (1865–1935).[22] In his writings, he analyzes the Jewish people's return to its ancient homeland as the initial stage of the Messianic era. The Zionist ideal also determined the Zionist movement's manner of conceiving *halachah*: first of all, the success of the project of settling the land and then the essentially eternal character of the State of Israel, which declared its independence on May 14, 1948, were elevated to the rank of the outer limits of the halachic process. The fiery polemics generated over the question of the observance of the sabbatical or *shmita* year (the seventh year, when Jews in the Land of Israel are biblically commanded to lay their lands fallow) graphically illustrates the generation of Zionist *halachah*.[23] In the late nineteenth century, when the Jewish people undertook to return to its ancient homeland, to settle the land and farm it, observance of the sabbatical year became a burning issue. The year 1889, which was a sabbatical year according to the Jewish calendar, was fast approaching. Should the sabbatical year be observed, or should it be ignored and should the land continue to be cultivated in order to prevent the collapse of a renascent and fragile agricultural economy? The Jewish farmers turned to the rabbinic authorities. Three respected halachic authorities met in Vilna (Vilnius) and decided to grant the farmers a *heter mechira* –

---

[21] Zoo Torah/Lambda Publishers, 2006; for other examples, see Marc Shapiro, "Of Books and Bans," 3.2 *Edah Journal* 1 (2003).
[22] See Yehudah Mirsky, *Rav Kook: Mystic in a Time of Revolution*, Yale University Press, 2014.
[23] For a detailed analysis of the issues, see Arye Edrey, "From Orthodoxy to Religious Zionism: Rabbi Kook and the Sabbatical Year Polemic," 26 *Dine Israel: Studies in Halakhah and Jewish Law* 45 (2009).

a permission to sell temporarily their lands to non-Jews; in this way, the prohibition would not apply and the farmers could thus continue to cultivate their lands. The decision was approved by one of the highest rabbinic authorities in that era, Y. E. Spector. During the sabbatical years 1889, 1896 and 1903, most of the Jewish farmers in Palestine used this authorization. However, a certain number of rabbinic authorities, who were also highly respected, vigorously opposed the authorization.

Just at that moment in history, Abraham Isaac Kook arrived in 1904 in Jaffa to serve as the city's rabbi. Although Kook was recognized for his creative thinking, he was also known for his conservative approach to halachic matters. Nonetheless, thinking about the next sabbatical year, he wrote an entire treatise, commenting on the laws relative to the sabbatical year and finding legitimation for the permission to sell one's lands temporarily. In both his treatise and his correspondence, Kook explained his position. When he lived in Russia, he was opposed to the suspension of the laws surrounding the sabbatical year; however, when he arrived in Palestine and saw the precarious situation of the Jewish farms, he understood that observance of the sabbatical year could place lives in danger and could threaten the entire enterprise of the Jewish people's return to its ancient homeland. A third argument that he presented and that is particularly interesting, because it touches on the very notion of authority in the Jewish law system, concerns the eternal nature of Judaism itself. If the rabbis were to refuse to authorize the suspension of the sabbatical year, the anti-religious Jews would use that refusal as an argument to underline Judaism's incompatibility with the modern world and with the Zionist movement. The authorization to temporarily sell Jewish lands to non-Jews tied in with the concept of the need of the hour (*hora'at sha'ah*; see earlier in this volume). Kook mentions other arguments to support his decision. The first is that, according to most rabbinic authorities, observance of the sabbatical year is no longer a biblical commandment but is now only a rabbinic one. The second is that the counting of years is not certain and that it was only by convention that the majority of halachic authorities adopted Maimonides' count. Kook also notes that, if the Jewish farmers stopped cultivating their fields for an entire year, the Arab shepherds would benefit and would use those fields for their flocks to graze. The farmers would then have to turn to the Ottoman justice system with the request that it recognize their property rights and that legal process would be long and costly. In the final analysis, these are classic arguments. However, Kook introduces a new parameter: the future of the Zionist movement must never be jeopardized, even if the farmers are, for the most part, secular, because the Jewish people's return to Zion constitutes the birth pangs of the Messianic era.

Rabbi Kook's ruling is still applied even today by the State of Israel's Chief Rabbinate. Nonetheless, some contemporary rabbinic authorities – Orthodox or ultra-Orthodox – are opposed to the continued granting of the authorization to sell, arguing that neither the prosperity of Israeli agriculture nor the enduringness of the Israeli economy in general justifies that authorization any longer. With the advent of Religious Zionism, we are witnessing the entry of politics into *halachah*.[24]

Further Reading

THE MAKING OF RABBINIC JUDAISM

Cohen, S. J. D. *From the Maccabees to the Mishnah*, 2nd edn., Westminster John Knox Press, 2006.
Fisch, M. *Rational Rabbis: Science and Talmudic Culture*, Indiana University Press, 1997.
Lapin, H. *Rabbis as Romans: The Rabbinic Movement in Palestine, 100–400 CE*, Oxford University Press, 2012.
Saiman, C. N. *Halakhah: The Rabbinic Idea of Law*, Princeton University Press, 2018.
Urbach, E. E. *The Sages: Their Concepts and Beliefs*, 2nd edn., Hebrew University Press, 1979.

BOOKS

Davis, J. "The Reception of the 'Schulhan Arukh' and the Formation of Ashkenazic Jewish Identity," 26 *Association for Jewish Studies Review* 251 (2002).
Leben, C. "Maïmonide et la codification du droit hébraïque," 27 *Droits* 113 (1998).
Sagi, A. *The Open Canon*, Continuum, 2007.
Steinsaltz, A. *Reference Guide to the Talmud*, 2nd edn., Toby Press, 2014.

---

[24] More could be said about the general conflict as to whether the State represents a new era for the *halakhah* (or *masoret yisra'el*): contrast the opinion of Justice Cohn with the opinion of Justice Silberg in the *Brother Daniel* case of the Supreme Court of Israel (*Rufeisen* v. *Minister of the Interior*, 1962, in Nahum Rakover, *Modern Applications of Jewish Law*, Library of Jewish Law, 1962, p. 46 seq.). See also Bernard Jackson, "Who Is a Jew?: Some Semiotic Observations on a Judgment of the Israel Supreme Court," 1.17 *International Journal for the Semiotics of Law/Revue Internationale de Sémiotique Juridique* 115 (1993).

Zeitlin, S. "Midrash: A Historical Study," 44 *Jewish Quarterly Review* 21 (1953).
Zelcer, H. *A Guide to the Jerusalem Talmud*, Universal Publishers, 2002.

HALACHIC AUTHORITY AND HALACHIC PROCESS

Berger, M. S. *Rabbinic Authority*, Oxford University Press, 1998.
Berkovits, E. *Not In Heaven: The Nature and Function of Jewish Law*, Shalem Press, 2010.
Bleich, J. D. "'Lo Ba-Shamayim Hi': A Philosophical Pilpul," in J. Sacks (ed.), *Tradition and Transition: Essays Presented to Chief Rabbi Sir Immanuel Jakobovits to Celebrate Twenty Years in Office*, Jew's College Publications, 1986.
Halberthal, M. *People of the Book: Canon, Meaning, and Authority*, Harvard University Press, 1997.
Hidary, R. *Dispute for the Sake of Heaven: Legal Pluralism in the Talmud*, Brown Judaic Studies, 2010.
Hollander, A. Y. "The Relationship between Halakhic Decisors and Their Peers As a Determining Factor in the Acceptance of Their Decisions," 20 *Jewish Law Association Studies* 96 (2010).
Jacobs, L. *A Tree of Life: Diversity, Flexibility, and Creativity in Jewish Law*, 2nd edn., Littman Library of Jewish Civilization, 2000.
Kellner, M. *Maimonides on the "Decline of the Generations" and the Nature of Rabbinic Authority*, State University of New York Press, 1996.
Koppel, M. *Meta-Halakhah: Logic, Intuition, and the Unfolding of Jewish Law*, Jason Aronson, 1997.
Levinson, B. M. "You Must Not Add Anything to What I Command You: Paradoxes of Canon and Authorship in Ancient Israel," 50 *Numen: International Review for the History of Religions* 1 (2003).
Lichtenstein, A. "The Human and Social Factor in Halakha," 36.1 *Tradition* 1 (2002).
Roth, J. *The Halakhic Process: A Systemic Analysis*, Jewish Theological Seminary, 1986.
Roth, J. "*Gufei Torah*: The Limit to Halakhic Pluralism," in J. Roth, M. Schmelzer and Y. Francus (eds.), *Tiferet leYisrael: Jubilee Volume in Honor of Israel Francus*, Jewish Theological Seminary, 2010, p. 207.
Sagi, A. "Halakhic Praxis and the Word of God: A Study of Two Models," 1 *Journal of Jewish Thought & Philosophy* 305 (1992).
Shapira, H. "Majority Rule in the Jewish Legal Tradition," 81 *Hebrew Union College Annual* 161 (2013).
Shapiro, M. B. "Is There a 'Pesak' for Jewish Thought?" in D. J. Lasker (ed.), *Jewish Thought and Jewish Belief*, Ben-Gurion University of the Negev Press, 2012, p. 119.

Sokol, M. (ed.), *Rabbinic Authority and Personal Autonomy*, Jason Aronson, 1992.
Walter, M. *The Making of a Halachic Decision*, Menucha Publishers, 2013.
Yuter, A. J. "Hora'at Sha'ah: The Emergency Principle in Jewish Law and a Contemporary Application," 13.3/4 *Jewish Political Studies Review* 3 (2001).

PARADIGMS OF AUTHORITY

Brown, B. "Orthodox Judaism," in J. Neusner and A. J. Avery-Peck (eds.), *The Blackwell Companion to Judaism*, Blackwell Publishers, 2000, p. 311.
Hacohen, A. "'Religious Zionist Halakhah': Is It a Reality or Was It a Dream?" in C. I. Waxman (ed.), *Religious Zionism Post Disengagement: Future Directions*, Yeshiva University Press/Ktav Publishing, 2008, p. 315.
Katz, J. "Da'at Torah: The Unqualified Authority Claimed for Halakhists," 11 *Jewish History* 41 (1997).
Silber, M. K. "The Emergence of Ultra-Orthodoxy: The Invention of Tradition," in J. Wertheimer (ed.), *The Uses of Tradition: Jewish Continuity in the Modern Era*, Jewish Theological Seminary/Harvard University Press, 1992, p. 22.
Yuter, A. J. "Is Reform Judaism a Movement, a Sect, or a Heresy?" 24.3 *Tradition* 87 (1989).

5

Hermeneutics

INTRODUCTION

Interpretation is a central element in the halachic process. Asking, "what is the Torah?" the Talmud immediately responds, "the interpretation of the Torah" (*BT Kid.* 49b). Thus, a chapter on exegesis or rabbinic hermeneutics is indispensable.

Rabbinic tradition is rich in hermeneutical principles that have been grouped under mnemonic titles: Hillel the Elder's Seven Rules, Nahum Ish Gamzu's Rules, Rabbi Akiva's Rules, Rabbi Ishmael's Thirteen Rules, Rabbi Yossi the Galilean's Thirty-Two Rules, Rabbi Elazar of Worms's Seventy-Three Rules, the Malbim's 613 Explanations, etc. We examine in the following developments the essential principles that emerge from these different groupings.

SECTION 1 EXEGETICAL APPROACHES: THE ORCHARD (HA-PARDES)

I FOUR APPROACHES

Four approaches have been developed in order to enable us to see all of the Torah text's abundance: the literal or obvious meaning of the text (*Peshat*), the text's allusive meaning(s) (*Remez*), its homiletic or aggadic meaning (*Derash*) and its esoteric meaning (*Sod*). These four levels of understanding of the biblical text are currently designated by the acronym PaRDeS ("orchard"; the Hebrew word is the source of the word "paradise").

The term *peshat* refers to the simple, literal, obvious meaning of the text. However, this term is not very satisfactory. A *peshat* interpretation extracts the meaning of the words being employed in the light of Hebrew grammar and the discursive context; thus, *peshat* is a contextual interpretation. Although it is possible to extract another meaning, whether allusive or esoteric, a verse should not be deprived of its obvious or literal sense. This is a hermeneutic principle that is held sacred by the Talmud (*BT Shabbat* 63a).

In contrast with *peshat*, the three other exegetical approaches are acontextual by nature.

The allusive meaning is a form of allegorical interpretation that is based on symbols or allusions hidden in the text. The homiletic or aggadic meaning is an interpretive tool that is based on *midrash*. *Midrash* (pl. *midrashim*) is a Hebrew term designating a hermeneutic, comparative and homiletic method of exegesis. The term *Midrash* also refers to a compilation of commentaries on the Torah, the Prophets and the Hagiographa: *midreshei halachah* (legal and ritual *midrashim*) and *midreshei aggada* (legends as well as moral, folkloristic and anecdotal *midrashim*). *Midrashim* constitute an oral tradition that has been taught ever since the granting of the Torah at Mount Sinai; they were written down after the closing of the Talmud, specifically, during the ninth and tenth centuries, and the Talmud cites *Midrashim* at length. There are many *Midrashim*: *Midrash Hagadol*, *Midrash Tanhuma*, *Pirkei de Rabbi Eliezer*, etc.

The last category of interpretation, *sod* ("secret" in Hebrew), is the esoteric, mystical part of the Torah.

Within these four categories of interpretative methods vis-à-vis the Torah, endless possible approaches exist. Thus, according to the *peshat* method of interpretation, there are numerous manners of understanding the Torah. That is why many commentators who focused on the *peshat*, such as Rashi, Ibn Ezra, Rashbam and numerous others, often disagree on the "literal" meaning of a verse.

II A FAMOUS CONTROVERSY: CAN THE *PESHAT* CONTRADICT *HALACHAH*?

Is the Torah the source of *halachah*? When they arrive at this stage of work, readers might reach a nuanced conclusion. If the Written Torah (or Written Law) is the central document of Jewish law, the Oral Torah (or Oral Law) is also of cardinal importance in the determination of *halachah* because the Oral Law contains details that complete the Written Law and provides the interpretation of the Written Law, even its interpretation as *peshat* (which means "conventional," "agreed," "obvious" rather than "literal"); in many cases, this leads to a result that is very different from what a literal reading of the particular verse or verses in the Pentateuch suggests.

This tension between the Torah and the Talmud and the manner in which it is resolved is expressed in a lively debate between Rashbam and Ibn Ezra. During the medieval period, and especially in the twelfth century, rabbinic literature evinced a powerful trend in favor of the *peshat*. The driving spirits behind this trend were two schools of thought: the French School, founded by Rashi (1041–1106), and the Rationalist School, formed by the Sages of Arab-speaking Jewish communities. The most eminent representative of the first school was Rashbam (Rabbi Samuel ben Meir [1085–1185], Rashi's grandson) and the leading representative of the second was Abraham Ibn Ezra (1089–1164). Among the numerous nuances of approach that distinguished these two commentators from one another, the most serious debate concerned the manner in which one should interpret verses in the Torah that have a halachic significance.

A basic question that must be asked is: is it permissible to interpret one or more verses in their context, even if the meaning that emerges conflicts with *halachah*, as it is understood by the Sages of the Talmud and their successors? Ibn Ezra deals with this question in the introduction to his commentary on the Torah:

> The way of *peshat* will not step aside for *derash*, for the Torah can be interpreted in a myriad of ways [lit., seventy facets]; however, when it comes to laws, statutes and rules, if we find two ways of understanding a verse, and one of the ways is in line with that of the Sages, for they were all pious, we will rely on the truth of their assertions, since without doubt they are reliable. Heaven forbid that we join with the Sadducees, who say that the Sages' interpretation contradicts Scripture.

Rashbam has a very different view. In the introduction to his commentary on the weekly Torah portion *Mishpatim* (specifically, *Exod.* 21:1–23, 33), he addresses the Sages, informing them that they must know and understand that he does not intend to explain the practical *halachah* here, although it is very important. He notes that, as he pointed out in his commentary on Genesis 1:1, the laws and legends are learned from supplementary words or letters present in the text. In the case of the weekly portion *Mishpatim*, he will explain the laws in a simple manner, although the practical *halachah* is of prime importance, as our Sages have said, "*Halachah* can uproot the Written Torah." In short, Rashbam regards the Torah as a polyvocal text and argues that the same verse can support simultaneously an obvious or literal meaning and a midrashic one, even though there might be a conflict between these two meanings. For his part, Ibn Ezra suggests that each verse has a correct meaning. When he comments on narrative passages, he does not feel obliged to accept the Sages' interpretations. However, when he comments on halachic passages, he feels duty bound, as a member of a long line of tradition, to respect the Sages' opinion. Any other attitude, in his opinion, would amount to a renunciation of the Oral Torah.

To illustrate these two approaches, let us take, for example, the commandment regarding phylacteries. The commandment to lay phylacteries appears four times in the Torah, according to the traditional reading of the text (*Exod.* 13:1–10, *Exod.* 13:11–16, *Deut.* 6:4–9, *Deut.* 11:13–21).[1] The Torah does not describe phylacteries nor does it issue any instructions as to how they should be made. According to the oral tradition, phylacteries are small sheets of parchment, written in a calligraphic style in black indelible ink and inserted into two square boxes. With the help of leather straps, male Jews wear one of the boxes on their arm and the other on their head during weekday morning services. However, does this reading correspond with the literal meaning of the relevant verses? Rashbam does not think so. In his gloss on *Exod.* 13:9, he comments: "It is written 'as a sign on your hand.' According to an obvious deep reading of these words, the meaning is that the Exodus from Egypt should always be in your memory, should always be on your mind as if it was written on your hand, in the same sense as the verse 'Let me be a seal upon your heart' (*Song of Songs* 8:6)." According to Rashbam, this verse does not command us to physically place that passage from the Torah "on your heart" (*Deut.* 11:18), that is, in practical terms, to place it on your left hand, as prescribed by *halachah*. Instead, this is a poetic expression commanding us to remember the Exodus; the verse appears in Deuteronomy because the commandment is intended to keep the pertinent passages in Deuteronomy in a prominent position. For Rashbam, phylacteries are the product of a homiletic interpretation and belong to the Jewish oral tradition.

Commenting on this same verse, Ibn Ezra adopts an interpretation that conforms with his own methodology:

> It is written, "And this shall be for you." There are those who disagree with our holy ancestors and who say that " being a sign and a remembrance" have the same meaning as "For they are a graceful wreath upon your head, a necklace about your throat" [*Prov.* 1:9]. They also suggest that the words "Bind them as a sign upon your hands" [*Deut.* 6:8] have the same meaning as "Bind them upon the tablet of your heart always" [*Prov.* 6:21]; they similarly understand that the words "inscribe them on the doorposts of your house" [*Deut.* 6:9]

---

[1] On the topic of phylacteries and the relation between Written Law and Oral Law, see also Chapter 4.

have the same meaning as "Write them on the tablet of your mind [lit., heart]" [*Prov.* 3:3]. In that case, what is meant by the idea that it [phylacteries] will be a sign and a remembrance? The answer is that the memory of the fact that "with a mighty hand the Lord freed you from Egypt" [*Exod.* 13:9] should be a familiar and frequent utterance on your lips. However, this is a mistaken approach for the Book of Proverbs opens with "The proverbs of Solomon," thus informing us that everything in that book is a proverb (not literal). However, the Torah is not a book of proverbs, God forbid; so that this verse retain its literal meaning and we will not remove it from its *peshat*. For its literal meaning doesn't contradict any logical principle, as is the case for, "Cut away, therefore, the thickening about [i.e., circumcise] your hearts" [*Deut.* 10:16], the understanding of which needs to be adjusted.

Ibn Ezra interprets these verses in accordance with *halachah*. Since it is not illogical to consider that they do in fact refer to phylacteries, one should not deviate too much from the generally accepted interpretation (i.e., the *peshat*). As Rashbam sees no problem in separating the literal meaning from the halachic meaning, he does not hesitate to deviate from accepted interpretation and to extricate from this verse its simple meaning.

SECTION 2 THE PRINCIPAL RULES FOR THE INTERPRETATION OF A BIBLICAL TEXT

In this section, we study only those methods of interpretation that permit us to extract the "literal meaning" of the text (that is, the *peshat*; see the previous section).

The thirteen hermeneutical rules presented by Rabbi Ishmael can be grouped under two headings:

- **Midrash hameikish**: Analogical interpretation, that is, the drawing of a conclusion from one domain and its application to another.
- **Midrash hameva'er**: Explicative interpretation, that is, the explication or elucidation of a text in the Torah.

I ANALOGICAL INTERPRETATION

A Rule No. 1: A Fortiori *Reasoning*

This kind of reasoning is known in Hebrew as *kal va-homer* and refers to the inference from a minor premise to a major one (*a minori ad majus*) or from a major premise to a minor one (*a majori ad minus*). The origin of *kal va-homer* is found in the Torah itself (*Gen.* 44:8, *Deut.* 31:27).

A majori ad minus: The laws concerning the prohibition on working on the Sabbath are stricter than those concerning work on Jewish festivals; thus, whereas cooking is forbidden on the Sabbath, it is permitted, to a certain extent, on a festival. If a certain action is permitted on the Sabbath, it is *a fortiori* permitted on a festival (*BT Beitza* 20b).

A minori ad majus: Conversely, if a certain action is forbidden on a festival, it is forbidden *a fortiori* on the Sabbath.

The usage of *a fortiori* reasoning is subject to certain principles that frame it. It is also subject to the principle *Dayo lavo min ha-din lehiyot kanidon*, namely, it is sufficient that the inference is equally severe vis-à-vis the premise from which it is derived but not severer: if A contains X, B cannot contain X and Y (*M Bk* 2:5). A *fortiori* reasoning can be used only for laws prescribed by the Torah (*de-oraita*), not for laws prescribed by the rabbis (*de-rabbanan*).[2] Nor can it be used for laws belonging to the category of "Laws that were directly transmitted to Moses at Sinai."[3] Similarly, a penalty cannot be

---

[2] On this distinction, see Chapter 2, Section 1, B.
[3] On this category, see Chapter 3, Section 1.

imposed on the basis of *a fortiori* reasoning (*BT San.* 54a); this also holds true for prohibitions (*BT Pes.* 24a).

B Rule No. 2: Analogy Based on Identity of Terms

This hermeneutical rule is known in Hebrew as *gezerah shawah* (lit., "identical decree") and entails an inference based on the occurrence of identical words. Even if the two cases with the identical words appear in two separate Torah passages and in different legal contexts, they are subject to the same laws. Sometimes the words are not just similar but also seem to be superfluous (*mufneh* in Hebrew), thus clearly indicating that they were placed there in order to point to a case of *gezerah shawah* (*BT Shabbat* 64a). There are two kinds of *gezerah shawah*: those that clarify the text of the Torah and those that give rise to a new law that is not included in the text. Tractate Kiddushin of the Babylonian Talmud (2a) offers an example of *gezerah shawah*: "How do we know that a woman can be betrothed with money? We learn this from the field of Ephron. It is written here, 'If a man takes a woman' [*Deut.* 22:13], while it is written there, 'Let me pay the price of the land; accept it from me' [*Gen.* 23:13], and, in that case, 'taking' means 'taking possession,' as it is written, 'the field that Abraham had bought' [*Gen.* 25:10]."

In other words, the Torah's use of the verb "to take" serves as the basis for the *gezerah shawah* between the verses dealing with *kiddushin* (*Deut.* 24:1) and Abraham's purchase of a field from Ephron (*Gen.* 23:13). A certain degree of precision is required here in order to prevent any misunderstandings: undoubtedly, the Torah regards marriage as an "acquisition" (*kinyan*), namely, the husband's "acquisition" of his wife.[4] However, the nature of this acquisition differs from the acquisition of property because the husband's "acquisition" of his wife does not mean that he owns her. Rather, this "acquisition" is the establishment of an exclusive marital tie that forbids the wife from marrying or having sexual intercourse with any other man.

Unlike *a fortiori* reasoning, which anyone can use as long as the guiding principles are adhered to, no one can deduce a *gezerah shawah* on his or her own authority (*JT Pes.* 6:11). In other words, in order to avoid any manipulation of the Torah's text that could lead to its destruction, particularly in view of the many repetitions that appear in numerous passages in that text, only those words that have been listed in accordance with the tradition of the Oral Law can serve as a base for a *gezerah shawah*. Moreover, there can never be a partial *gezerah shawah*. For a *gezerah shawah* to be valid, it must operate in both

---

[4] On *kinyan*, see also Chapter 3, Section 3.

instances; that is, we must be able to apply to B the law expounded in A, and vice versa (*BT Zevachim* 48a). The Sages are divided over the question as to whether a *gezerah shawah* implies the transfer of all the consequences of the law in one case to the second case or whether the joint law can be accompanied by specific laws, taking into account the particular nature of each case.

C Rule No. 3: Inference through Induction

The *binyan av* constitutes one of the cardinal rules of hermeneutics and appears as such in all the lists of exegetical principles. This interpretive rule breaks down into two rules:

- ***Binyan av mikatuv ehad***: Inference from a single verse.
- ***Binyan av mishnei ketuvim***: Inference from two verses.

The name given to this rule of interpretation stems from the fact that it is a construction (*binyan*) in which a verse or two serve as the basis for – or father (*av* in Hebrew) to – the conclusion that emanates from it.

The inference from a single verse can be illustrated by the following example. According to that verse, a "single witness may not validate against a person any guilt or blame for any offense that may be committed; a case can be valid only on the testimony of two witnesses or more" (*Deut.* 19:15). From the word "witness" we could deduce that the Torah is referring to only one witness. Thus, we must ask why the Torah explicitly uses the phrase "single witness." The word "single" appears to be superfluous. The Talmud teaches us that this preciseness is significant: whenever the word "witness" appears in a verse without being qualified by the adjective "single," the reference is to "more than one" witness. The term "a witness" serves as the basis (or "father") that allows us to deduce that the occurrence of the word "witness" without the qualifying adjective "single" should be interpreted as "at least two witnesses" (*BT San.* 30a).

An example of the deduction of a new norm from two verses can be seen in the rights that the Torah grants to agricultural laborers. The first verse allows the following: "When you enter another man's vineyard, you may eat as many grapes as you want, until you are full, but you must not put any in your vessel" (*Deut.* 23:25). The second verse allows the following: "When you enter another man's field of standing grain, you may pluck ears with your hand; but you must not put a sickle to your neighbor's grain" (*Deut.* 23:26).

Commentators note that the produce that an agricultural laborer is entitled to eat is not identical in these two verses and also note that these two verses deal with different rights: the verse concerned with vineyards deals with the law of gleaning, while the verse concerned with grain deals with the tithe that is due to the priest. We can deduce that the law common to the two verses (the construction or the father, *av*), both of which deal with produce in the field, is that agricultural employees can eat all the produce in the field once their work has been completed (*BT BM* 87b).

However, this principle can be limited by another principle (*shnei ketuvim haba'im k'echad*, lit., "two verses that come together"). If the same law appears in two or more cases, one applies the rule "two verses that come together cannot serve as a reference." If the Legislator felt the need to repeat a certain law in each of these cases, we are dealing here with exceptions and not with a general rule. According to some Sages, the extrapolation through *binyan av* remains valid as long as the rule is not mentioned in three different cases. However, this limitation is not systematic because the Talmud recognizes at least one case of deduction from four verses (*BT BK* 2a). In reality, the principle "two verses that come together" is intended to teach us that it is possible to challenge an inference when the suggested relationship between the verses is not decisive or, in other words, when there is an important difference that does not permit the transfer of a rule from case A to case B (see, for example, *BT Nazir* 40a–b).

II EXPLICATIVE INTERPRETATION

Several principles can be grouped under this rubric.

A Rule No. 4: A General Rule and a Particular Case

This principle is called *kelal uferat* (*kelal*, general rule; *perat*, particular case): if a halachic rule is presented in general terms and is then followed by particular cases, the rule applies only to those cases that are mentioned.[5]

The Torah states: "When any of you presents an offering of cattle [lit., animal] to the Lord, he shall choose his offering from the herd [lit., cattle] or from the flock [of sheep]" (*Lev.* 1:2). Whereas "animal" is a general term, "cattle" and "flock of sheep" are particular terms. Since the general

---

[5] Note: According to the rules of Hebrew grammar, certain consonants are pronounced differently when they are the first letter in a word and when they are not the first letter. Thus, in this section and in the following one, the words *kelal* and *perat* appear as *chelal* and *frat* respectively when they are preceded by a consonant.

term "animal" includes both domesticated and undomesticated species, the Torah excludes undomesticated species and authorizes the sacrifice of only domestic animals, specifically mentioning cattle or sheep. One could, of course, ask why the Legislator does not directly mention cattle and sheep and first makes an apparently superfluous detour by first mentioning "animal." The answer is that the proposition *min* (from) is used in a partitive sense: some of the species that are mentioned – but not all species – can be offered as sacrifices. Rashi is very precise in his commentary: the Torah excludes a domestic animal that has been used for the sin of bestiality, an animal that has been worshipped as an idol, an animal that has injured a human being and an animal one of whose organs has been torn out or torn away. Only those animals are included that are pure, whose bodies are intact and that have not been defiled may be offered to the Eternal (*BT Tem.* 28a). Moreover, if the verse had not begun with a general term, one could have applied another rule taught by Rabbi Ishmael, *binyan av* (see Rule no. 3), for example, which could have led us to include other animals belonging to these particular cases.

B Rule No. 5: A Particular Case and a General Rule

This principle is called *perat uchelal*: if the particular cases are presented first and are then extended by a general term, other cases are included in the rule, beyond the special cases that are mentioned. It is written, "If you see your fellow's ox or sheep gone astray, do not ignore it; you must take it back to your fellow ... You shall do the same with his ass; you shall do the same with his garment; and so too shall you do with anything that your fellow loses and you find" (*Deut.* 22:1–3). Whereas "ox," "sheep," "ass" and "garment" are the particular cases, "and so too shall you do with anything that your fellow loses and you find" is the general term. Since the particular cases are presented first, we understand that the obligation of returning a possession to its owner does not apply exclusively to these objects because the verse continues with a general expression that encompasses all lost objects (*BT Nazir* 35b). Again, we could ask why the Legislator does not simply state, "you must take back to your fellow anything that your fellow loses and you find." The reason is that, if the Legislator had done so, we might have applied another rule of interpretation and might have arrived at a result that was not intended by the Legislator.

C Rule No. 6: General Rule + Particular Case + General Rule (a General Law Limited by Specific Instances and Then Again Referred to in General Terms)

This principle is called *kelal uferat uchelal*. The normative schema is as follows. A general rule is limited by particular cases and is then once more expressed in general terms. In such a schema, we can only infer from similar cases to the particular ones. It is written: "When a man gives money or goods to another for safekeeping, and they are stolen from the man's house – if the thief is caught, he shall pay double; if the thief is not caught, the owner of the house shall depose before the judges that he has not laid hands on the other's property. In all charges of misappropriation – pertaining to an ox, an ass, a sheep, a garment, or any other loss, whereof one party alleges, 'This is it' – the case of both parties shall come before the judges: he whom the judges declare guilty shall pay double to the other" (*Exod.* 22:6–8).

In his commentary, Rashi explains that this passage deals with a *shomer hinam* – a person who is entrusted with an object for a certain period of time and who is not paid for this service – and who, in the case of a theft, is exempt from any responsibility. The term "in all charges of misappropriation" is a general expression, while the terms "ox," "ass," "sheep" and "garment" are the particular cases, which are followed by the general expression "any other loss." What is the common denominator shared by these particular cases? They are all examples of movable property that has patrimonial value (i.e., it is an object that has value and it can be bequeathed to someone). Thus, the Torah excludes here not only immovable property (such as a field or a house) but also movable property that has no intrinsic value but that does have monetary value (e.g., checks and other commercial means of payment). For such items, no oath can be taken.

There is also the principle of *perat uchelal uferat*: a particular case, a general rule and a particular case. This is a rule that is symmetrical to the preceding rule: when the general rule is situated between two particular cases, it applies only to cases that are analogous to the cases cited in the verse.

D Rule No. 7: The General Rule Requires a Particular Rule and the Particular Rule Requires a General Rule

This principle is called *kelal shehu tzarich li-frat u-frat shehu tzarich li-chlal*. Here, the general rule and the particular rule are independent of one another. Neither rule limits or extends the field of the other, although each of them permits us to define the other more precisely. Let us look, for example, at the following two verses:

> "Consecrate to Me every first-born; man and beast, the first issue of every womb among the Israelites is Mine" (Exod. 13:2).
> "You shall consecrate to the Lord your God all male firstlings that are born in your herd and in your flock" (Deut. 15:19).

"Consecrate to Me every first-born" is the general rule, while "all male firstlings" is the particular rule. From the words "every first-born" we could conclude that both male and female firstlings are included. However, the adjective "male" serves to exclude female firstlings. From the words "all male firstlings" we could deduce that the verse includes every male firstling that his mother gives birth to, even if he was born after his sister; however, the expression "the first issue of every womb" serves to deny the title of "firstling" to any male offspring that was not his mother's firstborn. In order to be accorded that title, the male offspring must be the "first to open the womb" (Rashi, *ad. loc.*). Finally, if the verse had not specified "the first issue of every womb," we might have thought that the title of "first-born" could be accorded to the offspring that is the "first to open the womb" after a firstling was born through a caesarian section. This is why the Torah specifies "first-born"; we can therefore conclude that an animal can be considered "first-born" only if that animal is a firstling in all respects: the "first to open the womb" and the mother's first offspring (*BT Bechorot* 19a).

E Rules Nos. 8–11: "A Law That Was Included in the Collective Term"

These rules, which are grouped under the rubric *davar shehaya bi-chlal*, relate to an everyday problem: when a general principle is presented in a verse and when particular cases are presented in other verses, what is the relationship between this general rule and those particular cases?

Three similar hermeneutic principles provide an answer to this question:

- "A law that was included in a collective term but which has been exemplified elsewhere in order to offer instruction is not only providing that instruction on its particular subject but also applies to the general principle as a whole." Let us examine the following two verses:

    > "But the seventh day is a Sabbath of the Lord your God: you shall not do any work" (*Exod.* 20:10).
    > "You shall kindle no fire throughout your settlements on the Sabbath day" (*Exod.* 35:3).

The prohibition stated in the second verse is included in the first one because the kindling of a fire is one of the thirty-nine categories of work that are prohibited on the Sabbath day. Then what is the purpose of this repetition? The Talmud deduces from the repetition that the sanction imposed on those who perform this particular category of work is similarly imposed in the general case, that is, for each of the other thirty-eight prohibited categories of work (BT Shabbat 70a).

- When a rule is included in a general principle and is then specifically mentioned in order to transmit information concerning that rule, the restrictions of that rule should be eased rather than tightened. Let us examine the following two verses:

  "He who fatally strikes a man shall be put to death" (Exod. 21:12).
  "For instance, a man goes with his neighbor into a grove to cut wood; as his hand swings the ax to cut down a tree, the ax-head flies off the handle and strikes the other so that he dies. That man shall flee to one of these cities and live" (Deut. 19:5).
  The first verse, which presents a general rule, makes no distinction between voluntary and involuntary homicide, which are both included in the phrase "he who fatally strikes a man." In the second verse, an exception is made in the case of involuntary homicide: a person guilty of involuntary homicide can flee to one of the cities of refuge and is thus not liable to the death penalty.[6]
  This interpretive rule differs from the preceding one: the specific case does not limit the general principle in its entirety but rather limits the specific example, excluding the general rule.

- "A law that was included in a general principle but has been mentioned explicitly once more with a detail not mentioned in the first law can lessen or tighten the restrictions of the general rule."

  Chapters 13 to 15 in Leviticus deal with a malady called *tsara'at* in Hebrew that is commonly, but mistakenly, translated as "leprous affliction" or "leprosy." This malady is the primary source of ritual impurity and can affect an individual's skin or hair or a garment or a house. In reality, this is a moral or social malady caused by certain kinds of

---

[6] Basically, the cities of refuge were six Levitical towns in the Kingdom of Israel and the Kingdom of Judah in which the perpetrators of accidental manslaughter could claim the right of asylum. See Jeffrey Stackert, "Why Does Deuteronomy Legislate Cities of Refuge? Asylum in the Covenant Collection (Exodus 21: 12–14) and Deuteronomy (19: 1–13)," 125.1 *Journal of Biblical Literature* 23 (2006); for a comparative perspective, see Craig A. Stern, "Torah and Murder: The Cities of Refuge and Anglo-American Law," 35 *Villanova Law Review* 461 (2000).

behavior that are unethical (especially, scandal mongering). Let us compare these verses:

"When a person has on the skin of his body a swelling, a rash, or a discoloration, and it develops into a leprous affliction on the skin of his body, it shall be reported to Aaron the priest or to one of his sons, the priests. The priest shall examine the affliction on the skin of his body: if hair in the afflicted patch has turned white and the affliction appears to be deeper than the skin of his body, it is a leprous affliction; when the priest sees it, he shall pronounce him unclean" (*Lev.* 13:2–3).

In verses 29 to 37 of this same chapter, the same law is presented when the "leprous affliction" is found in an individual's hair or beard. The "priest shall examine the affliction. If it appears to go deeper than the skin and there is thin yellow hair in it, the priest shall pronounce him unclean; it is a scall, a leprous affliction in the hair or beard" (*Lev.* 13:30).

Clearly, the specific case of "hair" or "beard" is included in the general case of "skin." However, the particular case displays a difference in comparison with the general case. In effect, in the general case, it is a white hair that is a sign of ritual impurity, whereas in the specific case, it is a yellow hair. In applying the rule that has been presented, the exegete will not say that both the white hair and the yellow hair are signs of impurity but will instead say that (1) a white hair is not a sign of impurity in the case of an individual's hair or beard (easing of the law's restrictions) whereas it is a sign of impurity in the case of an individual's skin; (2) a yellow hair is a sign of impurity in the case of an individual's hair or beard (easing of the law's restrictions) whereas it is not a sign of impurity in the case of an individual's skin (*Sifra* 1:3).

When a rule is first of all included in a general principle and is then specified elsewhere in order to determine an entirely new rule, the details of the general rule do not apply to this entirely new rule, unless it has been anticipated by the text itself.

Let us remain in the domain of the leprous affliction and let us now see one aspect of its process of purification: "The lamb shall be slaughtered at the spot in the sacred area where the sin offering and the burnt offering are slaughtered. For the guilt offering, like the sin offering, goes to the priest; it is most holy. The priest shall take some of the blood of the guilt offering, and the priest shall put it on the ridge of the right ear of him who is being cleansed, and on the thumb of his right hand, and on the big toe of his right foot" (*Lev.* 14:13–14).

The general rule concerning the guilt-offering requires the sprinkling of the animal's blood on the altar (*Lev.* 7:2), which is the case for sin-offerings, from which we can deduce that the same practice is required for the sacrifice offered in connection with leprosy. A question arises here: why does the Torah state "like the sin offering," uttering an assertion that appears to be superfluous? The response is as follows: given that, in the specific case of leprosy, a "new rule" has been introduced (the smearing of blood on the former victim of leprosy's right ear lobe, thumb and toe), we cannot know for sure whether the sacrifice offered by the former leprosy victim being purified is covered by the general rule regarding guilt-offerings – and requires the sprinkling of blood on the altar.

III A FEW COMPLEMENTARY RULES

A Chronological Order Is Not Always Respected in the Torah

This principle affirms that the Pentateuch does not necessarily present events and laws in chronological order, so much so that nothing requires us to interpret the events and laws according to the order in which they are presented. This principle applies only to the weekly portions of the Pentateuch but not to the verses in any given weekly portion.

This principle, which is reported by Rabbi Eliezer, son of Rabbi Yossi the Galilean, is the outcome of a principle of biblical legislative drafting, which we considered earlier (Chapter 2). The Torah is interested in general cases and does not go into the details of particular cases. As a result, the Legislator aims at cases occurring in daily life and not atypical ones, which does not necessarily mean that atypical cases should be excluded from the field of the norm's application. For example: "You shall be holy people to Me: you must not eat flesh torn by beasts in the field; you shall cast it to the dogs" (*Exod.* 22:30). We need not deduce from this verse that the consumption of a carcass found on a city street would be permissible. Here the Pentateuch cites what would be a habitual occurrence in an agricultural society (see Rashi, *ad loc.*, who provides other examples).

B The Torah Is Speaking the Language of Human Beings

Despite its very general phrasing, this rule is concerned only with the meaning that should be assigned in the case of the doubling of a verb in a verse. For example, *"Shale'ach t'shalach et ha-em"* ("Let [the mother bird] go"; *Deut.* 22:7), where the verb "to let go, send" is doubled (in a slightly different form) and serves to convey the injunction: "You must send [the mother bird]." According to Rabbi Ishmael, such a doubling of the verb is not a matter for hermeneutical interpretation but is rather a Hebraism, expressing an everyday turn of phrase; in this case, the Torah is speaking the language of human beings. Unlike Rabbi Ishmael, Rabbi Akiva attempts to draw legal conclusions from this doubling of the verb.

C The Consonantal Text of the Torah Is Authoritative/the Vocal Text of the Torah Is Authoritative

In ancient times, Hebrew writing was purely consonantal when it was still a spoken language. Hebrew ceased to be a spoken language 200 years before the start of the Common Era. The need to preserve the precise pronunciation of the Torah's text drove the Sages to produce a tool that would guide readers. Fundamental signs were inserted between the lines of text: diacritical signs (to indicate how the consonants should be vowelized) and cantillation tropes. The finalization of the biblical text was carried out by the Masoretes (Heb.: *ba'alei ha-massora*, the "Masters of the Tradition"). Different systems of vocalization developed until the one associated with the city of Tiberias, invented in the eighth century, became the accepted system four centuries later. The Masoretic text is thus the vocalized Hebrew text that is to be found today in printed Bibles. The text that is written on parchment (such as in Torah scrolls, phylacteries and *mezuzot*) and that is solely used for ritual purposes is a consonantal text.[7] This duality gives rise to a fascinating exegetical question: if the consonantal text can be subjected to a reading that was not adopted by the Masoretes and if that different reading has juridical implications (for example, singular in the Masoretic reading and plural in a different reading), what text should be given precedence? While the Sages might be in agreement in attributing meaning to both texts, they will differ on the authority that should be accorded either of the two readings.

Further Reading

Basta, P. *Gezerah Shawah: storia, forme e metodi dell'analogia biblica*, Editrice Pontificio Istituto Biblico, 2006.

Chernick, M. "Internal Restraints on Gezerah Shawah's Application," 80 *Jewish Quarterly Review* 253 (1990).

Cohen, B. "Letter and Spirit in Jewish and Roman Law," in Moshe Davis (ed.), *Mordecai M. Kaplan Jubilee Volume, on the Occasion of His Seventieth Birthday*, Jewish Theological Seminary of America, 1953 (English Section), p. 109.

---

[7] A *mezuzah* (pl. *mezuzot*) is a parchment inscribed with Torah paragraphs and attached in a case to the doorpost of a Jewish house as a sign of faith. To attach such a case is one of the 613 commandments.

Faur, J. "Law and Hermeneutics in Rabbinic Jurisprudence: A Maimonidean Perspective," 14 *Cardozo Law Review* 1657 (1993).
Garfinkel, S. "Clearing *Peshat* and *Derash*," in M. Saebo (ed.), *Hebrew Bible/ Old Testament: The History of Its Interpretation*, Vandenhoeck & Ruprecht, 2000, p. 129.
Goltzberg, S. "The *A Fortiori* Argument in the *Talmud*," in A. Schuman (ed.), *Judaic Logic*, Gorgias Press, 2010, p. 177.
Jackson, B. S. "On the Nature of Analogical Argument in Early Jewish Law," 11 *Jewish Law Annual* 137 (1994).
Jaffé, D. *Essai sur l'interprétation et la culture talmudiques*, Cerf, 2013.
Loewe, R. *The "Plain" Meaning of Scripture in Early Jewish Exegesis*, Institute of Jewish Studies, University College, 1960.
Mielziner, M. *Introduction to the Talmud*, 4th edn., Bloch Publishing, 1968.
Weingreen, J. *From Bible to Mishna: The Continuity of Tradition*, Manchester University Press, 1976.
Weiss Halivni, D. *Peshat and Derash: Plain and Applied Meaning in Rabbinic Exegesis*, Oxford University Press, 1991.

6

Jewish Law and the Law of Nations
The Administration of Legal Pluralism

INTRODUCTION

The ubiquitous character of the Jewish legal system naturally raises a question that is connected to legal pluralism and that touches on the relationship the Jewish legal system maintains vis-à-vis the systems with which it coexists in the same geographical space. *Theoretically*, all models are possible here – from isolationism accompanied by a proclamation of the Jewish law system's superiority to an unreserved recognition of the law of nations that could lead to the transformation of Jewish law into a subsidiary legal system – but that also includes more nuanced models.

Jewish law displays varying degrees of openness, depending on the nature of the external institution that it must confront. The judiciary system of a country is rejected, to the point that avoidance of any appearance before it is regarded as a cardinal commandment; the prohibition necessarily entails recourse to arbitration (Section 1). In contrast, Jewish law is conciliatory to the laws of a country, in accordance with the saying "the law of the state is the law" (*"dina d'malchuta dina"*) (Section 2).

SECTION 1 RABBINIC ARBITRATION

I A HISTORY RÉSUMÉ

The birth of rabbinic arbitration is closely connected to the history of the Kingdom of Judea and to the gradual loss of the Jewish people's sovereignty in its ancestral land. As one can read in the writings of Josephus Flavius (*Antiquities of the Jews*, Book XIV, ch. 10, Section 17), who presents Judea's history from 67 to 37 BCE, the Roman Empire allowed the local judicial system to continue to exist for a certain period of time, recognizing that system's authority as being on an equal par vis-à-vis the authority of the Roman courts that would henceforth be its rivals. However, the system's rabbinic judges were suspected of being in the pay of Rome and thus there was a parallel development of ad hoc arbitration, which became a necessity when the Roman occupier ceased to authorize the Jewish legal system to settle litigations on monetary matters. Deprived of *imperium*, the rabbinic courts, while retaining the title of *beit din* (rabbinic court of law) and continuing to follow the rules decreed by Jewish law, could operate only as arbitration courts to which Rome had granted the sword of justice.

However, the disappearance of the Kingdom of Judea did not mean the total disappearance of Jewish jurisdiction. In certain eras and in certain places, one of the aspects of the political autonomy of Diaspora Jewish communities was the existence of an official statute that concerned rabbinic courts and that fully recognized their judgments.[1] History teaches us that there was, however, a continual struggle waged by Jewish communities against a royal power that gradually reduced its support for the existence of parallel jurisdictions. In France, the conflictual relationship between the Parliament of Metz and the rabbinic court of that city is well known; this form of legal pluralism ceased to exist in France in 1789.[2] In Germany, for example, a "Jewish tribunal of first instance" – the Jewish tribunal of Altona (*das jüdische Niedergericht zu Altona*) – existed in Holstein; it was composed of three rabbis and its president was the chief rabbi of Altona. Its judgments were in accordance with the *Shulchan Aruch*, and its existence and competence were confirmed in 1699. Although it was constantly challenged by the political authorities, the rabbinic court of Altona remained in existence until 1863.

Today, authentic rabbinic courts exist only in Israel and Morocco and their *imperium* is restricted solely to personal status. Except for such cases, the award of a rabbinic court of law will be recognized and executed only if that court respects the laws of arbitration of the country in which it is situated. That is the case, for example, in the United States of America, in France or in the United Kingdom.

In reality, rabbinic arbitration is not necessarily *rabbinic* because the arbitrators are not necessarily rabbis. Instead, the minimum requirement for membership in a rabbinic arbitration court is sufficient knowledge of Jewish

---

[1] For an overview, see Israel Goldstein, *Jewish Justice and Conciliation*, Ktav Publishing House, pp. 1–83.
[2] Jay R. Berkovitz, "Acculturation and Integration in Eighteenth-Century Metz," 24.3–4 *Jewish History* 271 (2010); Jordan Katz, "'To Judge and to Be Judged': Jewish Communal Autonomy in Metz and the Struggle for Sovereignty in Eighteenth-Century France," 104.3 *Jewish Quarterly Review* 438 (2014).

law. Thus, the phrase "rabbinic arbitration" actually refers to *arbitration by a court that is basing itself on Jewish law*. Nonetheless, for the sake of convenience, we continue to use it here.

In Europe and in the United States, rabbinic arbitration is as old as the Jewish communities on the European and North American continents. In Europe, depending on the location and the era, rabbinic arbitration coexisted with Jewish jurisdictions recognized on the basis of privileges or licenses. In eras or locations where there was no autonomous Jewish jurisdiction, Jewish communities that were sufficiently important always applied rabbinic arbitration in civil matters. The recurrence of questions related to arbitration in the responsa attests to the fact that rabbinic arbitration was ever-present in all Diaspora Jewish communities. After a long period of decline, rabbinic arbitration has experienced a veritable renaissance in recent decades: it is practiced on all continents, it can be national as well as international and it is practiced in all those domains that Jewish law designates as *monetary* (see Chapter 2) – labor law, torts, corporate law, the laws of civil and commercial contracts, inheritance law, and, etc.

The other tendency of rabbinic arbitration is its institutionalization. In France, at the prompting of the chief rabbi of France, a rabbinic arbitration court (the Chambre Arbitale Rabbinique [CAR]) was created in 2007; its function is to settle disputes between members of the Jewish community and to arbitrate in lawsuits over monetary issues in accordance with the laws of the *Shulchan Aruch*. This rabbinic arbitration court has regulations for arbitration and includes permanent arbitrators. The court, which has experienced a growing degree of success, deals with 100 cases yearly, following the example of the Beth Din of America, which was founded in New York in 1960 by the Rabbinical Council of America (RCA).[3]

If rabbinic arbitration has in recent decades been enjoying a considerable degree of success, it previously experienced a certain decline. In the wake of the French Revolution and the rise of the Enlightenment, what is referred to as the "emancipation" of the Jews was accompanied by assimilation, which gave rise to growing disaffection among Jews toward their own legal system. As a result, in the early twentieth century, despite the continual exhortations of leading spiritual authorities, only a small minority of the members of European and American Orthodox Jewish communities turned to rabbinic courts of law with regard to issues that were not strictly connected to religious matters.

---

[3] https://bethdin.org/.

Why, we might ask, would the members of the Orthodox Jewish communities in Europe and America refrain from turning to secular courts of law? Do European and American courts not present sufficient guarantees for a satisfactory resolution of lawsuits, even between observant Jews? When we phrase that question in such terms, we are ignoring the fact that recourse to a rabbinic court is not an *option* but is rather a legal *duty* according to Jewish law. Other reasons – technical, economic, etc. – can motivate one to turn to rabbinic arbitration, but these are secondary (see Section 2). After we examine that question, we study the essential aspects of rabbinic arbitration: the arbitration agreement (*shtar berurin*), the composition of the arbitration court (see Section 3) and some procedural elements (see Section 4).

II RABBINIC ARBITRATION AS A LEGAL DUTY, TECHNICAL NECESSITY AND SOURCE OF SAVINGS

A *Rabbinic Arbitration As a Legal Duty*

We should recall here a fundamental idea: every Jew, irrespective of nationality or place of residence, is bound by specific civil and criminal laws; by its very nature, Jewish law is transnational and crosses international boundaries. The second fundamental idea, which we develop in what follows, is that, for the members of a Jewish community, arbitration is not an alternative mode of dispute resolution but is rather the normal mode because recourse to secular courts of law is, generally speaking, prohibited.

In order to define the nature and extent of the obligation to turn to the rabbinic arbitration system, let us study a number of verses in the Torah and engage in some exegesis. In one of the weekly portions in the Book of Deuteronomy, appropriately named "Judges" ("*Shoftim*"), specifically in verse 16:18, we read: "You shall appoint magistrates and officials for your tribes, in all the settlements that the Lord your God is giving you, and they shall govern the people with due justice." This of course presupposes an independent Jewish polity in the promised land. The commandment in this verse, the establishment of rabbinic courts, is one of the 613 commandments binding on Jews. Maimonides teaches us that this commandment is mandatory not only in the Land of Israel but also in the Diaspora (*MT, Laws Governing the Sanhedrin* 1:1). Not only does the verse command Jews to establish courts, it also commands the members of Jewish communities to present their litigations before these courts. In fact, some rabbinic authorities even argue that Jews who bring their legal dispute before a court belonging to the state that grants them a sum of money greater than what a rabbinic court would have allotted them are guilty of the sin of stealing from their neighbor. Moreover, and especially, Jews who act in this manner are violating an essential prohibition – *issur arka'ot*, that is, the prohibition against the presentation of a litigation before a Gentile court of law.

The roots of that prohibition can be found in one of the weekly portions in the Book of Exodus, entitled "Laws" ("*Mishpatim*"), specifically in verse 21:1. In this text, God transmits to Moses an entire corpus of civil and criminal laws; the portion begins: "These are the rules [or laws] that you shall set before them" (*Exod.* 21:1). Before *them*, that is, before *Jews*. God is essentially saying to Moses: I will teach you the laws and you will teach them to My people. This is the literal meaning of the verse. However, the Hebrew word *mishpatim* can be translated not only as "laws," "ordinances" or "statutes" but also as "lawsuits" or "legal actions." The two latter definitions are presented in the Talmud. In a *baraita* of the Babylonian Talmud, we read: "We learned the following: Rabbi Tarfon would say: 'Wherever you find the law courts of idol worshippers, even if their laws are like Israel's laws, you are not permitted to turn to their courts, as it is written, "These are the rules [or laws] that you shall set before them" – before them [i.e., Israel's judges] and not before [the judges of] idol worshippers'" (*BT Git.* 88b).

In other words, a literal meaning of the verse turns it into an introduction to a catalogue of the civil and criminal laws that Jews must observe. Rabbinic tradition interprets this verse as a reference to the legal proceedings that can be initiated on the basis of these laws or statutes and as an explicit commandment that litigations must be brought *before them*, that is, before the judges designated by Moses. This verse is thus understood as a reference to the judges whose nomination is related in the Book of Exodus, specifically in verses 18: 13–26. Rashi of Troyes (1040–1105) includes this talmudic interpretation in his commentary on *Exod.* 21:1:

> It is written, "before them" [i.e., before the judges of Israel] but not before [the judges of] idol worshippers. Even if you know that, with regard to one of our laws, they [the judges of idol worshippers] pass judgments that are similar to what would be judged in accordance with Israel's laws, you must not turn to their courts because any Jew who brings before a Gentile court a dispute with another Jew is desecrating God's name while honoring the name of idols and praising them [according to another version: augmenting their importance], as it is written (*Deut.* 32[:31]), "For their rock is not like our Rock, in our enemies' own estimation [or, our enemies are judging us]"; when our enemies judge us (i.e., when we turn to their courts), this is evidence of (i.e., we are attesting to) the superiority of their religion.

The *Shulchan Aruch* repeats these same terms almost verbatim (26:1). This law is a firm commandment. Many commentaries accompanying and elucidating the text of the *Shulchan Aruch* clearly state that the origin and nature of the legislation applied by Gentile courts are meaningless. Recourse to a Gentile court is prohibited even if the law guiding it on a given legal question is identical to what appears in Jewish law. It is irrelevant whether or not the religion of the members of the Gentile court is idol worship. The essence of the prohibition against recourse to a Gentile court is its rejection of divine law in favor of another legal system, whether or not that latter system is close to divine law in spirit or in substance. The prohibition has nothing to do with the nationality or religious beliefs of the judge. Thus, even if the parties know that the judge is a coreligionist, even an observant Jew, they must not present their litigation before that judge, who will inevitably apply either the civil code of the country or common law.

On the other hand, many rabbinic authorities admit that litigations can be presented before a non-Jewish *arbitration* court. These rabbinic authorities are essentially maintaining that the arbitrators in such courts are not bound by any particular body of laws and that recourse to their services is therefore not tantamount to a rejection of the Torah's laws. This holds true for American law, where the courts have often ruled that arbitrators are not bound by any particular substantive rules or by the rules of evidence but that instead an "arbitrator ... may do justice as it sees it, applying its own sense of law and equity to the facts" (*Silverman v. Benmor Coats*, Inc. 61 N.Y. 2d 299, 308 [1984]). Similarly, if the arbitration is subject to French law, it is permissible from the perspective of Jewish law to present a dispute before arbitrators deciding *ex aequo et bono*, i.e., who have the possibility of making decisions that do not have to conform to the rules of law.[4]

There are many exceptions to *issur arka'ot*. First of all, the defendant might refuse to appear after having received a summons from the rabbinic court three times. In this case, there is no prohibition against resorting to a secular court. Nonetheless, some rabbinic authorities insist that, in this case, the rabbinic court must formally authorize the plaintiff to issue a writ to the coreligionist defendant to appear before this secular court. A defendant who has been issued a writ by a coreligionist to appear before a secular court is authorized to appear in such a court and to resume the trial before it. According to some rabbinic authorities, even when the

---

[4] "Amiable composition" in French; "amicable composition" in Louisiana legal terminology. The arbitrator is then called "amiable compositeur" (amicable compounder).

opposing party in a legal action is non-Jewish, the legal dispute must be brought before a rabbinic court of law. However, since it is probable that a non-Jew will refuse to appear before a rabbinic court, it is permissible, argue most rabbinic authorities, to issue a writ to the non-Jewish litigant to appear before a secular court without any need for authorization from a rabbinic court. If there is the danger of imminent damage, it is permissible to turn to a secular court in order to obtain the necessary emergency protective measures: injunctions, expert opinions, etc. The permission here is rooted in the idea that, in such cases, the tribunal referred to does not, strictly speaking, hand down a "judgment" but instead is issuing a pretrial decision. The same holds true for the discovery process in the United States.

The other major exception to the need to turn to a rabbinic court is criminal trials. Ever since the Second Temple's destruction, rabbinic courts have ceased to deal with criminal cases (with very few exceptions). In any case, the idea of rabbinic courts being competent to judge in criminal cases would be incompatible with the monopoly of state-appointed courts in this matter, a monopoly that Jewish law recognizes in accordance with the rule "the law of the state is the law" ("*dina d'malchuta dina*"; see Section 2).

As a general rule, there is no prohibition against turning to secular courts when the arbitration award handed down by a rabbinic court cannot be implemented because of the particular domain in question – for example, matters that cannot be arbitrated under a specific legal system[5] in which the judgments of rabbinic courts must integrate themselves. Finally, it is permissible to turn to a non-Jewish court in order to recognize or implement a rabbinic arbitration award.

It is interesting to note here that all of the laws of *issur arka'ot* also apply to a lawyer who is a coreligionist of the plaintiff: legal representation of or legal assistance to a plaintiff before a non-Jewish court, when recourse to a rabbinic court is mandatory, is a violation of the biblical prohibition "you shall not ... place a stumbling block before the blind" (*Lev.* 19:14). This prohibition is essentially intended to prevent a lawyer coming to the assistance of someone who is unaware (that is, blind to the fact that) that he or she is violating the Torah.[6]

---

[5] In American or in French law, for example, all matters are not arbitrable.
[6] See Steven H. Resnicoff, "The Attorney–Client Relationship: A Jewish Law Perspective," 14 *Notre Dame Journal of Legal Ethics & Public Policy* 349 (2000). See also bibliography.

In practice, the prohibition against turning to secular courts is observed by few Jews. It appears that only a minority of the members of the French and American Jewish communities resort to rabbinic arbitration. In any event, we should add here that recourse to rabbinic arbitration can also be motivated by technical necessities.

B Rabbinic Arbitration As a Technical Necessity

In addition to being mandatory, recourse to rabbinic arbitration can sometimes be a technical necessity. In Jewish law, interest-bearing loans (interest, *ribit* in Hebrew) are strictly forbidden among Jews (*Exod.* 22:24, *Lev.* 25:35–38, *Deut.* 23:20–21). However, for reasons of pragmatism, the Sages, basing themselves on a passage in the Talmud (*BT BM* 94b), developed a legal mechanism called *heter iska* in order to allow loans between Jews but without colliding head-on with the prohibition against interest-bearing loans. We find here an example of inventiveness in rabbinic interpretation motivated by a desire to adapt to the socioeconomic context.[7] Schematically, the heart of the mechanism is a contract in which the borrower and lender agree to be partners in a business deal that is no longer a loan in which the lender brings into the deal a cash contribution, while the borrower brings his or her business into it. If the borrower's business prospers, the investor will receive profits, rather than interest, and the receipt of profits is legal in Jewish law. Evidently, if there are losses, the investor will have to share in them. Otherwise, it would not be an *iska* and would instead be an interest-bearing loan in disguise, and a legal dispute could arise as a result of such an agreement.

The manner in which secular courts, primarily those in New York, deal with *heter iska* shows that, generally speaking, they do not understand the mechanism presented before them or that they view it with contempt as an artifice. Not surprisingly, in most cases, they order the payment of interest, thereby arriving at a result that is contrary to the wishes of the parties. Thus, there would be here an obvious interest in recourse to arbitrators who are well versed in Jewish law.[8]

---

[7] Hillel Gamoran, *Jewish Law in Transition: How Economic Forces Overcame the Prohibition against Lending on Interest*, Hebrew Union College Press, 2008.

[8] Kenneth H. Ryesky, "Secular Law Enforcement of the *Heter Iska*," 25 *Journal of Halachah and Contemporary Society* 67 (1993); J. David Bleich, "The *Hetter Iska* and American Courts," 42.3 *Tradition* 49 (2009).

C The Economic Advantages of Rabbinic Arbitration

Finally, rabbinic arbitration can be advantageous for financial reasons because it is cheaper than the state-operated justice system. Thus, the CAR asks for only a fixed sum and for a modest amount for dealing with a lawsuit. The Beth Din of America has produced a detailed list of fees, which varies in accordance with the value of the litigation and the number of arbitrators sitting in session (one or three).

Another important factor in the reduction of costs is the fact that representation by a lawyer is not mandatory in cases brought before a rabbinic court. This can be explained by the fact that rabbinic tradition is reticent about lawyers in general.[9] Rabbinic tradition does not forbid the presence of an attorney in the court proceedings, with the result that the parties are represented by attorneys most of the time. Here the question arises as to the final burden of costs and fees between the parties. The general rule is derived from a discussion related in the Talmud (*BT San.* 31b). The debate revolves around the possibility of forcing a plaintiff to refrain from turning to a local court and to instead present the litigation before a tribunal that is geographically distant and that consist of judges who are more experienced, when there is the fear that the plaintiff will manage to influence the local judges. Rabbi Dimi reports that Rabbi Yohanan favors such a possibility. Rabbi Eliezer challenges Rabbi Yohanan's opinion and tells him, "My Master and Teacher, if a person lends money to his neighbor, should the lender have to spend additional funds? No, the borrower is forced to appear before a local tribunal" (*BT San.* 31b).

Rabbi Eliezer's opposition is undoubtedly motivated by the consideration that the rabbinic court will not grant any compensation covering the cost of the trial – such as the lawyers' fees and other expenses connected with the legal procedure – even to the party in whose favor the court has ruled. Thus, most of the Rishonim consider that the general rule should be that each party must bear the costs of the trial, whether the party has emerged victorious or whether it was defeated. This general rule has been codified in the *Shulchan Aruch*. Four recognized categories are exempted from this general rule: abuse of procedure by the plaintiff, abuse of procedure by the defendant, an agreement between the parties and litigations relating to the compensatory payment. Let us now take a look at the arbitration agreement and at the composition of the arbitration court in Jewish law.

---

[9] For an introduction, see Dov I. Frimer, "The Role of a Lawyer in Jewish Law," 1 *Journal of Law and Religion* 297 (1983).

III THE ARBITRATION AGREEMENT (*SHTAR BEIRURIN*) AND THE COMPOSITION OF THE ARBITRATION COURT

A The Arbitration Agreement

Jewish law requires, at the conclusion of an arbitration agreement, that it take the form of an arbitration clause or an arbitration contract. This agreement must determine the power of the arbitrators, designate the institution or name the arbitrators charged with the task of settling the litigation, etc.

Like the arbitration clause, the arbitration agreement must clearly show that the parties intend to submit their litigation to a rabbinic court, which will judge it in accordance with Jewish law. However, what might appear obvious in the eyes of experts in *halachah* might appear abstruse to laypersons, with the possible result that a secular court might deny the existence of an agreement. Thus, for example, an American judge refused to see an arbitration clause in a contract where the parties agreed that they would resolve their differences *"in accordance with the regulations of Speyer, Worms, and Mainz."* Whereas the appellant argued that this clause obliged the parties to seek recourse from rabbinic arbitration, the appellee argued the precise opposite. Undoubtedly, an expert explained to the judge the meaning of this reference: in these three German cities, during the medieval period, the highest Ashkenazi rabbinic authorities convened a synod and adopted a certain number of ordinances (see Chapter 3) applicable to their communities. Among the rules issued and related to several questions of civil law was the reiteration of the absolute obligation to submit all disputes to rabbinic courts and the strict prohibition against turning to secular courts. However, despite the expert's testimony, the New York judge refused to interpret the clause accordingly on the grounds that the First Amendment of the US Constitution forbids an American court from taking part in a religious dispute.[10] On the other hand, when the terms used in a clause are clear, the First Amendment does not place any obstacles in the way of secular courts that decide to order the clause's enforcement. Thus, the Court of Appeals of the District of Columbia has ruled that the meaning of the terms *"Beit Din"*, *"Orthodox rabbis"* and *"Din Torah"* were not disputed by the parties, that the Court of Appeals was not being called upon to settle a religious question and that, in consequence, the imposed enforcement of

---

[10] *Sieger v. Sieger*, 297 A.D.2d 33 (2002), 36–37.

such an arbitration clause would not constitute a collision with constitutional measures relating to religion.[11] In France, the principle of the separation of Church and state would certainly lead to the same results.[12]

B The Composition of the Arbitration Court

In principle, the arbitration court is composed of three arbitrators (*M San.* 1:3). This Mishnah relates a discussion between Rabbi Meir and other Sages. In this discussion, Rabbi Meir argues that each of the parties must choose an arbitrator and that the two parties must jointly choose the third arbitrator, while the Sages think that it is the task of the two arbitrators to choose the third. This procedure is traditionally referred to as *zabla*, which is a Hebrew acronym (*zeh borer lo echad ve-zeh borer lo echad*, this one chooses someone and that one chooses someone). On this point, *halachah* is unwavering. What happens if the two arbitrators are unable to decide on the third? Traditionally, the appointment was made by those who enjoyed the status of "Elders of the City." This institution ceased to exist after the Holocaust. Another method is to consider the rabbi of the city qualified *ipso jure* to serve as the third arbitrator.

Alternatively, the parties can agree to entrust the power to arbitrate to a single arbitrator. They can also plan to have more than three arbitrators. In principle, the disqualification of arbitrators is modeled on the disqualification of judges. The major grounds for disqualification are family ties and conflicts of interest. Ideally, the procedure of *zabla* could bring out the truth in the dispute. The two arbitrators appointed by the parties are going to investigate the facts and the law favoring one or the other of the parties, while the third arbitrator will arbitrate. In practice, at least in recent times, it appears that some individuals have sometimes confused the qualifications of an arbitrator with those of a lawyer, with the result that often litigations have not been settled satisfactorily or – in certain cases – have not been settled at all. This state of affairs explains why Jewish communities throughout the world are attempting to establish an institutionalized form of arbitration and to thereby avoid having to turn to ad hoc arbitration.

---

[11] *Meshel v. Ohev Shalom Talmud Torah*, 869 A.2d 343 (DC Cir. 2005). In the same vein, *Davis v. Melnicke*, 9 N.Y.3d 984 (2007), citing the leading case, *Avitzur v. Avitzur*, 58 N.Y.2d 108, 459 N.Y.S.2d 572, 446 N.E.2d 136 [1983], *cert. denied* 464 U.S. 817, 104 S.Ct. 76, 78 L.Ed.2d 88 [1983].

[12] French secularism is often misunderstood. For an introduction, see Michel Troper, "French Secularism, or Laïcité," 21 *Cardozo Law Review* 1267 (1999–2000); Patrick Weil, "Why the French Laïcité is Liberal," 30 *Cardozo Law Review* 2699 (2008); Blandine Chelini-Pont, "Is Laïcité the Civil Religion of France?" 41 *George Washington International Law Review* 765 (2009–2010).

IV SOME PROCEDURAL ELEMENTS

It is impossible to explain the arbitration procedure as it unfolds before a rabbinic court. We mention questions that appear to be essential and that could potentially have repercussions in terms of the recognition or enforcement of rabbinic awards.

Our presentation of the arbitration procedure will include the following elements: the issuing of a summons to appear before a *beit din*, the unique institution known as *siruv* (Hebrew for "refusal"), representation by a lawyer, the award and the precise role of the rabbinic court in the resolution of litigation.

A *The Summons to Appear before a Rabbinic Court and the Refusal* (Siruv)

1 The Principles

A rabbinic court has at its disposal an important means of pressure for bringing the recalcitrant to reach a binding arbitration agreement with the other party and to submit to the rabbinic court's jurisdiction. This means of pressure is the refusal (*siruv* in Hebrew), which can be compared to the concept of contempt of court in common law and which is situated on one of the middle rungs on the scale of coercive measures that are at a rabbinic court's disposal. Less drastic than *cherem* ("excommunication" or "anathema"), which is hardly used today, the refusal is harsher than *nezifa* ("rebuke"). It is linked to *nidui* (a milder form of excommunication that literally means "distancing").[13] The *beit din* writes a document declaring that Mr. So-and-So or Ms. So-and-So refuses to appear before it. Individuals who refuse to appear before a rabbinic court suffer a form of communal exclusion aimed at leading them to repent: they can no longer be included in various religious quorums (the ten-member *minyan* required for a prayer service, the trio required for the public recital of *birkat hamazon*, the prayer after meals), worshippers are forbidden to sit beside them in the synagogue, members of the Jewish community are forbidden to marry their children to the children of individuals in a state of *nidui* or to have commercial dealings with them, the name of the

---

[13] On these different forms of ban, see Michael Broyde, "Forming Religious Communities and Respecting Dissenters' Rights," in Michael J. Broyde and John Witte Jr., eds., *Human Rights in Judaism: Cultural, Religious, and Political Perspectives*, Jason Aronson, 1998, pp. 35–76; see also Asher Benzion Buchman, "Nidduy, Arur and Nezifah: Social Pressure," 13 *Ḥakirah* 213 (2012).

individual in a state of *nidui* appears in notices posted in communal buildings and newspapers, even on the Internet. The effectiveness of this ban depends on the more or less close ties existing among the members of the community in question and on the moral authority enjoyed by the members of the *beit din*. *Siruv* can sometimes be the object of an interesting dispute before state-appointed courts and illustrates graphically the relationship between Jewish law and the law of nations. The entire process involved in the imposition of a ban (*nidui*) is effective only in a community that is structured to a certain extent and where the rabbinate enjoys real authority. We consider certain aspects of a dispute prior to, and following, the pronouncement of a *siruv*.

2 The Refusal (*Siruv*) in Non-Jewish Courts

Initially, a person faced with the threat of a *siruv* can consider turning to the secular courts of law and to request that they order the rabbinic authorities not to enforce this grim sanction. The First Amendment of the US Constitution certainly hinders such interference on the part of secular courts in an internal conflict taking place in a religious community, as case law has often affirmed. In France, the principle of the state's neutrality would assuredly produce the same effect. Initially, American case law also reveals cases where an individual who had surrendered to a *siruv* or to the threat of one demanded the nullification of the arbitration agreement on the grounds that his consent would be vitiated by duress. This argument turned out to be unsuccessful because the appellant could not prove that he had been subjected to a degree of coercion that was greater than the degree of coercion resulting from obedience to the duties of one's conscience that are inherent in the fact of belonging to a religious community.[14]

---

[14] *Mikel v. Scharf*, 432 N.S.Y.2d 602, 606 (Sup. Ct. 1980): "[P]ressure is not duress." *Greenberg v. Greenberg*, 656 N.Y.S.2d 369 (App. Div. 1997), 370: "We find that the wife freely submitted herself to the jurisdiction of the Bais Din and that this was a manifestation of her having voluntarily undertaken obedience to the religious law which such tribunals interpret and enforce. The 'threat' of a siruv, which entails a type of ostracism from the religious community, and which is prescribed as an enforcement mechanism by the religious law to which the petitioner freely adheres, cannot be deemed duress" (see *Lieberman v. Lieberman*, 149 Misc.2d 983, 987). "The record in the present case does not support a finding that the wife was subjected to any particular coercion greater than that which is intrinsic in the case of any member of a religious community who, as a matter of conscience, feels obligated to obey the laws of his or her religious organization, or to follow the decrees of a religious court, and who consequently exposes himself or herself to the ecclesiastical sanctions available for the enforcement of such decrees or such law" (cf., *Golding v. Golding*, 176 A.D.2d 20; *Perl*

When the *siruv* is effective, it ostracizes the recalcitrant. This ban can ultimately ruin that individual's business. It can therefore happen that an individual on whom a ban has been placed will lodge a complaint concerning this situation with secular courts. Thus, in one such instance, the victim of a *siruv* attacked the three rabbis who had imposed the ban on him on the grounds that the *siruv*, in which his name appeared in notices in communal buildings and was disseminated on the Internet, constituted libel, ignored the principle of the due process of law and had inflicted emotional damage on him. The court dismissed the plaintiff's entire lawsuit. First, he noted that the tort of libel implies that a jurisdiction must take a position on the veracity of the elements contained in the *siruv* and must therefore state whether the *siruv* was justified from the standpoint of Jewish law – something that an American judge cannot do without violating the First Amendment of the US Constitution. Regarding the principle of due process, the court reminded that a *beit din* was is not an emanation of the state and, consequently, the appellant could not demand the due process's protection. Finally, the court decided that the appellant could not obtain damages because the tort of infliction of moral suffering supposes that a grave and insulting action has occurred. A member of an Orthodox community, who, by definition, adheres to that community's moral and legal system cannot complain about the system's activation.[15]

B *Representation by a Lawyer*

In Jewish law, a lawyer cannot be considered an essential component in court proceedings and thus a lawyer's representation of a client is not regarded as a fundamental right.[16] Quite the contrary, legal representation is perceived as a concession forced upon the Jewish community by the necessities of history. Thus, in the Talmudic trial, which is inquisitorial by nature, the lawyer is quite simply useless: the judge enjoys immense power, actively interrogates both witnesses and the disputing parties, and, in exceptional cases, even helps the parties to formulate their demands. Oath-taking is a frequent element and perjury is punished severely. Arbitration has the same schema, to which is

---

v. *Perl*, 126 A.D.2d 91; *Segal v. Segal*, 278 N.J.Super. 218, 650 A.2d 996; see also *Aflalo v. Aflalo*, 295 N.J.Super. 527, 685 A.2d 523). "In sum, the release signed by the wife was, as a matter of law and fact, voluntary." See also *Berg v. Berg*, 926 N.Y.S.2d 568, 570 (2011) et *Wydra v. Brach*, 2011 WL 4031513 (N.Y. Sup.), 8.

[15] *Thomas v. Fuerst et alii*, 345 Ill.App.3d 929 (2004). See also on libel *Berman v. Shatnes Laboratory*, 350 N.Y.S.2d 703 (1973).

[16] See *supra* note 9 and accompanying text.

added the procedure of choosing arbitrators (*zabla*), a procedure that is supposed to promote the emergence of the truth. While it recognizes some of the virtues of the adversarial system, Jewish law refuses to base that system on lawyers. It attaches great importance to the personal confrontation between the plaintiff and the defendant, and between the witnesses and the parties. Certain legal presumptions and the intensive use of oaths also contribute to a psychological involvement of the parties in the trial that the shield of legal representation would attenuate. Moreover, the Sages feared that the distance that legal representation creates might exacerbate passions and might even hinder the litigants from arriving at a compromise, which, as we see further on, is the ideal goal. The Talmudic tradition is also very cautious vis-à-vis the legal profession, which it regards more as an obstacle than as an aid to the manifestation of truth and justice, as attested in numerous sources in the Talmud (see, for example, *BT Shev.*, 31a). However, under the pressure of circumstances, *halachah* has slowly evolved and today lawyers play a central role in the rabbinic court. The destruction of the Second Temple and the dispersion of the Jewish people in the wake of that event rendered the appearance of litigants in person more and more problematic. The development of international commerce was another factor in the "softening" of *halachah*. The rules of the CAR make no mention of lawyers. When appearing before this arbitration court, the mission of lawyers is essentially reduced to the formulation of the litigants' demands in an intelligible manner for the arbitrators. The lawyers will in principle not discuss aspects that are strictly legal, because, in Jewish law, *jura novit curia* ("the court knows the law"). In its *Layman's Guide to Dinei Torah*, the Beth Din of America attempts to dissuade litigants from using the services of lawyers. Developments in previous centuries help explain this reticence.

C The Rabbinic Judgment (P'sak)

Majority decision prevails unless the arbitrators have been authorized to impose a compromise (*peshara*, see later in this chapter), in which case a unanimous decision is required.

Originally, the rabbinic judgment (*p'sak*) traditionally existed solely in oral form. Nowhere in the Mishnah do we see any mention of the *p'sak* being written down. When it describes the outcome of the procedure in a rabbinic court, the Mishnah states: "When the judges finished their deliberations ... the president of the court says: 'Mr. So-and-So, you are innocent; Mr. Such-and-Such, you are guilty'" (*M San.* 3:7). Although exceptions can exist, depending on the circumstances, they are always delimited and are never perceived as mandatory. When rabbinic judgments began to be written down, they had to be extremely brief and they functioned solely as the pronouncement of the judgment itself, because a rabbinic court is not obligated to cite the reasons for its decision. Whereas the Mishnah provides many details on the procedure to be followed (pretrial investigation of the case, witness testimony, etc.), it does not indicate that judges must explain their decisions. On the other hand, the Mishnah clearly specifies how the president of the court must pronounce its judgment: the president must communicate only the judgment itself. Generally speaking, the trial has a secretive character. In the case of a disagreement between the judges, they are not authorized to reveal the position they adopted before the deliberations; any judge who violates this prohibition is considered a slanderer (*M San.*, ibid.).

Similarly, these trials are held *in camera*. Apparently, the communication of the reasons for a court's decision was regarded as dangerous because that would mean the exposure of the court's reasoning and its decision-making process to the external world and to its possible criticism. Another risk was that the parties might construct their argumentation in order to make it more convincing – perhaps at the expense of truth and justice. Nonetheless, it is sometimes desirable to explain the grounds for the judgment in order to prevent anyone from accusing the rabbinic court of being partial.

In practice, the CAR issues its judgments in Hebrew. The arbitration award is then transcribed and translated into French in case a judicial approbation is required in order to enforce it. In conformity with *halachah*, the content is minimalist because, as we have already seen, an arbitration court is not obliged to explain the grounds for its award, even when requested to do so by the parties. In contrast, following the example of the majority of American rabbinic courts, the Beth Din of America issues its awards in English and detaches itself from the tradition by providing the reasons for every award – in accordance with the model of the judgments handed down by American courts – and including the authorities in support of that award. We undoubtedly see here evidence of a double influence: the practice of the rabbinic courts of the State of Israel and secular law. In addition, many American rabbis have studied law in university and have a PhD. In contrast, the course of study of the vast majority of members of the CAR is essentially in the field of Talmudic studies, which explains their strong loyalty to tradition. In various documents it has published, the Beth Din of America explains that one reason for this evolution is the desire to gain the assent of the parties and the public's support. Another evolution worth noting is the publication of some of its judgments (with the names omitted and with the parties' consent) in the *Journal of the Beth Din of America*.[17] This development constitutes an authentic innovation: whereas responsa (see Chapter 3) were published over the centuries, judgments were never published because they were usually not written down and, even when they were, they usually remained confidential. Contrary to what one might initially think, this publication of judgments is not intended to promote familiarity with precedents. In effect, Jewish law does not follow the principle of *stare decisis*, particularly because such a principle postulates a hierarchy between the courts, a hierarchy that does not exist in Jewish law.[18] In reality, as the editors of the *Journal of the Beth Din of America* claim, one of the aims of the publication of the awards is the education of the public by making it aware of the kind of litigations with which the Beth Din of America deals. Two other aims are to inspire confidence in the public and to display the professionalism of the Beth Din of America. Initially, rabbinic arbitration frequently bore the hallmark of amateurism; the publication of the judgments of the Beth Din of America can help erase that unpleasant memory.

The parties cannot appeal from a rabbinic award because, in rabbinic tradition, appeals do not in principle exist: "A rabbinic court does not closely examine the decision of another rabbinic court" (*BT BB* 138b). There is only one procedure that permits one to persuade a rabbinic court to revise its judgment completely or partially when it has committed an error or when a decisive piece of evidence has appeared after the pronouncement of the award and before it has been implemented (*SA HM* 20:1 and 25:1–2). This kind of change of award does not pose a theological difficulty: since the discovery of the truth is an aspect of justice in comparison with which all other aspects are subordinate, Jewish law cannot conceive that an erroneous judgment is irreversible and consequently rejects the notion of the authority of *res judicata*. However, in practice, this ideal perception of justice could cause the parties to run the risk that the dispute could reemerge at any moment. We can note here the interesting point that the parties have the possibility, within the framework of rabbinic arbitration, of waiving their right to a reexamination of their case, should a new piece of evidence be discovered, for example (for more detail on this point, see Chapter 3, Section 5). In this same spirit, the rules of the CAR, like those of the Beth Din of America, do not envisage the change of an award except in the case of a material error in the broad sense of the term.

---

[17] https://bethdin.org/journal/.
[18] On the absence of the *stare decisis* principle in Jewish law, see Chapter 3, Section 5.

D Strict Adherence to the Law (Din Torah) or Ex Aequo et Bono Decision (Peshara)?

In the law of nations, there are various ways of putting an end to a dispute. Arbitration is one of them, a compromise is another; generally, arbitration is used when a compromise is impossible. In Jewish law, these two modes for resolving disputes overlap: the arbitrator or the counsels of the parties must do everything possible in order to amicably end the dispute. Although arbitration is ideal, a mediation ending in a settlement (*peshara* or *bitzua*) is preferable because it restores peace between the litigants and also because it avoids the judiciary error that the judge or arbitrator and the parties fear above all else.[19] Among the numerous sources on this subject, we can cite a medieval commentary on the verse "do what is right and good in the sight of the Lord, that it may go well with you" (*Deut.* 6:18). In his exegesis of this verse, Rashi writes, "it is written 'what is right and good,' which means compromise." Apparently, this predilection for compromise appeared or began to develop after Bar Kochba's revolt against the Roman occupier (132–135 CE). The favor for compromise did not produce unanimity, far from it: three Sages of the Talmud debate this subject and each expresses a different opinion on the place the *peshara* occupies in the system of justice. For Joshua bar Korcha, recourse to the *peshara* is mandatory. In order to justify his view, he bases himself on a verse from Zacharia that instructs judges to issue judgments that promote peace and charity. For Rabbi Eliezer, son of Yossi the Galilean, an arbitrator who aims for a *peshara* is a blasphemer because only a strict adherence to the Law can enable us to achieve justice. He bases himself on a verse from Deuteronomy (1:17). Finally, Simeon ben Menassia is of the opinion that the *peshara* is neither mandatory nor prohibited but is only permissible. According to what has been established in *halachah*, a rabbinic court, before embarking on its mission, must ask the parties whether they wish to be judged in strict accordance with the Law or to enter a process of *peshara* (SA HM 12:2).[20] The arbitrators must make every effort to convince the parties to accept the

---

[19] Yuval Sinai, "Arbitration As An Ideal Procedure," 18 *Jewish Law Association Studies* 279 (2008); Itay Lipschutz, "'Biṣu'a' and 'Pesharah': Three Possible Interpretations," 31 *Dinei Israel* 105 (2016) (English Section).

[20] On the eminent place of *peshara* or compromise in Jewish law, see Menachem Elon, "Law, Truth, and Peace: 'The Three Pillars of the World,'" 29 *New York University Journal of International Law & Policy* 439, 440–446 (1997); Ytzchok Alderstein, "Lawyers, Faith, and Peacemaking: Jewish Perspectives on Peace," 7 *Pepperdine Dispute Resolution* 177 (2007); Haim Shapira, "The Debate Over Compromise and the Goals of the Judicial Process," 26 *Diné Israel: Studies in Halakhah and Jewish Law* 183 (2010); Joseph Reich, "Rethinking *Pesharah*: An Argument for the Increased Role of Mediation in the Contemporary *Beth Din*," in "Jewish Law," www.jlaw.com/Articles/RethinkingPesharah.pdf.

peshara, even if the procedure has commenced. Such is the practice today.[21] A rabbinic award can only ratify the agreement reached by the parties.

However, arbitrators can, in exceptional cases, dispense with the consent of the parties. In order to reinforce the foundations of this restriction on the consensual character of the *peshara*, halachic literature bases itself on the expression *"hatel peshara beneihen"* – "to arrange or place a compromise between them" (*BT San* 32b), but not to "make" a compromise. This means that an arbiter who proposes a compromise that is rejected by the parties can impose it on them. In what cases? There are two major categories. The first is one in which the rabbinic courts must, in strict accordance with the law, impose an oath on one of the parties. This is a fairly common practice. One wants to avoid the recourse to an oath because of the grave consequences of an eventual perjury. The second relates to *complex cases*: because of the facts or the law, the judges cannot determine who is right and who is wrong. The difficulty of a particular case does not authorize the judge to refuse to judge; however, in order to avoid a judiciary error, a judge might impose a compromise rather than opting for a judgment that strictly adheres to Jewish law.

There is an intermediary situation between strict law (Din Torah) and *peshara*: *"peshara karov l'din,"* literally, "a *peshara* that is close to the Law." In such cases, the arbitrators consider themselves obligated by the parties to judge in accordance with their (that is, the judges') sense of justice and not in strict accordance with *halachah*. Rabbinic arbitrators thus may find themselves in the position of deciding *ex aequo et bono*.

Whatever form of adjudication has been chosen by the *beit din*, it remains arbitration in the eyes of American law.[22]

---

[21] Haim Shine, "Compromise," in N. Rakover (ed.), *Jewish Law and Current Legal Problems*, The Library of Jewish Law, 1984, p. 77; Yitzchak Kasdan, "A Proposal for P'sharah: A Jewish Mediation/Arbitration Service," in N. Wolpin (ed.), *The Ethical Imperative: Torah Perspectives on Ethics and Values*, Mesorah Publications, 2000, p. 299; Moshe Taragin, "The Role of Pesharah within the Halachic Judicial System," in *Jewish Law*, http://jlaw.com/Articles/roleof.html.

[22] Comp. *Kozlowski v. Seville Syndicate, Inc.*, 314 N.Y.S.2d 439, 445: "Whether the proceeding be by Din Torah or by Pesharah, it is, of course, from the point of view of the law of the State of New York, an arbitration proceeding – statutory or common law."

SECTION 2 "THE LAW OF THE STATE IS THE LAW" ("*DINA D'MALCHUTA DINA*")

I THE GENERAL MEANING AND THE HISTORICAL BACKGROUND

The phrase "*dina d'malchuta dina*" is Aramaic and literally means "the law of the state is the law." It expresses the rule that the law of a country is binding and, in certain cases, may even supersede Jewish law. The problematic nature of this situation is comparable to – but not identical with – the problematic nature of conflicts between the laws of different legal systems (conflict of laws or, in European parlance, private international law).

This rule, established by the *amora* Samuel, can only be fully understood when placed in its historical context. The conquests of Ardashir I, king of Persia from 224 to 240 CE and founder of the Sasanian dynasty, which stretched from the Euphrates River to the Indus River, introduced a period of tranquility enjoyed by the Jews of Babylon. They had to adapt to the loss of their political autonomy caused by the centralism of the Sasanian regime. In 241, Shapur I, Ardashir's son, succeeded him and accorded to minorities a cultural and religious autonomy that was also granted to the Jews. Samuel, who was then the leader of the Jews in Babylon, convinced the Babylonian Jewish community that its members should be reconciled with the new government, and a personal friendship developed between Samuel and Shapur. In consequence, the rule decreed by Samuel assumed major political importance because it constituted recognition of the new Sasanian kingdom as a civilized state with good, equitable laws that Babylonian Jews must obey; he also called upon them to pay all the taxes that the king intended to levy.

II TALMUDIC SOURCES

The principle developed by Samuel is cited four times in the Babylonian Talmud (*Ned.* 28a, *Git.* 10b, *BK* 113a and *BB* 54b–55a). The rules reported in his name established the following: (1) Persian law relating to presumptions of ownership must be recognized even when, in certain matters, it is contrary to Jewish law. (2) The sale of land confiscated by the government because of nonpayment of the land tax is valid, but not when the sale is due to nonpayment of the poll tax (*BT BB* 55a and *BT BK* 113b). Other rules were adopted as a result of this principle: (1) Persian laws concerning the transfer of the ownership of real estate must be recognized even when they are not in accordance with *halachah* (*BT BB* 54b–55a). (2) The king has the right to sell a person into slavery for nonpayment of the poll tax, and that person may be purchased by a Jew from the government in order to serve him (*BT Yev.* 64a, *BT BM* 73b). (3) It is forbidden to lie to tax collectors and to conceal assets from them unless the tax in question is illegal for a reason stated in the Talmud (*BT Ned.* 28a, *BT BK* 113a). (4) The decisions of non-Jewish courts must be accepted even when they do not correspond to the canons of *halachah*. In this respect, the Talmud relates a controversy over the field of application of this last rule. According to one opinion, all categories of documents must be recognized except for acts of divorce and the enfranchisement of slaves. According to another opinion, recognition should be accorded only to declaratory acts like an acknowledgment of debt but not to constitutive acts such as deeds of gift (*BT Git.* 10b).

Despite the Talmud's liberalism regarding the laws of other nations, *halachah* remained the backbone of Diaspora Jewish communities. Its enduring dynamism is attested to by the thousands of responsa that have been issued in the course of centuries.

III A PRINCIPLE WITHOUT ANY LEGAL BASE?

The Talmud does not advance any legal base for the principle developed by Samuel. This question attracted scant attention among the *Geonim*. However, we do find an attempt to resolve the question in a responsum from the era of the *Geonim*. The Sage who was questioned, in light of the reality of Diaspora life – the Jews had already been living for a considerable period of time under a foreign legal system – states bluntly that it is God's will that the Jews must obey the laws of their rulers. To support his view, he cites a verse from Nehemiah: "Today we are slaves, and the land that You gave our fathers to enjoy its fruit and bounty – here we are slaves on it! On account of our sins it yields its abundant crops to kings whom You have set over us. They rule over our bodies and our beasts as they please, and we are in great distress" (9:36–37). Later, a certain number of explanations were proposed in rabbinic literature. According to a gloss by Rashi (*BT Git.* 9b), Jewish law allows Jews to accept, to a certain degree, the law of nations because the seventh law of the Noahide laws (concerning these laws, see Chapter 1) imposes on the nations the obligation of installing courts and, more generally, the obligation of establishing laws to preserve the social order. According to a gloss by Rashbam, the foundations of the principle are contractual because the subjects of the king accept the king's laws and ordinances of their own free will (Rashbam on *BT BB* 54b) or, as Maimonides puts it, "After all, the inhabitants of that land have agreed to accept him as their king and have acknowledged that he is their master and they are his servants" (*MT, Laws Governing Robbery and Loss* 5:18).

Later rabbinic authorities linked the rule of *dina d'malchuta dina* to the law by which a rabbinic authority is empowered to expropriate a member of the Jewish community (*hefker bet din hefker*) and especially to the fact that the halachic authorities, by virtue of their right to issue ordinances in the monetary domain (see Chapter 3) even when the ordinances are contrary to the Torah, have, in certain matters, recognized the kingdom's customs and laws (*Teshuvot Ba'alei ha-Tosafot* no. 12; *Devar Avraham* vol. 1, no. 1). Some commentators have compared the powers of non-Jewish kings to those of the kings of Israel (Ritba on *BT BB* 55a). Others are of the opinion that the legality of a kingdom's laws is rooted in the simple fact that the land belongs to the king, who can decide the conditions that must be met for residence there; if the Jews wish to settle in his kingdom, they must obey him (Ran on *BT Ned.* 28a, Or Zarua on *BT BK* no. 447). Still other commentators base the principle of *dina d'malchuta dina* on the concept of custom, which, as we know, is one of the sources of Jewish law (*Aliyot de-Rabbenu Yona* on *BT BB* 55a; on custom as a source of law, see Chapter 3, Section 3). The majority of these opinions reflect medieval socioeconomic concepts.

In the contemporary epoch, the debate has now shifted to the question as to whether the rule of *dina d'malchuta dina* is biblical or rabbinic in character.[23] The majority opinion is that the rule is of biblical origin.

IV CONDITIONS FOR THE APPLICATION OF THE RULE

Halachic authorities never recognized the laws of any kingdom, but they did specify the conditions under which the rule could be applied. However, some of these conditions have remained controversial up to the present day.

A *The Nature of the Political Regime*

According to some halachic authorities, the rule applies only when the regime is a monarchy (*Ora la-Tzadik* HM no. 1). Other authorities, on the other hand, are of the opinion that the rule can apply to other forms of government. With the gradual disappearance of monarchies throughout the world and their

---

[23] On this distinction, see Chapter 2, Section 1.

replacement by republican or democratic regimes, the second opinion has prevailed (*Knesset ha-Gedolah* Tur HM 369).

B *The Principle of* "Dina D'malchuta Dina" *and the Kingdom of Israel*

Another question is whether the principle of *"dina d'malchuta dina"* applies to Jewish kings whose kingdom is on the soil of the Land of Israel. According to Talmudic sources, a distinction must be made between Jewish and non-Jewish kings with regard to this principle; this is also the opinion of the early commentators. According to Rashba, those who believe that the principle does not apply to Jewish kings admit that it does apply if their kingdom is located outside the Land of Israel (Resp. Rashba vol. 2, no. 134). The exclusion of Jewish kings from the application of this maxim corresponds to one of the foundations we referred to earlier: whereas the monarchs of the nations are the owners of their kingdom, the kings of Israel are not the owners of their kingdom since after the Jewish people entered Canaan, the land was partitioned among the Twelve Tribes of Israel. However, over the centuries, the opinion that Samuel's doctrine was applicable to a Jewish king in the Land of Israel became increasingly popular (*Tashbez* pt. 4, section 1, no. 14).

C *The Principle of Equality*

All of the commentators agree that the rule does not apply if the law of the kingdom (or the republic) is not aimed at all of the subjects in the kingdom (or all the citizens in the republic). Thus, Maimonides writes: "The general rule is that every law that this king decrees for all his subjects and not just for one individual is not robbery" (*MT, Laws Governing Robbery and Loss* 5:14; see also SA 369:8).

However, in the light of the social reality of Diaspora life, the rabbinic authorities recognized the validity of certain laws that discriminated against Jews. In one responsum, a rabbinic authority went so far as to acknowledge the validity of a discriminatory law provided that it made no distinction between the Jews themselves (Rep. Maharik no. 195). Another rabbinic authority admitted the existence of special laws for foreigners (*Hochmat Shlomo* HM 369:8).

V THE DOMAIN OF THE PRINCIPLE'S APPLICATION

All of the laws of a kingdom are not recognized by Jewish law. Only certain domains are included in the rule's field of practical application.

A Monetary Law but Not the Ritual Domain

As noted earlier (Chapter 2, Section 1), one of the consequences of the distinction between the monetary and ritual domains relates to the rule under question here. All the commentators agree that the ritual domain can never be regulated by a non-Jewish sovereign. This is so evident that the principle is rarely referred to in rabbinic literature.

B The Interests of the King

Some opinions limit the application of the rule to the interests of the king, that is, to the interests of his kingdom, thus excluding private law from the application of the principle to apply it exclusively to public law (*Sefer ha-Terumot* 46:8). However, the majority of authors do not accept this restriction (ibid., *Maggid Mishneh*, *Malveh ve-Loveh* 27:1; Resp. Rashba vol. 1, no. 895).

C "Non-Jewish Ways" and the New Laws of the King

Some commentators are of the opinion that the Jews in the kingdom must recognize the laws of the king, but not "non-Jewish ways." This idea is not a shining example of clarity; in the medieval era, when it was introduced, it apparently referred to local customs having the force of law. Local customs could not acquire any force of law for Jewish communities because the "law of the king is mandatory, while the laws of his people do not obligate us" (Rashba, Resp. vol. 6, no. 149; *Beit ha-Bechira* BK 113b).

On the other hand, the majority of the commentators believed that the rule decreed by Samuel applied not to the laws that the kings themselves introduced but rather solely to the laws that preceded the law of the kingdom (*Teshuvot Ba'alei ha-Tossafot* no. 12; Ritba on BT BB 55a; Rashba on BB 55a). We can probably see here the influence of medieval legal thinking that valued only laws that were ancient or "immemorial." Insofar as Maimonides and the Rosh apparently disagreed with this commonly held opinion, Joseph Karo decided not to mention in his code this restriction to ancient laws. Karo's decision served as the basis for future rabbinic authorities in their extension of Samuel's rule. This extension of the rule was a critical necessity with the rise of nation-states that was accompanied by modern legislation that almost entirely erased all the ancient laws.

D State Law and Halachah

According to some rabbinic authorities, the law of the state is binding only if it does not run counter to *halachah*, that is, if it does not deal with questions that are explicitly regulated by *halachah* (A. Sofer [ed.], *Teshuvot chachmei Provintzia* HM no. 49; *Siftei Kohen* HM 73 no. 39; *Hatam Sofer*, Resp. HM no. 44). The distinction is not sufficiently clear because it is difficult to differentiate between what is contained in *halachah* and what constitutes a lacuna in the *halachah*, insofar as the majority of rabbinic authorities consider the Torah to have predicted everything and believe that every legal question contains a response that one should search for in one's heart (see above: the idea of "permanent revelation").

E Principal Applications

1 Taxes

As we have already seen, the king's right to levy taxes was recognized by the Babylonian Talmud and was extended by post-Talmudic literature. Tax fraud is clearly regarded as theft (*Tashbez* pt. 3, no. 46). Halachic authorities such as Joseph Karo continued to distinguish between justified taxes and confiscations, on one hand, and taxes and confiscations that are not (SA HM 369:6–11), on the other. In practice, the distinction is made for each individual case, depending on local conditions and the nature of the tax. In accordance with the *halachah* directly derived from the Talmud, an unlimited tax should not be recognized (see MT, op. cit., 5:11); nonetheless, the rabbinic authorities acknowledged later that this category of tax should be recognized if it is being raised for major needs, such as the financing of a war (*Hagahot Mordechai* BB no. 659). But what does the phrase "unlimited tax" mean? The concept has been interpreted as designating a regular tax where the amount is sometimes increased by the regime beyond the legal limit. On the other hand, when the amount of the tax has not been fixed *ab initio*, the king can impose an arbitrary surcharge on the population (MT, op. and loc. cit.; *Terumat Ha-Deshen* no. 341).

2 The Judgments of Non-Jewish Courts

From the period of the *Geonim* until the thirteenth century, *halachah* accorded recognition, but only in a limited sense, to the judgments of non-Jewish courts (MT, *Laws Governing Lenders and Borrowers* 27:1–2);

however, after that era, many commentators have extended the recognition given to non-Jewish courts (Ramban, gloss of BT BB 55a; Rashbi, gloss of BT Git. 10b). This approach can be observed in communal ordinances. In effect, however, the communities that chose to follow the Maimonidean code (MT) excluded three laws appearing in Maimonides's *Mishneh Torah*. One of them is the invalidity of the principle of donations sanctioned by non-Jewish courts. In light of this trend, the enforcement of such donations, including donations to assets already transferred by a debtor, was permitted, although, in the previous epoch, *halachah* allowed enforcement only for a debtor's free assets (Rashba, Resp. vol. 3, no. 69; *Piskei ha-Rosh* on *Git*. 1:10, 11). Similarly, recognition of the category of the tribunal making the judgment was extended as well. The need for ensuring the honesty of the members of a court – a point that is emphasized by the ancient halachic authorities (*MT Laws Governing Lenders and Borrowers* 27:1) – gradually vanished and the tendency to presume the integrity of non-Jewish courts ultimately triumphed (*Piskei ha-Rosh* on BT *Git*. 1:10, 11). Recognition was accorded not only to judges but also to public officials such as notaries (Ramban, Resp. no. 46). Finally, the most recent rabbinic authorities recognize every document generated by the non-Jewish legal bodies (*Be'er Yitzhak* EH 5:4; *Sho'el u-Meshiv* pt. 1, no. 10).

3 Changes in the Value of the Local Currency

Another question that is frequently discussed in connection with the principle of *dina d'malchuta dina* concerns changes in the value of the local currency. Here the rabbinic authorities rule that, if a regime decides that debts must be paid in a certain way, everyone must operate in accordance with that decision even if it creates the possibility that the prohibition of interest-bearing loans or theft might be violated (*Sefer ha-Terumot* 46:5; *Meisharim* 6:1; *Hatam Sofer* Resp. HM no. 58).

4 Government Appointments to Rabbinic or Judiciary Functions

In certain eras, the national or local government has intervened in Jewish communal affairs by appointing a rabbi or rabbinic judges. Some rabbinic authorities think that the national or local government has the right to do so and that such appointments are valid from the perspective of Talmudic law, by virtue of the principle of *dina d'malchuta dina*. Other rabbinic authorities think differently, and, as a result, there have been several famous disagreements between rabbis, where one of them was appointed by the government and the other was appointed by the Jewish community, each claiming the appointment's legitimacy from the standpoint of *halachah*. The opinion that prevailed was that, even if the principle of *dina d'malchuta dina* applies in this case, the official appointed by the government must not accept the appointment if it does not receive the Jewish community's approval (Ribash Resp. no. 271; Rema HM 3:4; *Tashbez* pt. 1, nos. 158, 162; Rema Resp. no. 123; *Hatam Sofer* Resp. HM no. 19).

CONCLUDING REMARKS

In the light of the preceding discussion, we may risk offering a few concluding remarks. Ostensibly, these two principles that serve to connect the Jewish legal system and the legal systems of the nations of the world appear to contradict one another to a certain degree. Is it logical for Jews to prefer their own tribunals and yet at the same time to accord considerable recognition to the law of nations? An initial response that is both historical and contextual can be given. The principle forbidding recourse to non-Jewish tribunals is rooted in the political context that gave rise to these laws: Rabbi Tarfon lived under the Roman occupation, which became increasingly oppressive. The avoidance of the Roman tribunals undoubtedly constituted a form of resistance. Moreover, we can easily draw a parallel with early Christian doctrine. Perhaps Paul of Tarsus, or, as is he is more commonly known, Paul the Apostle, had a certain Talmudic teaching in mind when he wrote:

> Dare any of you, having a matter against another, go to law before the unjust, and not before the saints? Do ye not know that the saints shall judge the world? And if the world shall be judged by you, are ye unworthy to judge the smallest matters? Know ye not that we shall judge angels? How much more things that pertain to this life? If then ye have judgments of things pertaining to this life, set them to judge who are least esteemed in the church. I speak to your shame. Is it so, that there is not a wise man among you? No, not one that shall be able to judge between his brethren? But brother goeth to law with brother, and that before the unbelievers. Now therefore there is utterly a fault among you, because ye go to law one with another. Why do ye not rather take wrong? Why do ye not rather suffer yourselves to be defrauded?" (1 *Corinth*. 6: 1–7)

In contrast with Rabbi Tarfon, Samuel, who lived in Babylon in the third century CE and who was a friend of the king and was also a political official, could not perceive the regime he lived under in the same manner that Rabbi Tarfon viewed the Roman conquerors.

From a technical standpoint, the conflict between these two norms was reduced by the introduction of the principle of the relationship between the two, a principle that even allowed the exclusion – or near exclusion – of one of them. Originally, the prohibition of recourse to non-Jewish tribunals fell under the category of the first norm, while recognition of the "law of the state" fell under the category of the second. The period of the Emancipation and the Great Sanhedrin installed by Napoleon in 1806 reduced Jewish law to the "smallest share of the banquet" and gave the law of the kingdom the lion's share.

However, it would appear that it was rabbinic arbitration that permitted respected halachic authorities to avoid recourse to non-Jewish tribunals and to settle their litigations in accordance with *halachah*. Among the teachings that we may draw from the Jewish legal tradition and its multi-millennial experience is the aptitude for permitting legal pluralism, an aptitude that could serve as a model for the Muslim communities that have recently established themselves in Europe or in the United States.[24]

Further Reading

JUDAISM'S RELATIONSHIP TO OTHER CIVILIZATIONS

Schacter, Jacob J. (ed.). *Judaism and Other Cultures: Rejection or Integration?* Jason Aronson, 1997.

THE PRACTICE OF SECULAR LAW ACCORDING TO JEWISH LAW

Biser, M. "Can an Observant Jew Practice Law? A Look at Some Halakhic Problems," 11 *Jewish Law Annual* 101 (1994).

Broyde, M. J. "The Practice of Law According to Halacha," 20 *Journal of Halacha and Contemporary Society* 5 (1990).

---

[24] Michael J. Broyde, Ira Bedzow, and Shlomo Pill, "The Pillars of Successful Religious Arbitration: Models for American Islamic Arbitration Based on the Beth Din of America and Muslim Arbitration Tribunal Experience," 30 *Harvard Journal on Racial & Ethnic Justice* 34 (2014).

PROHIBITION OF SEEKING RECOURSE FROM GENTILE COURTS

Bazak, Y. "The Halachic Status of The Israeli Court System," in *Crossroads: Halacha and Modern World*, Vol. 2, ZOMET, Torah and Science Research Teams: Alon Shvut-Gush Etzion, 1988, available at www.jlaw.com/Articles/israelcourt.html.

Bleich, J. D. "Litigation and Arbitration before Non-Jews," 34.3 *Tradition* 58 (2000).

Brand, Y. "Non-Jewish Courts and the Courts of the State of Israel: *Halacha*, Reality and Ideology," 8 *Daimon: Annuario di diritto comparato delle religioni* 111 (2008).

Bressler, D. "Arbitration and the Courts in Jewish Law," 9 *Journal of Halacha & Contemporary Society* 105 (1985).

Feit, Y. "The Prohibition against Going to Secular Courts," 1 *Journal of the Beth Din of America* 30 (2012).

RABBINIC ARBITRATION

Broyde, M. J. *Sharia Tribunals, Rabbinical Courts, and Christian Panels: Religious Arbitration in America and the West*, Oxford University Press, 2017.

Licari, F.-X. "L'arbitrage rabbinique, entre droit talmudique et droit des nations," *Revue de l'arbitrage* 56 (2013).

Sinai, Y. "Arbitration As An Ideal Procedure," 18 *Jewish Law Association Studies* 279 (2008).

Zelcer, H. "Two Models of Alternative Dispute Resolution," 4 *Hakirah* 69 (2007).

"THE LAW OF THE STATE IS THE LAW"

Jackson, B. "Jewish Law and State Law: 'Transformative Accommodation' and the JFS Case in England," 11 *Ecclesiastical Law Journal* 131 (2009).

Finkelstein, B. "'The Law of the State Is the Law': The Nature of Law in Jewish Jurisprudence," 19 *Review of Rabbinic Judaism* 256 (2016).

Graf, G. *Separation of Church and State: Dina de-malkhuta dina in Jewish Law, 1750–1848*, University of Alabama Press, 1985.

Povarski, C. "Jewish Law v. the Law of the State: Theories of Accommodation," 12 *Cardozo Law Review* 941 (1991).

Shilo, S. "Equity As a Bridge between Jewish and Secular Law," 12 *Cardozo Law Review* 737 (1991).

Smilévitch, E. "Halakha et code civil: questions sur le Grand Sanhedrin," 3 *Pardès* 9 (1986).

RABBINIC COURTS IN ISRAEL

Chigier, M. "The Rabbinical Courts in the State of Israel," 2 *Israel Law Review* 147 (1967).

Hacker, D. "Religious Tribunals in Democratic States: Lessons from the Israeli Rabbinical Courts," 27 *Journal of Law & Religion* 59 (2012).

Index

Aaron, 65
bar Abba, Samuel, 25
Abraham, 6–7, 113
Acharonim, 59, 70
Activities of Rabbis, 74–75
ben Aderet, Salomon, 84–85
Adimi (Rav), 18
Administration of law
   overview, 124
   dina d'malchuta dina ("the law of the state is the law") (*See* Dina d'malchuta dina ("the law of the state is the law"))
   rabbinic arbitration (*See* Rabbinic arbitration)
Aelia Capitolina, 69–70
A *fortiori* reasoning, 112–113
Aggada versus *halachah*, 68–69
Aggadic meaning, 108
Aggadic midrashim, 68–69
Aggadot (information), 77
Aharon of Barcelona, 38
Ahasuerus (Persia), 51
Akiva (Rabbi), 43, 68, 82, 107
Alfasi, Isaac, 70
Algazi, Salomon Nissim (Rabbi), 93
Allusive meaning, 108
Amoraic Era, 24
Amoraim, 24, 25, 61, 69–70
Amram (Rabbi), 24
Analogical interpretation
   overview, 112
   in Babylonian Talmud, 113
   a *fortiori* reasoning, 112–113
   identity of terms, analogy based on, 113–114
   inference through induction, 114–115
   in Jewish law, 24–25

   prohibition and permission versus monetary laws, 24–25
   Torah and, 24
Anathema, 135–136
The Antiquities of the Jews (Josephus Flavius), 97
Arbitration. *See* Rabbinic arbitration
Ardashir I (Persia), 143
Ashi (Rav), 61, 69
Asmachta (support), 27
Assimilation, 126
Astrolatry, 20
Attorney fees, 132
Authority
   binding, 72
   of books, 70–72
   deontic model of, 76
   epistemological model of, 76
   intellectual, 72
   persuasive, 72
   sources of, 76
Avot (Tractate), 72–73, 100

Babylonia, 143
Babylonian academies, 69, 70
Babylonian Talmud
   analogical interpretation in, 113
   authority of, 70
   criminal law and, 90
   dina d'malchuta dina ("the law of the state is the law") and, 143–144
   interpretation of law in, 69
   Maimonides on, 70
   pluralism and, 94–95
   rabbinic arbitration and, 128
Baraita, 57, 128

Index

Bar Kochba Revolt, 141
Bat kol (celestial voice), 80
Bava Batra (Tractate), 23
Beit Din, 73
Beth Din of America, 126, 132, 138, 139–140
Bible, 101–102, 122
Biblical canon, 67
Biblical Commandments. *See* Ten Commandments
Biblical law. *See* Jewish law
Binyan av (inference), 114–115
Blidstein, G.J., 8
Braitot, 68
British Mandatory Palestine, 9–10

Caesarian Talmud, 69–70
Canon law, 44
Case law, 58
Casuistry, 67–68
The Challenge of Creation (Slikfin), 101–102
Chamber of the Hewn Stone, 65
Cherem (excommunication or anathema), 135–136
Christianity, *dina d'malchuta dina* ("the law of the state is the law") and, 150
Chronological order, hermeneutics and, 121
Cities of refuge, 119
Civil Code, 1–2
Civil law, 57
Clothing, 28
Codification of Jewish law, 34, 60, 72
Commandments
  descriptive versus normative nature of, 17–18
  First Commandment, 17–18
  French law and, 31
  justificatory nature of, 19
  rabbinic legislation versus, 26–27
  Tenth Commandment, 36
Common law, 1–2
Communal legislation, 50–52
Comparative law, 1, 11, 12
Conflict resolution, 25–26, 27. *See also* **Rabbinic arbitration**
Consensual sources of authority, 77
Consonantal text versus vocal text, 122
Constantine (Emperor), 65
Contempt of court, 135
Contract, liberty of, 23–24
Conversion, 8, 44
"Counter-reform," 98–99
Creative authority in *halachah*
  overview, 82–83
  "by the pursuit of which man shall live," 89
  criminal law and, 89–91
  "it is time for God to act," 87–88
  "it is time for us to act on behalf of God," 87–88
  Maimonides and, 85–87
  "need of the hour," 89–91
  prophecy, rejection of, 83–84
  Sages and, 84–87
  Torah, prohibition on adding to or removing from, 83
Criminal law
  creative authority and, 89–91
  rabbinic arbitration and, 130
Critical Legal Studies, 12–13
Currency valuation, 149
Custom as source of *halachah*, 53–56

Da'at Torah ("Torah's point of view"), 100, 101–102
Damages
  compensatory damages, 132
  punitive damages, 13
David, 50
David, René, 1–2
Decisors, 72, 74
Defining *halachah*, 7
Dejuridicization of *halachah*, 98
Derogatory criminal laws, 89–91
Deuteronomy
  divine versus human judgments in, 42–43
  domain of *halachah* and, 78
  justificatory nature of, 18–19
  peshat versus *halachah*, 110
  prohibition on adding to or removing from Torah in, 83
  rabbinic arbitration and, 127
  sources of *halachah* and, 76
Diaspora
  criminal law and, 90
  dina d'malchuta dina ("the law of the state is the law") and, 146
  Gemara and, 55
  political autonomy of, 125
  rabbinic arbitration and, 125, 126
  rabbinic legislation and, 50–51
  transfer of ownership and, 55
Dietary laws, 22–23, 74
Digest of Justinian, 68
Dimi (Rav), 132

Dina d'malchuta dina ("the law of the state is the law")
  overview, 34, 143, 150–151
  conditions for application of, 145–146
  currency valuation, applicability to, 149
  domain of application of, 146–150
  equality and, 146
  government appointments, applicability to, 149–150
  historical background, 143
  interests of king, applicability to, 147
  judgments of non-Jewish courts, applicability to, 148–149
  Kingdom of Israel and, 146
  legal basis for, 144–145
  monetary law and, 147
  nature of political regime, effect of, 145–146
  "non-Jewish ways," applicability to, 147
  state law versus *halachah*, 148
  Talmudic sources, 143–144
  taxes, applicability to, 148
Discourse in *halachah*, 8
Discretion, 60–61
Divine versus human judgments, 39–43
Domain of *halachah*, 8, 35–37, 77–79
Doubt, 25–26, 27
Drawing of lots, 40
Due process, 137

Elazar of Worms, 107
"Elders of the City," 134
Eliezer (Rabbi), 80–81, 121, 132, 141
Elijah, 34
Elon, Menachem, 13
Emancipation, 98–99, 151
Emden, Jacob, 34
Enlightenment, 98
Entrustment of property, 117
Ephron, 113
Esoteric meaning, 108
Esther, 18, 51
Excommunication, 135–136
Exegesis, 94, 107, 108, 127
Exegetical approaches to hermeneutics, 107–108
Exemplum as source of *halachah*, 58–59
Exile, 7, 68, 88
Exodus, 26–27, 41–43, 128
Explicative interpretation
  overview, 112

davar shehaya bi-chlal (law included in collective term), 118
kelal shehu tzarich li-frat u-frat shehu tzarich li-chlal (general rule and particular case independent of each other), 117–118
kelal uferat (general rule—particular case), 115–116
kelal uferat uchelal (general rule—particular case—general rule), 117
perat uchelal (particular case—general rule), 116
perat uchelal uferat (particular case—general rule—particular case), 117
Ezra, 50

Feinstein, Moshe, 34
Feminist Legal Studies, 12–13
Fines, 24–25
Fire, kindling of, 118–119
First Commandment, 17–18
First Mishnah, 67–68
Flavius Josephus, 97, 124–125
Fluidity of *halachah*, 31
Forum shopping, 75
France
  Chambre Arbitale Rabbinique (CAR), 126, 132, 138, 139, 140
  Civil Code, 31
  comparative law in, 12
  jurisprudence constante, 71–72
  rabbinic arbitration in, 126, 129, 132, 134, 136, 138, 139, 140
  rabbinic courts in, 125
  Reform Judaism in, 98
  state of mind in French law, 36
  Ten Commandments and, 31
French School, 109

ben Gamla, Joshua, 50
Gamliel II (Rabban), 66
Gemara, 7, 69, 91
Genesis, 109–110
Gentile court proceedings, prohibition against (*issur arka'ot*), 127–131
Gentile courts, 129
Gentiles, 21, 83–84
Geonim, 59, 70, 144
Germany
  Civil Code, 1–2
  Neo-Orthodox Judaism in, 98–99
  rabbinic courts in, 125

Reform Judaism in, 98
die Wissenschaft des Judentums, 11, 12, 98
Get (divorce document), 1
Gezerah shawah (identical decree), 113–114
Grand Assembly, 67
Grand Sanhedrin, 50, 65–66, 91, 94–95, 101, 151
Grotius, Hugo, 2
Grundnorm, 48, 50, 88, 97–98
Guide for the Perplexed (Maimonides), 20, 78
Guilt offerings, 120–121

Hadrian (Emperor), 69–70
Hagiographa, 77, 84, 108
Halachah. See specific topic
Halachic authority
 creative authority (*See* Creative authority in halachah)
 domain of, 8, 35–37, 77–79
 hermeneutics (*See* Hermeneutics)
 pluralism (*See* Pluralism)
 Rabbis (*See* Rabbis)
 source of (*See* Source of *halachah*)
Halachic Man (J.D. Soloveichik), 37
Halachic midrashim, 68–69
Halivni, David Weiss, 18
Haman, 51
Hanukkah, 51
Hasmoneans, 50, 65
Haviva (Rabbi), 54–55
Hebrew law, 6–7. *See also* **Jewish law**
Heretics, 77, 88
Hermeneutics
 overview, 107
 aggadic meaning, 108
 allusive meaning, 108
 analogical interpretation (*See* Analogical interpretation)
 chronological order and, 121
 consonantal text versus vocal text, 122
 davar shehaya bi-chlal (law included in collective term), 118
 esoteric meaning, 108
 exegetical approaches, 107–108
 explicative interpretation (*See* Explicative interpretation)
 extent of hermeneutic authority, 79–82
 a fortiori reasoning, 112–113
 homiletic meaning, 108
 human language and, 121
 identity of terms, analogy based on, 113–114
 inference through induction, 114–115

 Jewish law and, 82
 kelal shehu tzarich li-frat u-frat shehu tzarich li-chlal (general rule and particular case independent of each other), 117–118
 kelal uferat (general rule—particular case), 115–116
 kelal uferat uchelal (general rule—particular case—general rule), 117
 Moses and, 82
 no superfluous words in Torah, 76–77
 perat uchelal (particular case—general rule), 116
 perat uchelal uferat (particular case—general rule—particular case), 117
 peshat (literal meaning), 107–111
 Rashi of Troyes and, 116, 117
 Sages and, 79–82
Herod (Judea), 66
Heter iska (business venture), 130
Hildesheimer, Ezriel, 98
Hillel, 21, 50, 53, 65–66, 91–92, 107
Hillel II, 73
Hindu law, 2
Hirsch, Samson Raphael, 79, 98
Historical background of *halachah*, 6–7
History of the People of Israel (Renan), 11
Holocaust, 100
Homiletic meaning, 108
Hora'ah (instruction), 74
Hora'at sha'ah ("need of the hour"), 89–91
Horayot (Tractate), 94–95
ben Houchiel, Hananel, 93
Hughes, Charles Evans, 93
Human language, hermeneutics and, 121
Human versus divine judgments, 39–43
Hungary, Neo-Orthodox Judaism in, 98

Ibn Ezra, Abraham, 20, 108–111
Identity of terms, analogy based on, 113–114
Ideology of *halachah*, 32–33
Idolatry, 20, 21–22, 89
Ijma'a (consensus in Islamic law), 70–71
Imperative character of *halachah*, 8
Induction, inference through, 114–115
Infallibility, 101
Inference through induction, 114–115
Inheritance, 23–24
Interpretation. *See* Hermeneutics
Involuntary homicide, 119
Ishmael (Rabbi), 107, 116
Islamic law, 70–71

Israel
  comparative law in, 13
  halachah, Israeli law versus, 9–10
  rabbinic courts in, 125, 139
  Religious Zionism, 102
Israeli law, 9–10
Issur arka'ot (prohibition against Gentile court proceedings), 127–131

Jeremiah, 81
Jerusalem Talmud, 69–70
Jethro, 41–42
Jewish law
  overview, 7
  analogy, use of, 24–25
  Babylonian Talmud (*See* Babylonian Talmud)
  customs and, 53
  dina d'malchuta dina ("the law of the state is the law") and, 143–144
  Gemara, 7, 69, 91
  hermeneutic authority and, 82
  Jerusalem Talmud, 69–70
  ma'aseh (exempla) in, 58
  Mishnah (*See* Mishnah)
  pluralism and, 91–92, 94–95
  property transfers and, 54–55
  prophecy and, 83–84
  scriptural sources of authority, 76–77
  sevara (logic) and, 57
  severance pay and, 38–39
  taxes and, 148
Jewish Legal Studies, 12
Jewish philosophy, 77
Jewish Scriptures, 71
Jewish thought, 77
Joshua, 50, 67
ben Judah Crescas, Hasdai, 17–18
Judah the Prince, 66, 68
Judaic law. *See* Jewish law
Judaism
  Liberal Judaism, 97–98
  Neo-Orthodox Judaism, 98–99
  Orthodox Judaism, 98–99
  Progressive Judaism, 97–98
  Rabbinic Judaism, 66–67
  Reconstructionist Judaism, 97–98
  Reform Judaism, 97–98
  "Ultra-Orthodox" Judaism, 99–102
Judea, 124–125
Judges, 41–43, 60–61, 76–77, 128, 138–139

Juridicity of *halachah*, 7–8, 17–18
Justificatory nature of commandments, 18–19

Kabbalah, 22, 34
Karaites, 97
Karo, Joseph, 34, 70, 93, 147, 148
Kelsen, Hans, 2
Kiddushin (Tractate), 113
Kindling of fire, 118–119
Kinyan (acquisition), 54–56, 113
bar Kochba, Joshua, 141
Kohen (priest), 85, 96
Kook, Abraham Isaac, 102, 103

Lack of scholarly interest in Jewish law, 2
Lactantius, 35
Lacuna in Jewish law, 47, 50, 64, 148
La fonction du droit civil comparé (Lambert), 12
Lambert, Edouard, 12
Law and Economics, 12–13
"The law of the state is the law." *See Dina d'malchuta dina* ("the law of the state is the law")
"Leaders of Their Generation," 101–102
Legal pluralism, 124
Legislation
  communal legislation, 50–52
  legislative drafting, 29–30, 121
  rabbinic legislation (*See* Rabbinic legislation)
Legistics, 29–30
Leprosy, 119–121
Levirate marriage, 23–24
Leviticus, 83–84, 119–120
Lex talionis, 94
Liberal Judaism, 97–98
Liberty of contract, 23–24
Literalism, 97
Literal meaning, 107–111
Living law, *halachah* as, 9
Loans, 130
Logic as source of *halachah*, 57
Luria, Isaac, 34

Ma'aseh (exemplum) as source of *halachah*, 58–59
Maccabees, 51
Maharal of Prague, 100
Maimonides (Moses ben Maimon)
  generally, 70
  on Babylonian Talmud, 70

Index

Commandments versus rabbinic legislation, 26, 27
creative authority and, 85–87
on criminal law, 90–91
on *dina d'malchuta dina* ("the law of the state is the law"), 144–145, 146, 147, 149
divine versus human judgments, 43
legislative drafting and, 29–30
on martyrdom, 89
on Moses, 33–34
on pluralism, 91
prescriptive nature of Commandments and, 17–18
on prophecy, 84
on rabbinic arbitration, 127
on rabbinic legislation, 50, 51–52
on sacrificial worship, 20
on Sages, 77
on science, 78
on state of mind, 36
on Torah, 21–22
Majority rule, 71–72
Malbim, 107
Mamzer (illegitimate child), 96
Mara d'atra (master of the place), 72–73, 101
Marriage, 23–24, 113
Martyrdom, 89
Masoretes, 122
Mechilta, 68–69
Meir (Rabbi), 134
ben Menassia, Simeon (Rabbi), 141
Mercaz Ruhani, 102
Mezuzah, 122
Midrashim, 68–69, 108
Mishnah
overview, 67–69
apodictic character of, 69
as compilation or anthology, 68
on documents, 24
First Mishnah, 67–68
on inheritance, 23
ma'aseh (exemplum) in, 58
Oral Law, 7, 47
organization of, 68
pluralism and, 91
property transfers and, 54–55
rabbinic arbitration and, 138–139
tractates of, 68
on trial by ordeal, 41
Mishneh Torah (Maimonides), 70
Mishpatim (weekly Torah portion), 109–110

Mishpat ivri (Hebrew law), 12–13
Mizrahi, 102
Modus operandi of *halachah*, 37–43
divine versus human judgments, 39–43
orientations of behavior, 37–39
Monetary laws
dina d'malchuta dina ("the law of the state is the law") and, 147
prohibition and permission versus (*See* Prohibition and permission versus monetary laws)
Monotheism, 20
Morocco, rabbinic courts in, 125
Mosaic law, 6. *See also* **Jewish law**
Moses
administration of justice by, 41–42
hermeneutic authority and, 82
Maimonides on, 33–34
Oral Law and, 67
prophecy and, 83–84
rabbinic arbitration and, 128
rabbinic legislation and, 50
revelation of law to, 6, 31, 33–34, 47
ritual purity and, 92, 93

Nahmanides (Moses ben Nahman), 17–18, 20, 26, 27, 79–80
Nahum Ish Gamzu, 107
Napoleon (France), 151
Nathan of Rome, 7
Nehemiah, 144
Neo-Orthodox Judaism, 98–99
Nezifah (rebuke), 135–136
Nidui (distancing), 135–136
Nissim Gaon, 81
Noahide laws, 6

Opinions
majority, 71–72
minority, 68, 71
unanimous, 138
Oral Law, 7, 47–48, 67
Ordeal, trial by, 40–41
Ordinances. *See* Rabbinic legislation
Ordination, 65, 73–74
Orthodox Judaism, 98–99
Ottoman law, 9–10

Palestinian Talmud, 69–70
Panjurism, 101
Pappi (Rav), 54–55

Paul of Tarsus, 150
Penalties, 24–25
Pentateuch. *See* Torah
Persian Empire, 51, 143
Personal status, 9–10, 44, 125
Peshara (*ex aequo et bono* decision), 141–142
Peshat (literal meaning), 107–111
Pharisees, 97
Phylacteries, 110–111
Pilgrimage, 68
Pirkei Avot, 72–73
Pluralism
  overview, 124
  affirmation of, 91–93
  Babylonian Talmud and, 94–95
  Jewish law and, 91–92, 94–95
  legal pluralism, 124
  limits of, 94–96
  Maimonides on, 91
  Mishnah and, 91
  rabbinic arbitration (*See* Rabbinic arbitration)
  Sages and, 91, 92, 93
Politics, 102
Poskim (decisors), 72, 74
Precedent, 58, 60, 140
Presumptions, 57
Priest *(Kohen)*, 85, 96
Progressive Judaism, 97–98
Prohibition and permission versus monetary laws
  overview, 22–23
  analogy and, 24–25
  conflict resolution and, 25–26
  inheritance and, 23–24
  liberty of contract and, 23–24
  marriage and, 23–24
  rabbinic legislation, 24
  systemic principles of, 24–26
Property
  entrustment of, 117
  transfers of, 54–56
Prophecy
  Maimonides on, 84
  rejection of, 83–84
Prophets, 67, 77, 80, 83–84, 90–91, 108
Proverbs, 40
P'sak din (rabbinic court judgment), 138–140
P'sak halachah (rabbinic ruling), 74, 79
Psalms, 87–88
Purim, 51

Qualifications of Rabbis, 72–74

Raba, 57
Rabbah, 24
Rabbenu Hananel, 93
Rabbinical Council of America, 126
Rabbinic arbitration
  overview, 150–151
  appeals, 140
  arbitration agreement, 133–134
  Babylonian Talmud and, 128
  in camera nature of, 139
  composition of arbitration court, 134
  criminal law and, 130
  Diaspora and, 125, 126
  domain and, 130
  economic advantages of, 132–133
  in France, 126, 129, 132, 134, 136, 138, 139, 140
  heter iska (business venture), 130
  historical background, 124–127
  infrequency of use, 126
  institutionalization of, 126
  issur arka'ot (prohibition against Gentile court proceedings), 127–131
  lawyer, representation by, 137–138
  as legal duty, 127–131
  loans and, 130
  Maimonides on, 127
  Moses and, 128
  nidui (distancing) and, 135–136
  non-Jewish arbitration versus, 129
  peshara (*ex aequao et bono* decision), 141–142
  p'sak din (rabbinic court judgment), 138–140
  Rashi of Troyes and, 128, 141
  requirements, 125–126
  res judicata and, 140
  right to counsel, 137–138
  Sages and, 134
  secular courts and, 127–131
  settlement, 141–142
  siruv (summons), 129–130, 135–137
  statutes, 125
  strict adherence versus amicable composition, 141–142
  summons, 135–137
  as technical necessity, 131
  Torah and, 127
  in United States, 126, 129, 133–134, 136, 137, 139–140
  zabla (selection of arbitrators), 134
Rabbinic courts, 125

Rabbinic Judaism, 66–67
Rabbinic law. *See* Jewish law
Rabbinic legislation
　on clothing, 28
　Commandments versus, 26–27
　on conflict resolution, 27
　Diaspora and, 50–51
　on family, 51
　legislative drafting, 29–30
　on loss of money, 27–28
　Maimonides on, 50, 51–52
　Moses and, 50
　on national awareness, 51
　prohibition and permission versus monetary laws, 24
　on religion, 51
　on respect and deference to teachers, 28–29
　Sages and, 50, 51–52
　on society, 51
　as source of *halachah*, 50–52
　Ten Commandments versus, 26–27
　Torah versus, 50, 51
Rabbis. *See also specific Rabbi*
　overview, 72
　activities of, 74–75
　forum shopping, 75
　qualifications of, 72–74
　Rabbi as title, 72
　role of, 72–74
　semicha (rabbinic ordination), 73
　yadin yadin (rabbinic license), 73
　yoreh yoreh (rabbinic license), 73
Rashba, 84–85, 144–145, 146
Rashbam, 108–111
Rashi of Troyes
　dina d'malchuta dina ("the law of the state is the law") and, 144
　on divine versus human judgments, 43
　French School and, 109
　hermeneutics and, 116, 117
　on phylacteries, 83
　rabbinic arbitration and, 128, 141
　on sacrifice, 96
Rationalist School, 109
Rav, 25, 78
Rava, 18, 54–55, 84
Rav as title, 72
Ravina, 61
Reconstructionist Judaism, 97–98
Red heifer, 19
Reform Judaism, 97–98

Religious legal system, *halachah* as
　divine versus human judgments, 39–43
　domain of, 35–37
　fluidity of, 31
　ideology of, 32–33
　modus operandi of, 37–43
　orientations of behavior, 37–39
　parameters of, 33
　relative nature of religious character, 32
　sources of, 33–34
　worldview, promotion of, 32–33
Religious Legal Theory, 12–13
Religious Zionism, 102
Renan, Ernest, 11
Res judicata, 140
Respect and deference to teachers, 28–29
Responsum as source of *halachah*, 59
Revelation
　Moses, revelation of law to, 6, 31, 33–34, 47
　as source of *halachah*, 47
　in Torah, 47
Ribit (interest-bearing loan), 66–67. *See also Heter iska* (business venture)
Rif, 70
Right to counsel, 137–138
Rishonim, 59, 70, 75, 132
Ritual purity, 80–81, 92, 93, 119–121
Ritva, 92
Role of Rabbis, 72–74
Roman Catholic Church, 44
Roman Empire, 7, 124–125
Romano-Germanic law, 1–2
Roman Palestine, 69–70
Rosh, 70
Rov (majority rule), 71–72
Ruth, 54

Sabbath, 27–28, 94–95, 112, 118–119
Sabbatical year, 102
Sacrifice, 94–96
Sacrificial worship, 20
Sadducees, 95, 97
Sages
　creative authority and, 84–87
　domain of *halachah* and, 77–79
　French Sages, 92
　hermeneutic authority and, 79–82
　ma'aseh and, 58
　Maimonides on, 77
　on martyrdom, 89
　pluralism and, 91, 92, 93

Sages (cont.)
  rabbinic arbitration and, 134
  rabbinic legislation and, 50, 51–52
  Rationalist School, 109
  sources of *halachah* and, 77
  Tannaim, 67
Samuel (Amora), 143, 144, 146, 147, 150
Sanctions in *halachah*, 8
Sanhedrin, 34, 50, 64–66, 79, 90
Sasanian Persians, 143
Scholarly interest in Jewish law, 2
Science, Jewish law as, 11
Scripturalism, 97
Scriptural sources of authority, 76–77
Scroll of Fasting, 89–90
Second Temple, 7
Secularization, 41–43
Settlement, 141–142
Sevara (logic) as source of *halachah*, 57
Severance pay, 38–39
Shammai, 21, 50, 65–66, 91–92
Shapur I (Persia), 143
Shoftim (weekly Torah portion), 127
Shulchan Aruch (Karo), 70, 125, 126, 129, 132
Sifra, 68–69
Sifrei, 68–69, 79
Sifri, 68–69
Sinaitic law, 6. *See also* **Jewish law**
Siruv ("contempt of court"), 129–130, 135–137
Situmta, 54–56
Slikfin, Natan, 101–102
Sofer, Moses, 34
Solomon, 19, 50
Soloveichik, Joseph B., 37
Sotah (woman suspected of adultery), 41
Source of *halachah*
  overview, 33–34
  case (judgment) as, 58
  consensus, 77
  custom as, 53–56
  dreams as, 81
  ma'aseh (exemplum) as, 58–59
  rabbinic legislation, 50–52 (*See also*
    Rabbinic legislation)
  responsum as, 59
  revelation, 47, 80–81
  scriptural sources, 76–77
  sevara (logic) as, 57
  tradition, 53–56
Spector, Y.E., 102–103
Stare decisis, 60–61, 140

State of mind, 36–37
Systemic principles, 24–26

Talmudic law. *See* Jewish law
Tannaim, 67
Tannaitic Era, 22–23
Tarfon (Rabbi), 150
Targum Yonatan, 83–84
Taxes, 148
Taxonomy of commandments, 22
Teleology of commandments, 18–22
Ten Commandments. *See* Commandments
Tenth Commandment, 36
Terminology, 30
Tertullian, 35
"Third family" of law, 1–2
Torah. *See also* **specific book**
  analogy and, 24
  chronological order and, 121
  consonantal text versus vocal text, 122
  domain of, 35–37
  goals of, 21–22
  human language and, 121
  justificatory nature of, 18–19
  lacunae in, 64–65
  Maimonides on, 21–22
  mishpatim (weekly Torah portion),
    109–110
  no superfluous words in, 76–77
  oral, 7, 47–48, 67
  prohibition on adding to or removing
    from, 83
  rabbinic arbitration and, 127
  rabbinic legislation versus, 50, 51
  revelation in, 47
  scriptural sources of authority, 76–77
  sevara (logic) and, 57
Tosefta, 23, 68
Traditio clavium (delivery of keys), 55
Tradition as source of *halachah*, 53–56
Transfers of property, 54–56
Transnational legal order, *halachah* as, 44
Trial by ordeal, 40–41
Typology of books, 67–70

"Ultra-Orthodox" Judaism, 99–102
Unique features of *halachah*, 2–3
United Kingdom
  British Mandatory Palestine, 9–10
  common law in, 1–2
  rabbinic courts in, 125

United States
  common law in, 1–2
  comparative law in, 12–14
  First Amendment, 133–134, 136, 137
  rabbinic arbitration in, 126, 129, 133–134, 136, 137, 139–140
  rabbinic courts in, 125
  Reform Judaism in, 98

Vanderlinden, Jacques, 33
Vocal text versus consonantal text, 122

Weltanschauung, 32–33
Western legal tradition, 12–14
die Wissenschaft des Judentums, 11, 12, 98

World Zionist Organization, 102
Written Law, 47–48. *See also* **Torah**

Xerxes I (Persia), 51

Yavneh academy, 66
ben Yechiel, Asher (Rabbi), 70
Yeshivot (Talmudic academies), 100
bar Yochai, Simon, 34
Yohanan (Rabbi), 69–70, 89, 132
Yossi the Galilean (Rabbi), 107, 121, 141

Zabla (selection of arbitrators), 134
ben Zakkai, Yochanan, 41
Zeitgeist, 97–98
Zionism, 9–10, 102
Zohar, 34